THE PIRATE QUEEN

BARBARA SJOHOLM

THE PIRATE QUEEN

In Search of Grace O'Malley
and Other Legendary Women of the Sea

SEAL PRESS

Published by **Seal Press**
A member of the Perseus Books Group
1700 Fourth Street
Berkeley, CA 9 4710

Portions of this book appeared in *The North American Review*,
Spring 2003 ("The Lonely Voyage of Betty Mouat"), and in
A Woman Alone: Travel Tales from Around the Globe, Seal Press,
2001 ("Halibut Woman").

Cataloging-in-Publication data has been applied for.

ISBN-10: 1-58005-109-x
ISBN-13: 978-1-58005-109-5

Designed by PDBD
Cartographer: Suzanne Service

Distributed by Publishers Group West

To my mother
in memoriam

"I'm going to be a pirate when I grow up," she cried. *"Are you?"*
—Astrid Lindgren, *Pippi Longstocking*

CONTENTS

LIST OF ILLUSTRATIONS

(LIST OF ILLUSTRATIONS, CONT'D)

LIST OF MAPS

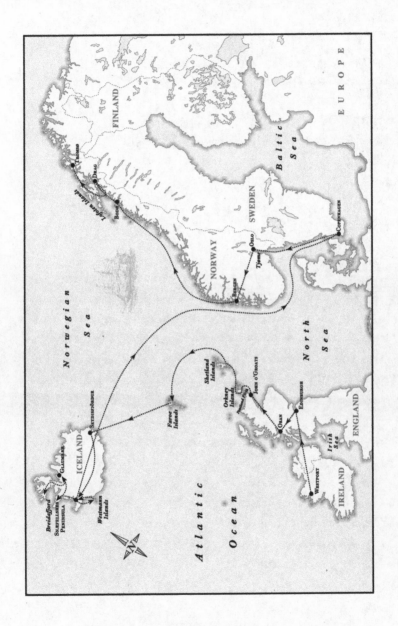

The author's journey

INTRODUCTION

CROSSING CLEW BAY

ONE AFTERNOON in May I found myself in the stern of the *Very Likely*, a motor launch ferrying me and four other passengers across Clew Bay on the west coast of Ireland. We were bound for Clare Island, where the sea captain, clan chieftain, and pirate Grace O'Malley had lived in the sixteenth century. Born in 1530, Grace grew up to become a rover, a raider, and such a scourge to the English that her name appears regularly in Elizabethan state papers. "This was a notorious woman in all the costes of Ireland," wrote Sir Henry Sidney in 1583. Another English governor, Lord Justice Drury, called her "a woman that hath impudently passed the part of womanhood and been a great spoiler and chief commander and director of thieves and murderers at sea." Queen Elizabeth put a price of five hundred pounds on her head.

The inner reaches of Clew Bay are riddled with hidden reefs and rocks, dotted with hummocks and holms, those small islands that are sometimes exposed and sometimes submerged. Its currents are fierce; any invading force would think twice about trying to navigate it. Grace O'Malley knew it like the back of her hand. She grew up on its shores and for years made Clare Island, just outside the entrance to Clew Bay, her stronghold and base for raiding the coast.

Her pirate galleys and the English ships that pursued them

are long gone, but ferries and launches make the crossing several times a day from Roonagh Pier, on the mainland. I'd just arrived in Ireland from Seattle, and was now on the first of what would be many voyages around the North Atlantic in search of the stories, lost, forgotten or otherwise misplaced, of seafaring women like Grace. It was a brisk, sunny day, and the midday light winked up from the choppy waves like tiny mirrors on an Indian bedspread patterned in aqua and dark green.

An elderly, tweed-capped gentleman called Paddy leaned over the railing of the *Very Likely*. The seagulls keened in swoops above, the whitened green water boiled under us, and Paddy clung in misery to my arm. From the small cabin forward his wife called anxiously, "Paddy, if you feel the urge, remember to hold on to your teeth, will you now?"

He nodded weakly in her direction and confided to me, "I'm not a good sailor. Are you?"

"Yes, except for the very worst weather." The short voyage of the *Very Likely* across the island-flung channel was a heart-leaping, wave-skidding pleasure to me.

"You're a seafaring woman then?" Paddy asked.

Aye, matey! I wanted to say, though kayaking around Lake Union in Seattle and off the rocky coastlines of the Pacific Northwest wasn't exactly like commanding a pirate galley in the North Atlantic. But I'd always loved the ocean, whether I was in it or on it. I'd grown up in Southern California swimming in the ocean, and though I never had a boat, I did have a surf-board. More importantly, I'd always dreamed of ships and the sea. Long Beach was a port city, filled with sailors, tattoo parlors, and blood banks. Our next-door neighbor was a long-shoreman; school field trips were to the harbor to watch the cargo being hoisted on and off the ships. Growing up, I liked to read about cabin boys on clipper ships and was much taken by the adventures of Pippi Longstocking, whose father had been a sea captain before he became a cannibal king, and who dreamed of becoming a pirate herself.

I'd first become interested in Grace O'Malley the year before, while on a writer's residency in another sea-smashed landscape, Cape Cornwall in England. Passing through London, I'd picked up a book on women pirates. *Bold in Her Breeches*, edited by British writer Jo Stanley, had a whole chapter on Grace, and it was this pirate who most captured my imagination, for everything she was, and everything she wasn't. Commanding vessels at sea and a fighting force of two hundred men, engaging in piracy and swordplay, looting, destroying, murdering—the captain of a pirate ship must be, hands down, the most transgressive role to which a woman could ever aspire. Dirty, greedy, sensual, tough, and charismatic; a gambler, a wife, and a mother; a leader of men, a politician when necessary, Grace comes down to us as that rare woman who claimed freedom as her birthright. For to go to sea is to feel that ordinary boundaries cannot hold you; to be a pirate is to assert that whatever you fancy belongs to you. The boldness of Grace's adventurous life long past youth was something that appealed to me particularly; she had, after all, remained a pirate into her seventies.

Grace O'Malley was only one among many pirates in *Bold in Her Breeches*. Jo Stanley had collected material on women as disparate as Alfhild, a Viking princess who commanded a fleet of longships for battle and piracy, the Chinese pirate Cheng I Sao, and Mary Read and Anne Bonny, who plied the trade in the Caribbean in the 1700s. It was Grace O'Malley who interested me most, however, and not just because she was a pirate, but because she was, from all accounts, a great seafarer, and stories of women and the sea were sparse. After reading Anne Chambers's biography, *Granuaile: The Life and Times of Grace O'Malley*, I began searching for other stories of seafaring women from the past and was disappointed, though perhaps not surprised, to find so few.

The scraps I discovered here and there often seemed to be more mythic than historic. Creation stories told of Tiamat, the Babylonian goddess of salt water, whose waters commingled with the fresh waters of her consort, Apsu, to engender all the gods. Norse myths sang of Ran, the sea god's wife, who captured the drowned and carried them to her watery kingdom. Legends from many northern European countries described underwater creatures—mermaids, seal people, Finfolk—while more recent folklore mentioned "sellers of the wind" and sea witches, who had the power to create storms and calms. The more I poked around in the library, at used bookstores, and on the Web, trying to satisfy this new, consuming interest, the more curious I became. When mythology told us there once had been sea goddesses who ruled the watery depths, why did it seem that women had so rarely rowed and sailed the ocean's surface? Or, if they had, what had happened to those histories?

Like most people I'd been raised to believe that women never went to sea, and a glance at some of the best-known anthologies of sea literature bore this out. Their names simply weren't there. Yet, with just a bit of research, I found references to women who passed at sea as sailors and marines, to fishers and fishwives, to ship owners, stewardesses, and navigators, to wives and daughters who sailed with their families on whalers and merchant ships. Why didn't their intriguing stories figure more prominently in maritime history and literature?

I kept looking and found tantalizing fragments in histories, sagas, and old travelogues, fragments that only whetted my appetite. Many of them seemed to come from the European North Atlantic, from Ireland, the British Isles, and Scandinavia. With source materials so hard to obtain from the other side of the world, I decided that to really get a picture of women's maritime lives in history and myth, it would be far easier to travel there myself than to keep requesting interlibrary loans. I wanted to see those same coastlines I was reading about, to sail those same seas.

I decided that my pilgrimage would take me, as often by sea as I could manage, from Ireland to Scotland, to Orkney, to the Shetlands, to the Faroes, to Iceland, and finally to Norway. Although many other parts of the world—Africa, Brazil, the Mediterranean countries, and Polynesia—claim sea goddesses, and although women have fished, rowed, swum, and sailed off every inhabited coastline on the planet, I knew that the North Atlantic has an ancient tradition of myth and folklore about the sea, as well as a long, recorded seafaring history. I suspected I was most likely to find written material in the local libraries and bookshops of the British Isles and Scandinavia. Other northern countries—France, Germany, the Netherlands—all with rich mythic and maritime cultures, seemed beyond my ken, language-wise. On the other hand, I read and spoke Norwegian from many visits to that country. I was particularly interested in stories from Norse myths and sagas, as well as the sea-going culture of coastal Norway. It had often struck me in my reading of maritime literature how infrequently Scandinavia was mentioned. Yet the Vikings were some of the greatest sailors in world history, and in times past the Norse influence was strong all through the region I proposed to travel.

The northern waters were my heritage, too. With a grand-father born in Ireland and a grandmother from Sweden, I some-times wondered if I carried an inborn love of cold gray waves and blustery winds. I might have grown up under sunny skies, along white sand beaches in Southern California, but there was nothing I liked more than a rocky coast and a howling gale, and I'd settled in the Pacific Northwest as a young woman in part because it had a salt-wet climate and a maritime history.

I'd once been to sea in the North Atlantic. The summer I was twenty-two I worked as a dishwasher on the *Kong Olav*, one of the Norwegian coastal steamers that plied the long and tor-tuous fjord country from Bergen around the North Cape to the Russian border. Every third trip we crossed the Norwegian Sea to Svalbard. Although I'd been far from keen on dishwashing, I'd loved the ship itself, and everything about being at sea. I'd always wanted to take the trip again—as a passenger. I was looking forward to that voyage, at the end of my journey, in late August. Now, however, it was mid-May, and I had leagues and centuries to travel first.

I'd wanted to begin the trip in Ireland because of Grace O'Malley. She was one of the very few seafaring women to be remembered so heroically in ballad and story. She had castles as her monuments and a growing contemporary interest in her life not only as a pirate, but as a powerful female leader in a frac-turing society. Whatever I might find as the weeks went on, Grace would be my touchstone: the one maritime woman who really was remembered, in folklore and song, if not always in the history books.

Grace O'Malley even had a small museum now—the only one in the world dedicated to a seafaring woman. I'd been there this morning, before embarking on the *Very Likely*. Dim, mysterious,

**Grace O'Malley at the
Granuaile Heritage Centre**

and cold, the Granuaile Heritage Centre in Louisburgh smelled of cleaning fluids and old carpet. A life-size figure of Grace O'Malley met me at the entrance to the exhibition room. She wore a long auburn wig, like a transvestite, and had a saber in a leather belt slung around her waist. Her arms, in a white shirt with vast sleeves, were arranged awkwardly, as if she were dancing the Swim. Perhaps, over the winter, her posture had slipped. One hand, I was sure, was meant to be shading her brow as she looked into the distance for doubloon-laden galleys to plunder.

The museum wasn't yet open for the summer season, but I'd arranged with caretaker Mary O'Malley (a common last name in these parts) to let me in for a look around. Fortyish, quick stepping, with her cardigan held close around her neck, Mary was apologetic about the state of the museum, which had been closed up since the previous September. The building, a former Anglican church, was unheated and mildewy. The electricity was dodgy. The spotlights on the exhibits kept shorting out. Boxes of post cards and books had yet to be put on shelves. "We need to Hoover! We need to wash windows!" They had so much to do before next week! She explained it all in a hopeless but jolly rush. They were all volunteers here, and very proud of the place.

"You'll show yourself around?" she asked. "I've a few things to do at home and then I'll be back." She sidestepped a pair of tourists who were hammering at the door, "We're closed, my dears. Come back in June," and drove off.

I hadn't expected to be left to myself here. I walked past erratically lit maps of sixteenth-century Ireland and found myself in front of a model of a typical castle of the time, four stories high, with ramparts and a wall walk. Storage was on the lower floors, and quarters for the chieftain's family on the upper. Green branches, animal skins, and antlers decorated the whitewashed walls; bits of hay and rushes were strewn about the flagged floor. Along with fireplaces on each level, narrow, recessed windows opened in the thick stone walls. On the ground floor someone had placed a few model sheep and pigs. More sheep and cows ruminated outside, in between the beehive-shaped huts of the clan's followers and local peasants. These tiny, barefoot figures with disheveled hair milled around in worsted trousers and overshirts.

This was Ireland in the early sixteenth century, a tribal society that had hardly changed for centuries. Unlike the rest of Europe, where the humanistic ideals of the Renaissance were flourishing and nations were on the rise, Ireland was fragmented into warring fiefdoms, each controlled by a clan. Raiding and cattle stealing were the norm. There was no central government, no head of state who could have gathered the loyalties of the chieftains and parleyed with other European rulers. In the Europe that was shaping itself, this decentralized, tribal society had no chance. The world Grace O'Malley was born into would be almost gone by the end of her lifetime. Paradoxically, it was the very disorder of the sixteenth century that allowed Grace to assume a powerful role that few women in history have matched. As the clan system disintegrated under the increasing colonial control of Henry VIII's and Elizabeth's governors, space opened up for an enterprising and wily woman who could play both sides, and keep her own counsel.

O'Malley coat of arms

When Grace was born, the O'Malleys, whose motto was *terra marique potens*, "powerful by land and sea," were still wealthy and strong, a law unto themselves. They controlled Clew Bay and the region around it, and had for centuries. Unlike many of the other Gaelic clans, the O'Malleys made a living from the ocean; they fished, traded, and licensed fishing rights in their waters. They hired their crew out as sailors and ferried Scottish mercenaries, the fabled gallowglass, to fight in clan battles. They also raided the coastlines of Western Ireland, including the international port of Galway Town, and robbed merchant ships of their cargoes of silks and spices, damask and wine.

They are the lions of the green sea
men acquainted with the land of Spain
when seizing cattle from Cantyre
a mile by sea is a short distance to the O'Malleys.

GRACE'S FATHER, Dubhdara, or "Black Oak," was chieftain of the O'Malleys, and by all accounts he raised Grace, if not to carry on the family line—for she would have to marry—then to be an experienced seafarer with an eye for the main chance when it came to trading and raiding. Her mother, Margaret, had lands of her own, which Grace eventually inherited. Once there had been warrior queens in Ireland, like Queen Maeve of Connaught, and descent was through the female line, but with Ireland's conversion to Christianity in the fifth century, Roman law had gradually influenced traditional Gaelic, or Brehon, law, and that had meant a downgrading of women's status. Still, even in the sixteenth century, women in Ireland had more rights than women in England. They could keep their family name and hold and administer property, for instance. Even though we know little of Grace's mother, we know that Margaret had the right to pass on land and property to her daughter.

Grace wasn't an only child, but her biographer Anne Chambers has suggested that her brother, Dónal, may have been illegitimate, or at least not the son of Margaret. Importantly for Grace, he seems not to have been inclined to the seafaring life. If he had been, it's more likely he would have carried on the family's tradition of trade and piracy, and no one would have thought anything of it. But just as Grace's birth in the sixteenth century made an opening for her in Ireland's shifting power structure, so did being her parents' sole offspring. The girl with a weather eye and an aptitude for life at sea was early given the chance to show what she was made of.

The Granuaile Heritage Centre cheerfully mingled fact and legend in its telling of Grace's story, and indeed, it couldn't be any other way. The English had been most assiduous about recording Grace's pirating and raiding; letters and documents attest to their interest in her, a mixture of respect and frustration. On the contrary, in the comprehensive Irish history, the *Annals of the Four Masters*, Grace's two husbands are mentioned, as are her sons, while her name is not recorded. Until Anne Chambers began looking through English state papers and other old manuscripts and forgotten records, stories about Grace had mainly survived in ballads and local folklore—and a few enjoyable, but not necessarily accurate, historical novels.

I circled around the exhibit hall to the entrance again, where Grace, in her long wig and doublet and hose, stood watch. I took out my almost blank journal, the notebook I hoped to fill with stories of northern maritime women by the end of a few months, and wrote some notes and made some sketches. Dissatisfied with her drooping posture, I took Grace's left arm in mine and joggled it back up above her shoulders, so that her hand was firmly above her eyes. Now she looked a proper sea captain again, bold and farseeing. In this pose she was a good subject for a picture. *Grace O'Malley Looking Out to Sea*, I scribbled in my journal underneath the sketch.

ON THE *Very Likely*, Paddy and I found ourselves awash in spray as we approached Clare Island. Paddy was utterly miserable, bent over the railing, while I was, in spite of my jet lag, terribly exuberant. I made out a stone tower in the mist. "Look, there's the castle!" I said to Paddy, to distract him. "Grace O'Malley's castle! Still standing after all these centuries."

"D'you still have your teeth, Paddy?" his wife shouted, hearing my excitement and seeing me point.

"Grace O'Malley's castle!" I shouted back.

The castle on Clare Island now hove firmly in sight, a smallish, squared stone fortress on a slight hill overlooking the bay. The *Very Likely* entered the harbor and tied up at the dock. Paddy's wife and I each took hold of an arm and helped him up the ladder. He had a decidedly pale and dejected expression and his bandy legs shook. I knew that they were only on Clare Island for the day. They planned to take the six o'clock launch back to the mainland. Paddy confided that he was dreading the return.

"What about you, dear?" asked his wife, as I shouldered my pack and began walking away in the direction of land. "Just a short trip? Or a long one?"

"A few months," I said, suddenly overwhelmed to find myself in Ireland, actually on Clare Island, instead of in Seattle, paddling past houseboats on Lake Union and simply reading books about women and the sea. The moment that stuns us in life is the moment when dreams become reality.

But as I stood looking down the tar- and seaweed-scented wharf, and felt the unaccustomed weight of my possessions on my shoulders, my courage returned. These were the times, these days of new beginnings in foreign places, when I'd always felt most awake and alive. I took a deep breath and started down the dock.

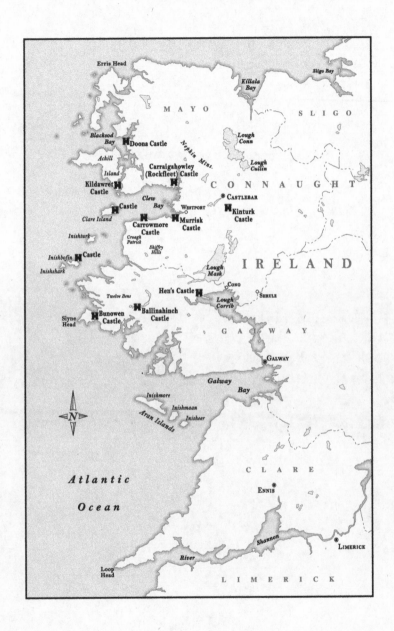

Grace O'Malley's Connaught

CHAPTER I

GRACE O'MALLEY'S CASTLE

Clare Island, Ireland

My home on Clare for two nights was a converted lighthouse
at the western edge of the island. One of the Belgian owners,
Monica Timmerman, her shrewd face topped by an angelic frizz
of blond curls, was waiting at the curve of the harbor with a
large and muddy dog in tow, to drive me in her Land Rover
three miles across the island up to the lighthouse. The afternoon sun blazed as Monica walked me across a neatly pebbled
courtyard to my room. I was the only guest, though two others
would turn up later, in time for dinner. Even Monica's husband
wasn't around. He was in Brussels being interviewed for a television program called "Far-Flung Belgians." The lighthouse
and its outbuildings reminded me of a convent—in the
Caribbean. The thick curved walls dazzled with whitewash, the
doors were bright reds and blues, and inside my room aqua,
orange, and crimson made a tropical splash. When I walked a
few steps outside my door to the wall at the edge of the cliff, I
looked out into the fierce immensity of the Atlantic.

Grace was born on the mainland, probably at Belclare
Castle, the seat of the O'Malley clan, but she would have spent
many summers out here on the island. The fishing was good,
and the moorage closer to the sea lanes; it was the custom to
graze animals on Clare and the other islands of the bay in
warmer months. Some of the legends that relate to Grace's

3

youth take place on Clare, including one where a determined young girl climbed up these cliffs to kill the eagles that had been carrying off O'Malley lambs from the valleys. She was small, the eagles were large and angry; their talons gashed her forehead, leaving scars. There are no pictures of Grace, so novelists have felt free to describe her as a fiery redhead, or "tiny and dark." With a father called Black Oak, I imagine her as raven-haired and firmly planted on her feet.

In the Granuaile Heritage Centre yesterday I'd seen a painting of a young girl hacking at her long hair. One story has it that when Grace's father told her she could no longer sail with him because she was a girl, she immediately chopped off her hair. Some say that her Irish name, Granuaile, came from the nickname Gráinne Ui Mhaol, or "Bald Gráinne," the word *maol* meaning bald and the reference being to her shorn locks as a child. More likely is it that Granuaile was related to the Gaelic Gráinne Umhall (the Umhalls were the territory over which her father ruled). Over the years the English used many variant spellings of her name in their letters and papers: Grany Imallye, Grany Ne Maly, Grainy O'Maly, and, finally, Grace O'Malley.[1]

I stood looking out into the Atlantic, and the wind blew my own hair back in a banner. Seagulls and terns shot up and down the cliffs like tiny living elevators. It's said the O'Malleys had the gift of weather prophecy, and that it was Grace, not her brother, who inherited the ability to recognize a shift in wind, a scent of thunder. How many of these childhood stories can we

---

1 I have held to the conventional nomenclature for Grace because, although she would not have called herself Grace O'Malley, we are not completely sure what she did call herself. Her nickname Granuaile, widely used in the Clew Bay region, is not well known outside Ireland. Anne Chambers, her biographer, calls her both Granuaile and Grace O'Malley. Other writers have referred to her as Grania, a contemporary Irish spelling of Gráinne.

trust? Perhaps the important thing is that the legends of Grace were told and retold; she flourished in folklore as a wild and resourceful young girl during centuries in which women lived cramped, restricted lives. One story tells of how she climbed up into the rigging of her father's ship when the O'Malleys were fleeing Algerian corsairs; pulling down her trousers, Grace wickedly mooned the infidel pirates. On another occasion, it's said, when the family galley was boarded by sailors from an English man-o'-war, Grace jumped, cursing and shrieking, from the yards on to the back of a knife-wielding sailor, in order to alert her father and save his life. It's with bravery like this that a girl can endear herself to a crew. However Grace managed it, she learned the sailor's craft early on, and never let it go.

Like the adventurous childhoods of many headstrong, free-spirited girls, Grace's ended, at least temporarily, in marriage. In 1546, when she was sixteen, she was married to Dónal O'Flaherty, the son of a chieftain. Although the O'Flahertys were more warlike than the O'Malleys, the two clans had more often been allies than opponents, and this marriage was meant to solidify the link. Grace left Clew Bay and moved south to Connemara, to Bunowen Castle. She had three children with Dónal, two sons, Owen and Murrough, and a daughter, Margaret.

If Grace had had a different husband, her story might perhaps have ended there. With reluctance she might have accepted her role as the wife of a powerful man, in line to become a chieftain. She might have spent her days organizing the castle's household, entertaining guests, and rearing children. The O'Flahertys had some ships, but they were not a great seafaring clan like the O'Malleys; their wealth, as was typical, came from land and cattle. As an O'Flaherty wife and mother, Grace might never have put to sea again.

But Dónal of the Battles, as her husband was called, had a
fierce temper and reckless ways that led him into trouble. He
was more interested, apparently, in feuding with the neighboring Joyces than in providing leadership and income. As the
years passed, Grace grew to assume authority not only over the
household, but over the O'Flaherty fighting men. It's after her
marriage that historical sources begin to mention her raids on
ships bound for Galway. She cornered them, demanding either
tribute or part of the cargo in return for allowing them further
passage. Dónal, on the other hand, was eventually murdered by
the Joyces, who'd nicknamed him "the Cock," for his high-
handed, posturing ways. "Cock's Castle" they came to call the
island fortress on Lough Corrib that had once been a Joyce
stronghold and that Dónal had taken away from them. After his
death, they came to reclaim it, but found Grace O'Malley
installed. She defended it so vigorously it was rechristened
"Hen's Castle." It's still called that today.

Grace defended it again from English soldiers who came to
force her surrender. After days of siege she had her followers
strip the lead off the castle's roof and melt it down, the better to
pour over her enemies' heads. Then, when the English retreated
off the island, she sent one of her men for reinforcements. Hen's
Castle remained hers, at least for a time.

For although many of the traditional Brehon laws gave
Gaelic women a more equal role than their counterparts in the
rest of Europe—and Grace had been able to keep her maiden
name and her right to O'Malley lands—Grace could not legally
inherit the O'Flaherty title or lands after Dónal's murder. With
no other means of support, Grace retreated home to Clare
Island to, in effect, create her own independent chieftaincy. It's
a measure of her charismatic leadership that a number of

disaffected O'Flaherty men chose to follow her, assuming that her skill at sea would translate into wealth and security for them. When her father died, the ships that had belonged to the O'Malleys came to her. She began to assemble a force of two hundred seafaring and fighting men, drawn from many of the clans of Western Ireland. Along with trading and the licensing of fishing rights, piracy grew more important to her, and with it, control of the passage into Clew Bay.

Piracy, which is essentially robbery, only romanticized because it involves ships at sea, has taken many forms over the centuries. In sixteenth-century England it was to some degree state sanctioned, as Elizabeth I sought to divert the gold and silver flowing from the New World to Spain away from King Philip's coffers and into her own. Sir Francis Drake and others were semi-officially hired by the crown as privateers to attack Spanish galleons. This century also saw the rise of the pirates of the Barbary Coast, who, after terrorizing Mediterranean waters, had begun to venture into the North Atlantic. Often called Turks, they were in reality mostly Algerians living under the rule of the Ottoman Empire, which stretched from Hungary to the Middle East and North Africa and whose capitol was Istanbul. During Grace's lifetime, and especially in the seventeenth century, Algiers became a great slave market, where European captives who'd been abducted from coastal villages and ships were taken to be sold or ransomed. The piracy of the Algerian corsairs was thus doubly threatening—your money *and* your life—and Grace herself had to steer clear of their ships.

Her own form of piracy seems almost benign, though her victims, mainly the merchants who owned the French, Portuguese, and Spanish caravels and galleons that had a long history of trade with Galway Town, were none too happy when they saw her ships on the horizon. Sometimes she only charged a percentage of their cargo as a tax for allowing them to pass; sometimes she took the whole cargo—and the ship to boot.

Outside my room at the lighthouse, I leaned forward into the freshening wind (the time when I'd be heartily sick of constant Atlantic blows was still before me). The captain of a ship passing off this rocky coast would hardly guess that on the other side of the island lay a pirates' lair, the harbor sheltering Grace O'Malley's growing collection of vessels: the wooden, clinker-built Gaelic galleys, with thirty oars, a single mast, and a lateen sail, whose shallow draughts, like those of the Viking longships, helped with maneuvering around Clew Bay's reefs and shoals. Stolen Mediterranean caravels and "baggage boats," the yawls and longboats that carried fish, cattle, goods, and the spoils of plunder, lay there as well. Those sailing offshore would never imagine that a widow and mother of three had put aside domestic duties for a second chance to relive her childhood dreams of seafaring and swashbuckling.

DINNER THAT night was in the elegant dining room of the lighthouse. Monica's restrained service hinted that endive salad with goat cheese and spring lamb with new potatoes were a bit wasted on three Americans, two of whom were wearing T-shirts that said "Make Mine a Guinness!"

He was from Fresno; she was originally from Tennessee. He worked for the Bureau of Alcohol, Tobacco and Firearms and had the look of someone used to smashing down doors. She had a cowed expression (I imagined) and kept on about how beautiful Ireland was, and how friendly everyone was, and how green it was, while Mr. Fresno interrogated me: What was I doing here? How long was I planning to be gone? What did I do in America?

At first I was vague about my trip, and what I was looking for, but finally I broke down, only to recall how dreams are diminished when shared with the wrong people. I was traveling for a few months, just on my own, to collect material about women and the sea. I was a writer, in Seattle, and hoped to eventually tell some of the stories.

"What's that going to prove?" asked Mr. Fresno, his eyes skeptical, his jaw hard, while Ms. Tennessee cut her lamb into dainty pieces. She was faded underneath her makeup, an over-the-hill country singer perhaps, in her forties, wearing cowboy boots and silver hoop earrings, a ring on every finger.

"It's not to prove anything," I said mildly. "It's just an interest." A consuming interest, I could have added, one to have made me come all the way here.

"But you want to make a point, right?" He had the straggly hair and stubble of a man on vacation, but the bloodhound perseverance of a working detective. "Like, that a few women were sailors or something?"

"Well, there was Grace O'Malley," said Ms. Tennessee. Her long dark hair fell in her face, and she didn't look at him as she spoke. "You know, that pirate lady they talk about. I bet that's why you came to Clare Island, isn't it?" She smiled at me, with an encouraging nod. "To learn more about that pirate lady, Grace O'Malley?"

He ignored her. "What's your methodology?" he asked.

"My methodology?" I said.

"You know, your *plan*. Are you doing interviews and tabulating results?"

Now he sounded like a dissertation committee member. In

fact, my methodology was somewhat random. I had some leads, some hunches, and boundless curiosity. Where was the fun in knowing what I would find before I set off? Did I dare mention *fun*? Or passion for the subject? I wasn't so naive as to expect to discover that women had actually been the majority of seafarers. I'd be happy if I found a few more than Grace O'Malley. In fact, I was happy with what I'd been finding out about Grace O'Malley in the last two days. Who was Mr. Fresno to disparage her? She'd skewer him with her cutlass. Fortunately Monica came in with apple tart and coffee. The conversation shifted, to lighthouses, and Monica, warming, told us the story of the renovation. I left my companions leafing through a book of photographs that showed the progress of turning the decommissioned lighthouse into an inn.

Still, after dinner as I went to my room, and laid out my journal and books, I wondered at my hesitancy. Why hadn't I made larger claims for women's connection with the sea? I was still uncertain, I supposed, what that might mean. Had we only stood on shore, waving goodbye? How many female captains, sailors, fishers could there have been? How many myths would it take to make a satisfying statistic? Instead of looking through my notes, as I'd meant to, and describing what I'd seen today, I opened the red door of my room, and went out to the thick, whitewashed wall at the cliff's edge. The sun was setting, familiarly, in the west. Even though I'd grown up on the Pacific, not the Atlantic, my travels over the years in maritime Europe had always pointed me in the direction of my childhood ocean view. The clouds had a stronger whiff of rain now, blood orange and carmine against the flame-blue sky.

It was easy for me to imagine young Grace scanning the same horizon I had when young, for, though she looked toward what would become Canada and I toward Japan, neither country was visible; there were only waves and more waves.

The ocean off Long Beach, California, was already much tamed when I came along midcentury. There was a breakwater and a port; the shoreline had been reshaped in places and over the years much more of that would happen, as the city struggled to overcome its tawdry amusement park image and attract back those who'd fled to the suburbs. Nevertheless, to me the ocean was a vast wilderness of water, especially compared with Alamitos Bay, where I often spent summer days when I was small. The bay was the baby beach, separated from the ocean by a thin peninsula of sand, a road with houses on either side. That strip of dividing land was like a curved arm, and in the warmth of that embrace my younger brother and I spent long days splashing in the shallow waters of the bay or making sandcastles on the shore. My mother and her two good friends, Vina and Eleanor, sat under an umbrella, gossiping and keeping an eye on all us children through harlequin-tipped sunglasses.

The mothers didn't like to go to the real beach across the road. It was windier, for one thing, and a long, hot trek down to the water's edge. The waves, though subdued by the breakwater, were tall to a child. But once I reached a certain age, six perhaps, I begged relentlessly to go to the real beach, at least part of the day. I relished the cold slap of the Pacific in my face, loved to feel lifted off my feet and carried into shore by the waves. I even loved—though this was frightening too—to be dragged back into the sea by a powerful force, the most powerful natural force I'd ever known.

The ocean was huge and even as a child I loved that hugeness and didn't fear it. The salt water was less a bridge than a world between worlds. If you were a fish, you could swim to

Japan. If you were a mermaid, it would be your home. But all this, my mother, raised in the Midwest, swimming and canoeing the Michigan lakes, didn't understand. The ocean for her was a closed door, the end of the road. She stood on the shore, up to her ankles, complaining that the water was freezing and she just couldn't understand how the Pacific could be so cold when it was *ninety-five* degrees in the shade, for goodness sake. She splashed her arms and legs, but not her face or hair, and returned to towel and book, with the firm injunction to me to watch my little brother, and for neither of us to go in too deep or too far.

But deep and far was just where I'd longed to go.

The NEXT morning the Americans were already gone. After breakfast I set off for a walking tour of the island. It was wet but not raining; rills and streams trickled through lumpy fields. Before the Great Famine two thousand people had lived on Clare, and these had been their potato fields. The hills and trenches were grown over now, and turf had spread over the fields, making the landscape resemble a series of rusty-green bundles placed in rows. Bright marsh marigolds were abundant, and wild yellow iris shot up from boggy rivulets. A pair of peregrine falcons soared overhead. Near the few houses along the road bloomed raspberry lipsticks of fuchsias, white-pink rhododendrons, and purple foxgloves. Clare Island had 150 inhabitants now. During the era when the O'Malleys and their retainers summered here, the land must have teemed with cows, for the Irish clans counted wealth in castles and cattle, and in her heyday Grace owned a thousand head.

After a few hours I arrived down at the harbor and the

Clare Castle

castle. The square little fortress had looked better from the sea. Some sheep grazed outside on the grassy headland. Inside, the ground floor was dark and rubbishy with beer cans littering the dirt floor. Irish castles were originally the idea of the Norman invaders in the twelfth century; the warring Gaels continued the tradition of military strongholds in which the tower kept enemies out. These castles were the essence of romance: four or five stories high, rounded or square, with slit windows from which to shoot arrows. Some had turrets and crenellations. Family life took place upstairs, where the thick walls were kept whitewashed and hung with skins and furs to keep out the cold.

But this castle had a sour, fusty smell, the mortared walls pee-stained and scarred with initials. The stone stairs that led to the rooms above had broken off at head level; a ladder lay in several pieces below. Even with the diorama from the Granuaile

Heritage Centre in my mind's eye, it was hard to imagine the castle and outbuildings full of life, as the O'Malley clan entertained friends, relatives, and wandering bards and feasted on mead, buttermilk, oatmeal, mutton, game, and wild garlic. I tried to picture young Grace running through the yard, into the castle, shouting that there were ships entering Clew Bay, and could she sail out with her father and his men and attack them? I tried to imagine her living upstairs as a newly widowed sea captain, plotting her future at a window that overlooked the harbor. But—perhaps it was the smell—I couldn't. The castle seemed less sinister than neglected, hardly a fitting memorial to Clare Island's most famous past inhabitant.

Castles often look more romantic from a distance, just as meals of oatmeal and buttermilk or mead and mutton were perhaps tastier described than eaten. But thinking of the stout meals of the O'Malleys, I grew hungry.

In the bar of the Bay View Hotel, on the other side of the harbor from the castle, I ordered a cheese sandwich and a pot of tea. An elderly couple sat down next to me and we struck up a conversation. They were curious about the converted lighthouse. "The rumor is that they only advertise in Continental papers," the man told me with a twinkle. "They don't want the Irish." Liam was from Belfast, his female companion, Pat, some years older, from Dublin. I'd run into them the afternoon before, when I first arrived on Clare, up by the lighthouse. They'd been scampering around the hillside. Pat was an amateur botanist; they were birders, too. "Though on this trip we call ourselves the Naked Ornithologists," Liam said. "We don't have our binoculars."

"I'm at the beginning of a long trip," I said, when Liam asked, and I told them about the voyages I planned to make over the next few months.

"And why Clare Island? Why Clew Bay?"

"I suppose a journey needs to start at the right place, and Grace O'Malley is probably the greatest woman seafarer ever."

Oh, but they knew all about the Pirate Queen. Liam quoted:

She unfurled her country's banner
High o'er battlement and mast
And 'gainst all the might of England
Kept it flying 'til the last.

"They were singing that song in the rebellions against the English in the late eighteenth century," he said. "That's almost two hundred years after Granuaile's death."

"Of course," said Pat, "Granuaile wasn't exactly an Irish heroine, but they made her so."

"Well, she stood up to Queen Elizabeth," Liam reminded her.

"Yes, but eventually she accepted English rule. She *did*, Liam," Pat said fondly. "You know yourself that her descendants are still aristocrats. There's a lord right across Clew Bay there, owns Westport House. You don't get a peerage by standing up to the English!"

"There wasn't really an Irish state then," Liam explained to me. "It was her clan that she cared about. She made sure she and her family did all right. And Granuaile—it was only later she became a kind of symbol like, to the Irish rebelling against the English."

"*Now* we think it's grand she was a pirate," mused Pat. "Pirate Queen this, and Pirate Queen that, but have you ever thought exactly what a pirate does? She was a thieving, murdering old woman now, wasn't she?"

"Ah, woman, will you take the romance out of everything?"

"Let's have a glass to her anyway, the old girl," said Pat.

The bar was a festive place, even on a weekday afternoon. The three of us had a pint, and joked, and told stories for quite a while and then went outside and took photographs of each other, before I started the three-mile hike back up to the lighthouse. I was sorry to leave them and the easygoing friendliness of the Bay View. The rooms were half the price of the lighthouse and the atmosphere more convivial. Tonight I'd dine in solitary splendor at the huge oak dining table on rich Belgian food. All the same, as I crested the last hill and saw the thick, whitewashed walls of the lighthouse, I found myself walking more quickly.

Soon I stood at the cliff wall outside the red-painted door to my room. From here I had a sweeping view of Achill Island to the north. It was off Achill Head that Grace saw a ship foundering one gale-riven day. She and her crew immediately set off from Clare, not to rescue the survivors, but to claim the salvage. Among the wreckage on the rocks, she found washed up a handsome young man. His name was Hugh de Lacy, the son of a wealthy merchant from the other side of Ireland. Grace brought him back with her to Clare and the two of them reputedly fell in love. Not long afterward Hugh was murdered by members of the clan MacMahon. Grace took her revenge by killing those responsible for Hugh's death, and eventually she captured the MacMahon's castle as well.

Standing in the stiff breeze at the edge of the high cliffs of Clare, I squinted my eyes and imagined I saw a galley off the coast, sailing close to the wind. A woman with rough-cut hair and a scarred forehead stood at the helm, a spyglass raised to her eye, a knife ready to hand. She was looking for trouble.

Oaths spewed from her mouth and all the men rushed to do her bidding. The waves beat high against the bow, and the wind took them south to Galway Town and past. If they saw an English man-o'-war, they would run before the wind. If they found a Spanish caravel low in the water with a cargo of silks and spices, they would board her and take whatever they pleased.

A pirate in the prime of life! Not only did Grace O'Malley awaken memories of my bold and energetic childhood, a time before my mother became ill, when I dashed through the waves imagining myself a sea creature who could breathe underwater, or when I ran through our neighborhood with a pack of boys and could climb trees, roller-skate, and play softball all summer long; Grace O'Malley offered a possible picture of the future. Why stop being a vigorous adventurer at any stage in life? I'd be fifty in October. Two years ago I'd gone on an Outward Bound trip in the desert that had just about killed me, but that had convinced me that, with encouragement, even a cowardly middle-aged woman could learn to rock climb, rappel off hundred-foot cliffs, and sleep by herself in the wilderness.

> And no warlike chief or viking
> E'er had bolder heart than she.

This was nothing anybody was ever likely to say about me, but I repeated the words from an old ballad about Grace, and drew strength from them as I walked away from the cliff and back to my cozy room. Heroines make us braver, for whatever we have to do.

◎   ◎   ◎

I FELL asleep that night reading in bed and hearing the crash of waves below. The next morning it was pouring and Monica offered me a lift back to Westport, where she had shopping to do. We boarded the larger passenger ferry, *The Pirate Queen* painted on her bow. The late spring rain lashed the island-strewn bay, and the holms and hummocks were invisible in the mist.

On the way past Louisburgh, Monica complained about the Irish. "You come to Ireland because it's freer than Belgium, and because you love the people. But of course the Irish are . . . the Irish. They really are hopeless, you know. Lazy and all that. They take money from the EU; they set up these heritage centres everywhere. But they don't keep them running. They're not interested. It's just a strategy to get free money."

I didn't agree. The Granuaile Heritage Centre, despite its faulty electricity and mildewed cold, was obviously a great labor of love. The Clew Bay Heritage Centre, on the quay at Westport, was even less a candidate for an EU scam. I'd visited it two days ago. It was one of those jumbly little museums of local history whose treasures included the cradle of Lord Haw Haw, a sash once belonging to Yeats's great love, Maud Gonne, some eighteenth-century coins, Neolithic quernstones, memorabilia from the Easter Uprising, skates taken from the body of a local boy who drowned in a pond, and many photographs of Princess Grace of Monaco, who had once climbed Croagh Patrick. She got to the First Station, anyway.

"Don't get me wrong, they're lovely people . . ." Monica said. "But they don't take pride in their heritage. They make a big noise about this Grace O'Malley, but have you been inside that castle on Clare? There are always beer cans and trash. My husband goes in there sometimes and cleans it up. Does it shame them? No."

"I'm Irish myself," I said, to dissuade her from going on in this vein. "One of the far-flung Irish. A grandfather of mine was born in County Cork."

"Wilson, that's not an Irish name."

"I'm Irish on my mother's side." But in fact none of my family names, the Lane of my Irish relatives, the Swanson of my Swedish grandmother, were particularly ethnic sounding. As for Wilson, my father's adopted name, it was hardly a name at all. It was like a glass of tasteless water. It was a drab jacket I wore because it was familiar.

Monica sighed. "I love Ireland, of course. And my husband wouldn't live anywhere else."

We drove along in silence for a bit, as the rain gushed down the windows.

This was the fifth time I'd been to Ireland, and as I always did, I thought about my grandfather who'd left when he was fourteen, in 1902. John Lane was born in Kilronane, outside Dunmanway, a market town in the heart of West Cork. Other relatives must have gone to Boston over the years, for he joined them, then moved on. He traveled to Oregon and joined the cavalry, I've heard, then turned up in Detroit. He was a cook in France during the First World War, and sent post cards to his new wife, Faith, a nurse from Battle Creek, Michigan. After the war they moved to Brooklyn and had my mother. He ran an Automat and wore a bowler hat on walks in Prospect Park. They became vigorous Christian Scientists, and during the depression returned to Battle Creek. Both my grandparents became pillars of the church there, and practitioners. My grandfather was especially renowned for his ability to heal. He went from being a poor Irish Catholic to a respectable Midwesterner, known for his elegant pinstriped suits. I remember him well, though he died when I was only six.

For years, in my early travels to Europe, I'd avoided Ireland, from some peculiar, misplaced resistance to turning into an Irish American looking for her roots. But as soon as I'd come to West Cork, on a scouting expedition to Dunmanway to retrieve my grandfather's baptismal certificate in order to get an Irish passport, I was immediately taken in by the Irish, including, of course, my own relatives. They made me feel at home, made me feel as if I were recovering some piece of myself I hadn't known I'd lost.

Perhaps because I was in equal measure Swedish, and had spent so much more time in Scandinavia, I found it hard to think myself a true Irish American, even with my passport. Yet Grace O'Malley's story stirred in me more than just fascination at her exploits. I was Irish enough to feel that her story had something to do with my own relatives' history. I knew why they had kept her story alive for so many centuries, why she belonged to the Irish and no other people.

WE PULLED into the small town of Westport, where I'd be staying for another day or two. Monica asked me, "Where are you going?"

She meant, I realized later, where should she drop me, but I answered, dreamily, "North. To Scotland and Shetland and Iceland and Norway. I'm looking for stories about women and the sea."

"Women and the sea," she said, wondering. I would hear that wondering in voices for weeks to come.

CHAPTER II

THE PIRATE QUEEN

Clew Bay, Ireland

No one knows what Grace's second husband looked like, but his nickname was Richard-in-Iron, or Iron Dick, for his habit of wearing a suit of armor left over from his Anglo-Norman forebears. Richard Bourke was a chieftain in the northern reaches of Clew Bay, in line to become the MacWilliam, a title with even greater status. Legend has it that Grace appeared one day at the door of his castle at Rockfleet to propose marriage. Legend also has it that it was really his castle she wanted. It's easy to see why.

The stone castle of Carraigahowley stands nearly at the edge of bronze seaweed-covered rocks, deep within the island-crumbled waters of Clew Bay. Unlike the now neglected fortress on Clare Island, the castle at Rockfleet, as it's now called, is far from passing ships at sea, and still seems to hold the romance of the past intact. This square tower keep, four stories connected by a spiral staircase, came to be Grace's favorite of the many homes she had around Clew Bay. A taxi driver dropped me there early one morning, and I stood gazing out into the lightly choppy waters where I'd soon be cruising with local angler Mary Gavin Hughes on her boat, *Shamrock I*. I could see Mary now across the small cove on the dock, pumping diesel.

According to folklore, Grace wasn't married long. Traditionally, Brehon law held that either party could divorce

21

Carraigahowley (Rockfleet) Castle

after a year, merely by uttering the words to dissolve the marriage. Trial marriages were frequent and fashionable, and after a year and a day, it's said that Grace locked herself in the castle when he arrived, and shouted down from the battlements, "Richard Bourke, I dismiss you!"

Adding, "And I'm keeping the castle!"

But history shows that they continued together, if not as traditional marriage partners, then as allies, and they presented a united front to the English, who treated them as husband and wife. While Grace was generally conceded to be the more politically astute, there are many instances of mutual support. Richard doesn't seem to have objected to Grace's continued piracy and ownership of the castle. And after his death, unlike what had happened with Dónal O'Flaherty, when she lost all claims to his property, Grace took a third of Richard's property

and made sure her son from the marriage, Tibbot-ne-Long
("Toby of the Ships" as he was called), received his inheritance.

LIVING GEOGRAPHY, that's some of what travel is, especially a
pilgrimage undertaken with a biography or history book in hand.
It was one thing to read that Grace coveted Carraigahowley
Castle for its strategic location; another to slide my hands over
the stone walls damp with sea wind, to breathe in the iodine tang
of kelp, to see how a scatter of islands and shoals stretch out to
protect the castle in this backwater inlet from any surprise attacks
by sea.

Rain and gusty winds would come in a few hours, but this
morning, sun spackled the mortar of the castle stones and but-
tered the blue waves as I went to join Mary on the dock. She ran
a one-woman sea-angling business, but I'd talked her into
taking me out into Clew Bay for a few hours so that I could see
Grace's castle from the water and get a sense of the shape and
feel of the bay itself.

Mary was trim but sturdy, brawny in the arms and narrow
in the hips. Her skin was smooth and tan, her curly dark hair cut
short. She wore sunglasses with leopard-patterned frames.
They were the only flashy thing about her, and she didn't take
them off until later in the day. It may have been as much a question of initial shyness as of glare. Later I saw her eyes were a
soft, bright blue. She had on a navy fleece jacket and tall rubber
boots.

We set off, at first with me standing at the back of the
thirty-six-foot Aquastar, so I could snap some photographs of
the castle. As it receded dramatically behind us, I came forward
into the cabin and perched on a seat next to her. The cabin was

comfortably dusty and cluttered, like the dashboard of a beloved old Chevy, but Mary was precise and firm in her handling of the *Shamrock I*. No surprise that she'd grown up around boats, on one of the inner islands, and had learned seafaring and weather reading from her grandfather and father. She'd begun fishing with her grandfather at age three and at age ten had taken up sport angling, eventually winning dozens of championships in Ireland and Europe. Like Grace, Mary knew Clew Bay, down to every shoal, reef, and tricky current. As we threaded our way through the islands, Mary pointed out the shallows and other areas to watch out for. Below the surface were other little islands, submerged. All the islands, down to the rocky clusters, were named.

"That one's Frenchman's Rocks," she said. "There was a French merchant ship coming out of Westport that came to grief there. Sunk entirely."

The island where she'd grown up, Clynish, was one of five that were inhabited. In the past, more families had made their home out in Clew Bay. But over the last century, in particular, people began to leave, either for the mainland or England or America, more because of isolation than anything else.

"No one went hungry here," said Mary. "It was a rich life, between the fishing, the animals, and your potatoes and vegetables. We always had fish to eat, and raised cows and sheep, too, which we sold. We used to put halters on the cattle and put them in boats or lead them across to the mainland during low tides. Islanders would also gather seaweed and sell it on shore."

Mary and her brother were first taken to school on the mainland by their father in a small boat with an outboard motor. Later she and her brother went back and forth by themselves. "There were days when the motor didn't work. It was a long row." She learned to navigate the reefs and currents of Clew Bay early on, and to read the weather and waves. "My father would say, 'Slow down when you see a big wave coming, Mary.'" Her grandfather used to take her out sailing, in a yawl with a brown sail. "I remember his hand on the tiller. The other hand held a pipe." Her father taught her to be careful going out to sea, to make sure that nothing was wrong with the boat. "I'm famous for having three of everything." She added, "Many fathers wouldn't be happy with a girl managing a boat, but mine was."

Her father used to take tourists out fishing occasionally on the weekends, and Mary had done it for about fifteen years now. She mostly ferried small parties of men, serious deep-sea fishermen, to the lee of Clare Island or around Achill Island. If the weather turned bad, she could head back into the more protected waters of the bay. The sandbanks, along with the combination of deep and shallow waters, mean productive fishing. "We've caught seventeen species of fish," she told me: blue shark and skate, conger, whiting, John Dory, ling, coalfish, and mackerel among them.

The *Shamrock I* was packed with gear, and idly, I wondered if I should turn my hand to catching fish. But I was more interested in talking to Mary. I told her my interest in Grace O'Malley. I said the taxi driver who'd brought me to Rockfleet wasn't impressed by the O'Malleys. "Great thieves," he'd called them, only half-joking, and had gone on, "Of course everything around here is named O'Malley this and O'Malley that. Is anything named for the common people, for a family like mine? We're the ones who had our land trampled and taken, our fields burnt, our houses knocked down."

But Mary had named her daughter Grania, and took pride in being a woman of the sea. "Europe's only lady skipper," she

told me. She betrayed her pride in this with only a slight tightening of the lips, as if holding back a smile. "Some people call me
the modern-day Granuaile," she said. "Men don't mind sailing
with me. They know I'll take care of them and lead them to a
very successful day of fishing." Her husband wasn't much for
the sea, she added. He was a roofer, and liked to stay on shore.

Most of the islands of Clew Bay were near the mainland,
but now we headed out into rougher waters. I hoped for dolphins, but didn't see any. The boat bucketed, and Mary told stories of storms that had forced her over to Achill Island to tie up
for a few days. I'd been supremely happy while we'd been
making our way around the small islands—the empty pasture-
lands with crumbling stone walls here and there, the white
sandy beaches, the colonies of seals basking or swimming, steel
gray heads like helmets flashing—but I also liked riding the
foaming green waters farther out, bracing myself in a corner of
the cabin as Mary, as she had learned, slowed to take the big
waves slugging our bow.

I could imagine Grace looking something like Mary at
around forty, though probably more weather-beaten, both of
them steady at the tiller, energetic and unflappable. Middle age
was the time of some of Grace's most outrageous exploits,
undocumented in history books, recalled in traditional stories in
Connaught, burned into the memories of some of the unlucky
families who lived through them. The O'Boyles, the Mac-
Sweeneys, the O'Loughlins all knew her raiding parties first-
hand, as did the inhabitants of the islands off the coast:
Inishbofin and the Aran Islands, Inishmore, Inishmaan, Inisheer.
She stole their ships; she stole their cattle; she attacked castles all
along the coast. At Carradh Castle her men fired a cannonball
from their ship and knocked down part of a wall. Her gambling

was as legendary as her bravery in battle. She was notorious for swearing and sex, too: perhaps another reason she lived on in popular memory but not in Irish history books.

Given the stories of Grace's physical toughness and courage, it's not surprising that there's even an admiring tale about the birth of her fourth child, Tibbot-ne-Long, the son of Richard Bourke. Legend has it that she was out at sea when she felt the first contractions. Seeing no need to turn toward shore, she simply went below and delivered him. The day after he was born, as Grace lay in her cabin recuperating, Algerian corsairs attacked the galley. The second-in-command came below and asked her to lead the men against the pirates. "May you be seven times worse off this day twelve months, who cannot do without me for one day," she said. Half-dressed, she climbed on deck, swearing loudly and blasting the Algerians with her musket while she rallied the men. "Take this from unconsecrated hands," she shouted. Reputedly, the Algerians were so overwhelmed by her fierceness and dishevelment that they abandoned their attempt to board Grace's galley and fled.

Those years were halcyon for Grace, but they weren't to last. The English had first noticed Grace O'Malley when she was married to Dónal O'Flaherty and exacting tolls from merchant ships off Galway. They took greater notice when she beat them back at Hen's Castle. But for a long while she was only one of many Irish irritants to England's grand plans for the country, a curiosity perhaps because she was a woman.

Although the Anglo-Normans had nominally conquered Ireland in the thirteenth century, they'd intermarried and become as Irish as the Gaelic clans, given over to the pleasures of cattle stealing, jockeying for power, and feasting and drinking. Richard Bourke's family, for instance, came from

Anglo-Norman stock that had turned Irish. The only part of Ireland that England could be said to control fully was the former Viking town of Dublin and its environs, called "the Pale." The west and north of Ireland, especially, was boggy and thick with trees, difficult to penetrate. That was how the O'Malleys and other clans had held out so long. With the reign of Henry VII came new policies aimed at subduing and colonizing the wild Irish, but it was Henry VIII who decided to call himself King of Ireland. Within a few years of his death, Elizabeth I took up where her father and grandfather had left off.

The insidious system of "surrender and regrant" played on the fragmentation of Ireland and was far less expensive than wholesale warfare. The chieftains were offered a bargain. All they had to do was submit to the authority of the English crown. They'd then be "regranted" their lands, with titles to boot. Many also received favors and financial advantages from the English crown. The catch was that in doing so they agreed to give up traditional Brehon law for English law, and to accept the right of sheriffs and justices to enforce it. Some chieftains surrendered quietly and others tried to work both sides. But for many, the notion of paying rents and taxes on estates that had been in their clans for centuries was intolerable, as was giving over many of their quasi-regal powers and privileges to Elizabeth's agents.

The conquest of Ireland proceeded erratically, but unstoppably, throughout the sixteenth century. Elizabeth sent provincial governors to offer terms to the chieftains, and began establishing bastions of the English legal system. There were many rebellions, of course, and outright battles, not all of which the Irish lost. But Elizabeth's deputies played a divide-and-conquer game, inserting themselves into the rivalries between and

among the clans. One chieftain after another became either an
English peer or a corpse.

Lord Deputy Henry Sidney (the father of poet Sir Philip
Sidney) paid his fourth visit to Galway in 1577, intent on "colonization by persuasion." Along with many others, Grace
appeared before him to voluntarily submit to Elizabeth. She
impressed Sidney, as was her intention, with an account of her
many ships and fighting men. Sidney later wrote:

> There came to mee also a most famous femynyne sea capten
> called Grany Imallye, and offred her service unto me,
> wheresoever I woulde command her, with three gallyes and
> two hundred fightinge men, either in Ireland or Scottland,
> she brought with her her husband, for she was as well by
> sea as by land well more than Mrs Mate with him. . . . This
> was a notorious woman in all the costes of Ireland.

Grace had little intention of actually giving up power, and
shortly after meeting Sidney, she launched a raid on the estates
of the earl of Desmond, one of the Gaelic chieftains who had
taken an English title in the south of the country. He captured
her, however, and turned her over to the English in an attempt to
curry favor with the new rulers. She spent months imprisoned at
Limerick before being transferred to the dungeons of Dublin
Castle. Lord Justice Drury, who dealt with her then, called her "a
woman that hath impudently passed the part of womanhood and
been a great spoiler and chief commander and director of thieves
and murderers at sea to spoil this province. . . ." But he also
described her as "famous for her stoutenes of courage and
person, and for some sundry exploits done at sea."

Grace spent eighteen months altogether in the dungeons of

Limerick and Dublin castles, cruel punishment for a woman who'd ranged far and wide across the seas. Soon after she was released, the castle at Rockfleet was attacked, and the next years required much cunning. She and Richard Bourke took titles in 1581, and though Richard died in 1583, "Lady Bourke" continued as the de facto head of the clan, supported by Bourke relatives and her own children, two of whom, Owen and Margaret, had also married Bourkes. She was then fifty-three, already long past the life expectancy for a woman in those times. Her most difficult years lay ahead.

In 1584 Sir Richard Bingham became governor of Connaught. Unlike Sir Henry Sidney, Bingham believed more in "colonization by the sword" than "colonization by persuasion." Bingham came to take a hard line with the clan leaders who were resisting English power, by laying waste to their estates, putting them in prison, and isolating them from their followers. He pursued Grace O'Malley with single-minded zeal. To his way of thinking, she had no legal entitlement as a widow to the Bourke property, and absolutely no right to rule. Not only had she been attacking and plundering English ships for the last twenty years, but this "nurse to all rebellions," as he termed her, was still fomenting mischief among the clans. Lady Bourke was no more subject to the queen than she had ever been.

Bingham set out to destroy her, and very nearly succeeded. Several of the Bourke clan, including Grace's stepsons, were executed by martial law, and her oldest son, Owen O'Flaherty, was murdered underhandedly, even though he had not joined his clan's rebellion against Bingham's government. Bingham also kidnapped her youngest son, Tibbot, and sent him to his brother, George Bingham, as a hostage, so that Tibbot could learn the English language and be tutored in the ways of the

English. At one point Bingham imprisoned Grace herself:

> She was apprehended and tied with a rope, both she and her
> followers at that instant were spoiled of their said cattle and
> of all they ever had besides the same, and brought to Sir
> Richard who caused a new pair of gallows to be made for
> her where she thought to end her days.

Bingham could have killed her; instead, her daughter
Margaret's husband, whom the English called the Devil's
Hook, offered himself as hostage, and Grace was set free. She
fled north with her ships and continued to foment mischief.
Bingham killed the cattle on her estates and burned her crops.
He found his way into the treacherous waters of Clew Bay, and
impounded her fleet, thus destroying her livelihood.

The loss of her cattle and crops was misery, but the loss of
her ships was intolerable. With cunning amplified by desperation, Grace, now sixty-three, composed a courteous and politically wily letter to Queen Elizabeth, dated 1593, thus opening a
correspondence with the English state. Her petition didn't challenge Elizabeth's right to rule Ireland, but was, in effect, a sort
of special pleading for herself and some of her relatives. Her aim
was to protect herself from Bingham, to procure the release of
her son Tibbot, captured and imprisoned by Bingham a second
time, and to get back to her business at sea. After establishing
contact with the court, Grace set off by sea, evading Bingham
and making her way up the Thames.

In London, like multitudes of petitioners, she waited for an
audience with the queen, and found herself a friend at court,
Lord Burghley. This statesman and close advisor to the queen
had been aware of Grace O'Malley for twenty years and was

intrigued enough to send her a sort of questionnaire, the
"Eighteen Articles of Interrogatory to Be Answered by Grany
Ne Maly."

I try to picture this Irish chieftain and pirate queen sitting
in Shakespeare's London giving detailed answers (in the third
person, and doubtless through a scribe and/or interpreter) to
such questions as "Who was her father and mother? Who was
her first husband?" and deftly fielding the query "How she hath
had maintenance and living since her last husband's death?" by
answering humbly that after returning to Carraigahowley and
fleeing Bingham, "she dwelleth in Connaught a farmers life very
poor . . . utterly did she give over her former trade of maintenance by sea and land." The questionnaire and her answers are
a historian's dream come true, and I can only imagine Anne
Chambers's thrill when she discovered the parchment pages in
the Public Record Office in London, and began to decipher the
difficult English script. For in Grace's answers, not only do we
learn important facts about Grace O'Malley's life and her relations, but we can also see the construction she has put on them,
her way of emphasizing her harmlessness and skating over her
part in any rebellions against the English rulers.

The eventual meeting between Grace and Elizabeth at
Greenwich Palace is the stuff of legend, the centerpiece of many
a ballad and historical novel about the Pirate Queen. Although
some chieftains of Ireland had previously gone to England to
parley with the queen, most ended up in the Tower of London.
Grace was one of the few to find the queen's favor and to sail
back to Ireland with everything she sought: freedom for her son
Tibbot, an end to Bingham's pursuit of her, and, most importantly, a return to what Grace euphemistically called "maintenance by sea and land," that is, piracy.

Before the English Queen she dauntless stood,
And none her bearing there could scorn as rude;
She seemed as one well used to power—one that hath
Dominion over men of savage mood,
And dared the tempest in its midnight wrath,
And thro' opposing billows cleft her fearless path.

And courteous greeting Elizabeth then pays,
And bids her welcome to her English land
And humble hall. Each looked with curious gaze
Upon the other's face, and felt they stand
Before a spirit like their own.

Of course no one knows exactly what went on at their meeting. It's said they spoke in Latin, the only language they had in common, and that when Elizabeth offered to make Grace a countess, she refused, apparently feeling she had already attained the same status as the queen. There's also a story that Queen Elizabeth offered Grace a handkerchief when she sneezed. After blowing her nose heartily, Grace tossed the embroidered cloth into the open fireplace. The court was shocked to see this. "In England," a courtier rebuked her, "We do not throw handkerchiefs in the fire." "What do you do with them then?" asked Grace with interest. "We save them for another time." "What! You save a dirty piece of cloth? The queen may do this, but not I."

Amusing as this is, it's probably unlikely that Grace would have done anything to insult Elizabeth. Yet imagining an encounter between two such similar women, more or less the same age, who operated in a man's world, has fascinated many. The Granuaile Heritage Centre has an elaborate diorama of their meeting at the Tudor court—Queen Elizabeth with whitened face set off by a huge ruff and red wig and Grace, gray-haired and bent over, disguised in a shabby simple cloak, an elderly mother asking only for her beloved son's freedom.

This scene suggests that Elizabeth thought Bingham must have been dreaming, to believe such a worn old woman could be a threat to the crown, and in fact later Elizabeth wrote to Bingham ordering him "to have pity for the poor aged woman."

Eventually, with Lord Burghley's influence, Elizabeth commanded Tibbot's release and recommended that Grace O'Malley and her son be able to live undisturbed the rest of their lives. I imagine Grace throwing off the shabby cloak as soon as her ship was out of the Thames, and raising her saber high as she set off for the wilder shores of Ireland again. Elizabeth had given Grace and her clan permission to fight the Spanish and French on behalf of the English crown. Grace, of course, interpreted this in her own way, as license to return to plundering ships off Ireland's coast.

Not long after, she was reported to have built three large galleys, each big enough to carry three hundred men. Sir Richard Bingham continued to make life miserable for her and her clan, however; two years after her first visit to Queen Elizabeth's court, she returned to England with a petition for Lord Burghley, complaining that Bingham made it impossible to claim her property and go about her business. Grace's persistence in claiming her rights was rewarded. In 1595 Bingham's own followers conspired against him, and he was forced to flee Ireland for England, where he found himself in prison.

Now there was little to hinder Grace from returning to the sea with her pirate galleys, and one of the last written references to her comes from an English captain who skirmished with one

The meeting of Grace O'Malley and Queen Elizabeth I

of her ships and got the better of the crew: "This galley comes out of Connaught," he wrote of the encounter, "and belongs to Grany O'Malley." At the time she was seventy-one.

She died in Rockfleet Castle, it's said, in 1603, the same year as Queen Elizabeth. The old Ireland was gone; Grace's son Tibbot-ne-Long, as astute as his mother, saw which way the wind was blowing, and came out on the side of the English in the Battle of Kinsale, which put an end to serious Irish resistance. For his loyalty to the crown, Tibbot-ne-Long was knighted Sir Tibbot, and amassed the greatest estate in Mayo. Charles I later made him Viscount Mayo and it's this line, of Bourkes and Brownes, that still owns Westport House, even though the clan of O'Malleys is legion. Grace disappeared from history, though not from memory. She was kept alive in family stories, and in legends told around Clew Bay for centuries.

The *Shamrock I* was approaching Clare Island. Again I saw Grace's castle, and felt a thrill, though, like Grace, I now preferred the fortress at Rockfleet. Mary pulled into the harbor and dropped me off. I planned to walk to the abbey to see the spot where Grace was said to be buried, and then to make my own way back to Westport. Mary said she'd pick me up in town the following day and drive me to Mulrany, for an evening of local music away from the tourist venues. I watched the *Shamrock I* motor out to sea again. Another storm was coming, and Mary wanted to get the boat to Achill Island. She'd be up at four tomorrow morning to take out a party of anglers.

AFTER THREE or four, I stopped counting, but Mary and her friend Geraldine continued to put away Bacardi-and-Cokes. They had stronger heads than I did. Myself, I stuck with what the men at the bar had lined up in pints before them: Guinness with a creamy head, expertly pulled and a new one plunked down as the last of the old went down. I managed one pint for every three of theirs.

I'd taken a short nap today in my hotel, knowing the evening would go late. Mary and I arrived at Neven's Pub, on the north side of Clew Bay, around eleven, shortly before the Mulloy Brothers started up in the back room. As Mary had promised, there were none of the German tourists that you'd find in the pubs in Westport, nursing a Heineken, good-naturedly and stolidly enjoying the Irishness of it all. This was the real thing, lots of music and lots of drink, and everyone lived nearby. The Mulloy Brothers, beloved locals, were in their fifties and looked not at all related: one round-faced, another black-bearded, a third thin and wrinkled.

"Let's have a dance, Geraldine," Mary urged. Even though she'd been up since dawn, her feet were tapping. Her friend was a youthful-looking mother of seven, red-haired, brown-eyed, cigarette-voiced, a willing dreaminess about her. She teased Mary for a bit, then got up without a word. Mary had said they were both mad for set dancing, whether any partners turned up or not. Mary took off her short leather jacket, the one her son had just brought back from his trip to India, and stepped out onto the small space in front of the musicians. Geraldine smiled indulgently and tossed her red hair. She wore a white blouse and skirt and heels. The two of them crossed their arms high on their chest and lifted their feet. They were quick and precise, circling shoulders or kicking in time. Mary had the same serious face I'd seen yesterday on the boat: modest pride at doing something perfectly. After the jig they waltzed, with narrow-hipped Mary taking a proper lead. They were a joy to watch (though most of the men just quietly drank their beers), their faces flushed and shining.

After a few sets, Geraldine bowed out for a cigarette. I had the feeling Mary could have danced for hours. She turned instead to one of the men and they began to discuss fishing.

Geraldine and I got on the topic of religion, and that led to her telling me about a recent pilgrimage to Lourdes. She'd gone with her sister, not because they were sick or crippled, just because it was a long-held dream. "It's something I just can't describe . . . the way it made me feel to see Bernadette's Grotto, to bathe in the waters," she said, looking about fifteen as she finished another drink and smoked another Winston. I wondered how old her children were. She had also climbed Croagh Patrick, the Holy Mountain, overlooking Clew Bay.

"So have I, many times," said Mary, coming over for another round. "My brother and I thought nothing of running up it of a summer evening, just to see the view."

I asked if they'd ever climbed without shoes, the way people used to, to show their faith. "I haven't done anything bad enough to go barefoot for penance," said Mary, but Geraldine, said smiling, "I'd like to go up it barefoot. I may yet do that."

I thought about the Gaelic phrase, *an thuras*, "the journey," which I'd come across in reading about Celtic pilgrimages. The notion of this particular kind of pilgrimage was still current in certain holy places in the Celtic world, such as Iona, and belonged to an earlier form of Christianity, before such popular Catholic stations-of-the-cross hikes like the one up Croagh Patrick. *An thuras* meant to make a circuit, usually counterclockwise, around a number of related sites. Each site—a cross, a stone, a chapel, or a shrine—was intended to be a trigger for a certain ritual or prayer. "Mnemonic devices," they've been called, *mnemonic* meaning to aid the memory. Perhaps it was the Guinness, but I suddenly thought I could see my upcoming journey around the North Atlantic in that light. Beginning with Grace, her castles and even the dioramas and paintings of the Granuaile Heritage Centre, I'd be looking not only for stories but for physical clues about the lives of maritime women from myth and history. My journey wasn't religious, but it was a pilgrimage of sorts, from site to site in search of relics, statues, homes, castles, and coastlines.

The evening was breaking up. It was now after two. The nondrinking, singing Mulloy brother, Tom of the black beard, the one who'd once been a carpenter and then had fallen and broken half the bones in his body, began taking people off in his taxi. In fifteen minutes he came back for me, and waving goodbye to Mary and Geraldine, I got in. Tom ran me at high speed back to Westport and gave me a tape from a box in the trunk.

The night porter showed no sign of disapproval at a woman on her own getting in after three in the morning. Instead he asked if I'd had a good time.

I told him about my evening in Mulrany with the Mulloy Brothers.

"Ah," he nodded. "They're grand."

I WENT back to Carraigahowley Castle at Rockfleet the next day. This time the tide was low, the boulders covered with crinkled ochre and bronze leaves and bulbs glistening wet. Sea gulls sat in all their pristine whiteness on the tangle of seaweed. I'd borrowed a key to the castle, and I went inside, up the cold steps to the fourth floor. The view was excellent, in spite of the fact that castles lacked picture windows in those days. There was a hole in the stone up there, even smaller than the slits that passed for windows in Irish castles. It's said this was the opening through which Grace threaded the rope that anchored her favorite ship to the leg of her bed. As she slept, she must have felt the galley moving in her dreams.

I climbed down from the top floor of Carraigahowley, and walked around the castle as the wind freshened. I was still a little tired from my late night with Mary and Geraldine, still a little overwhelmed from all the traveling to get here; yet, in touching the old stone of Grace's castle, new energy coursed through me. I imagined the Pirate Queen staring out to sea from her tower, or sleeping with her ship tied to her bedpost. The name of this bay abounding in islands came from the Irish god, Cuan Mo. But I thought that *clew* in the old meaning suited it best. For a clew was a ball of thread, the thread that Ariadne gave Theseus to guide him through the labyrinth, the source of our word *clue:* anything that points to the solution of a mystery.

I felt as if, by starting the first stage of my journey, *mo thuras*, here on Clew Bay, where a fierce little girl had grown up and a wild, canny woman had remained a pirate until late in life, I'd taken hold of a thread, and was ready to follow it, wherever it led. If it was tied to a pirate's galley, so much the better.

CHAPTER III

AT THE EDGE OF THE
SEA CAULDRON

From Oban to the Pentland Firth

LEAVING IRELAND, I flew to Edinburgh to visit friends, then traveled by train to Oban on the west coast of Scotland. I wanted to slip back in time, further back than Grace O'Malley's day, to the mythological realm, where sea goddesses stirred up cauldrons of whirling water, storm kettles of surge and drag. In Gaelic these cauldrons are called *coire*, and one of the most famous of them lies not far from Iona and Mull in the Hebrides, between the sparsely inhabited islands of Scarba and Jura. There, the Atlantic tide comes and goes so quickly and voluminously that the narrow gap between the islands becomes a watery conflagration of currents, creating waves that slap up twenty feet tall. It is called Corryvreckan or *coire breckan*, "the cauldron of the plaid."

This tub of violence is where the great winter hag Cailleach was said to wash her cloak. When storms came on, especially in autumn, people told each other, "The Cailleach will tramp her blankets tonight." She washed her plaid and when she drew it up, it was white and the hills were covered with snow. They used to say that, before a good washing, the roar of the coming tempest was heard by people on the coast for a distance of twenty miles. It took three days for the cauldron to boil.

Oban is the end of the rail line from Glasgow, the terminus for ferries to the Inner and Outer Hebrides. I looked longingly

41

at the harbor, where the white ships of the Caledonian MacBrayne line were moored, but they couldn't take me close enough to catch a glimpse of Corryvreckan. At the Oban tourist office I found an appealing brochure for a small cruise operation farther down the coast, run by a young man and woman. They ran tours out to the whirlpool in the tourist season. I called and reached a machine, left a message, then turned my attention to finding a room for the night.

It was raining—no, not just raining, but pissing down. I stood dripping in the tourist office with other wet visitors to Oban while a staff member fixed me up with a room for the night. I made my way along the dreary esplanade to a group of tall guesthouses built in the town's Victorian heyday. Ten days into my trip, my green rain slicker was beginning to feel like a second skin.

The prospect of viewing a thundering whirlpool in this rainstorm seemed unlikely, as well as perhaps unwise; however, it was perfect weather, I thought as I took off my wet clothes and settled myself into a chair in my garret room at the top of six flights of stairs, to think about storm goddesses. I put on the kettle and blessed the Scots for having the right idea about comfort: plenty of tea, biscuits, and tiny containers of milk.

LEAN AND mean, that's the Cailleach, blue-faced, rust-haired, one-eyed, with a single tooth. Stories of this ancient goddess are found in the west of Ireland and the Highlands of Scotland, and are particularly common around the firths of Oban. It's said that she created the mountains and the islands by dropping stones from the creel she carried on her back. Many mountains have their own Cailleach. The Cailleach nan Cruchan is said to have lived on the summit of Ben Cruchan, not far from Oban. When anything put her in a temper, she gathered a handful of whirlpools and descended the mountain in a fury. She crossed Loch Etive in a single stride, and doing so, lashed it into a tempest that prevented all passage at Connel Ferry. Connel, from "cona thuil," which means whirling floods, was also said to be the place through which the Cailleach drove her goats, that is, her frisky waves. The Cailleach is much connected with the Isle of Mull in the Inner Hebrides. The frothy swells off its coast are called her sheep and goats. Where waves billow and the coastline seethes white is her stomping ground.

Donald Mackenzie, who collected Scottish folklore in the first part of the twentieth century, has an entire chapter about the Cailleach in one of his books. He calls her the Scottish Artemis, who roamed the mountains with her animals, and carried a magic wand to control the weather. As with most ancient goddesses, her early power was elemental and to be revered as much as feared. Later she turned into a sea witch responsible for storms and drownings. But she was always associated with the coldest, stormiest part of the year. Her strength grew as autumn arrived; she reigned supreme until spring. Some later stories sentimentalize her as a beautiful girl who turned into a hag in winter, then succumbed each spring to another beautiful girl who replaced her. Other stories tell how she kept her youth by never failing to drink from the waters of life in the moment before the sun rises, once a year. When once she was prevented or forgot, she fell dead, and didn't rise again.

I prefer the older stories, of the Cailleach and her ocean form, Muileartach, who appears in Irish poetry and lore. Muileartach came from the west, over the waves; she lived in the ocean with her lover, and enjoyed having her body massaged by sea merchants. The only way to kill her, it's said, was to bury her up to her shoulders in soil.

> Her face was blue-black of the luster of coal,
> And her bone-tufted tooth was like red rust.
> In her head was one pool-like eye.
> Swifter than a star in a winter sky.

Like the Cailleach, Muileartach often took the shape of an old woman. It's said she visited a house on shore to ask for lodging, pretending to be a cold and weary traveler. When the door was slammed in her face, she kicked it open furiously. This is something I could imagine the real Irish sea queen Grace O'Malley doing. In fact, there's a story about Grace that has her asking for hospitality at Howth Castle north of Dublin. Turned away at the gate, she retaliated by kidnapping the owner's grandson, whom she encountered on the beach. She took the boy back with her to Clew Bay, refusing to return him to his frantic relatives unless a single condition was met: No one should ever be turned away from Howth Castle again. For four hundred years this tradition has been observed. The gate to Howth Castle is always open now, and a place laid at the table.

The Cailleach and Muileartach faced no opposition in their line of work; they were omnipotent forces, unchallenged in a world where the violence of wind and waves could only be worshipped and revered, never controlled. But as the later stories of the Cailleach as a beautiful girl who turns into a hag attest, that ancient power flagged over the centuries. The storm goddess, who did her washing in the whirlpool of Corryvreckan and lashed her frothy sheep and goats into a tempest of white wool, became a worn-out old woman. Prevented from drinking at the stream where she traditionally renewed her energy, she gave up, and withered to nothing.

The northern waters have another sea goddess, the benign sea deity and summer spirit, the Mither o' the Sea, often invoked by fishermen in Orkney and Scotland. She brought warmth to the ocean and stilled its storms; she filled the waters with fish. Her enemy was the winter spirit, Teran, and each March, around the vernal equinox, they fought each other. It was Teran's voice in the howl of the March gales and the thunder of the waves. When the storms subsided, the fishing folk knew the Mither o' the Sea had defeated Teran, wrapped him tight as a baby in swaddling clothes and thrown him to the bottom of the ocean. Sooner or later, in autumn, Teran escaped again and fought the Sea Mither in a series of shrieking storms known as the *gore vellye*, or "autumn tumult." In winter he was victorious and she was bound and banished. In this story it was the male who created storms, and the female who stilled them, quite the opposite of the Cailleach, whose calendar corresponded to Teran's. In some tales the Cailleach turned to stone April 30 and came alive again October 31. This year she seemed to have missed her deadlines, for it was May and she was still kicking the waters into a froth and bringing the fury of the clouds down upon us.

MIDAFTERNOON I went out again, braving the howling winds coming at me over the esplanade. I made another phone call to the small cruise company, left another message. There was a library across the street from my guesthouse, a tiny one upstairs in a municipal building. I went in to ask about using their computer to access my email, and met the first of many librarians who would answer my question, "Do you have anything on women and the sea?" with complete aplomb. This one had a sense of humor. I had titled my email message "From Bonnie Wet Scotland." Passing by, he remarked, "May I call you Bonnie?" He helped me find some books of folklore with stories of the Cailleach. The library was a busy place, not exactly with individuals reading books, but with people crowding in to exchange gossip. In a room off the corridor opposite, a screech of little girls in school uniforms practiced the violin for a coming concert.

Later I wandered around Oban, dipping into shops to get out of the persistent downpour. On a summer's day the shops advertising ice lollies and shellfood (winkles and cockles) would be doing a brilliant trade. Today people were huddled inside teashops or bakeries, eating, if the signs in the windows were any indication, delicacies like Jap Fancies and Chelsea buns. Tartan-vending establishments were selling everything from thimbles to throw rugs in the family clan motif. One shop was promoting "Kilts for Hire." Standing inside a woolen blizzard of green, red, black, and yellow, I had a sudden memory of my father. How, as our world fell apart with my mother's illness and death, he used to tell me stories of his own childhood, the early death of his mother, his unrecalled first years in an orphanage, his adoption by the Wilsons when he was five. His real father was named Walter Stewart. "Stewart was the name of the royal house of Scotland," he told me. "So that means we're related to the former kings and queens of Scotland." Even as an eleven-year-old, I was skeptical of this assertion, an orphan's fairy-tale dream of having secret royal blood.

I bought my father a tie nevertheless, and when the clerk

said, "Ah, the Stewart clan. Are you a Stewart?" I answered, "Er. Yes, I guess I'm a Stewart," tasting it on my lips. I remembered at sixteen trying on the identity of a writer, practicing a new signature on lined notebook paper: *Barbara Stewart. Barbara Stuart.* Even then I seem to have had my doubts about Wilson. In fact, my father's relatives were more Swedish than Scottish. His mother, who died in childbirth at age twenty, was born in Stockholm. In the one photograph we had of her, from her wedding when she was sixteen, I looked almost exactly like her at the same age.

Bonnie Stewart? Bonnie Stuart? Was it too late to change?

Around six o'clock, I finally made contact with the cruise-company couple. "We're not going out again till next week," the young woman apologized. "Aside from the weather forecast, we need to replace a part. The motor."

I had a vision of being at the lip of the whirlpool and the motor suddenly failing. Down, down we'd be pulled, as helpless to stop our suction as the paralyzed narrator in Edgar Allan Poe's story, "A Descent into the Maelström."

> How often we made the circuit of the belt it is impossible
> to say. We careered round and round for perhaps an hour,
> flying rather than floating, getting gradually more and
> more into the middle of the surge, and then nearer and
> nearer to its horrible inner edge.

"You won't be around next week?" she asked. "It should be fixed by then."

"I'm on my way to Orkney," I said regretfully, but with some sense of having postponed death for yet a little while. The rain lashed against the plastic walls of the phone booth, and when I stepped out onto the quay at the end of the esplanade, the wind came at me horizontally. All day I'd heard people grumbling, "It's winter again, isn't it?"

Again I had the sense, feeling the icy rain on my face, that the Cailleach was still at large this May. Along the coast she was taking huge strides, her face blue-black and her one tooth rusty and red; she was peering at her tubs of washing with her goggle eye, and giving them a stir with her magic weather wand. I walked again through the streets, which were mostly empty, and passed a variety of eateries, including one that touted "Steak Mince Bridies" on a card in the window, before settling on a take-away of chicken curry from an Indian restaurant. "I'm sorry about the weather," said the young woman who took my order. "Global warming, I expect." In earlier times she would have said, "The Cailleach is tramping her blankets tonight."

I DIDN'T much like the look of the water between me and the Orkney Islands. All day the rain had flailed against the windows of successive buses, from Fort William to Inverness and now to John o' Groats. While some of the loveliest lochs and glens of the Highlands slipped by, I felt as if I were in a gray tunnel. The towns looked depressed and bleak. Inverness is not best appreciated from the environs of the bus station. The waiting room consisted of two benches, and the café next door reeked authentically of bacon, fish, and boiled tea. A sign on one of the local buses summed up my sense of being a superfluous tourist here: "Come too close and I'll smack you in the mouth." It was an advertisement for a biscuit called "Hit."

Yet when we pulled up to John o' Groats at five-thirty in the evening, I, like the handful of other passengers, all women with

shopping bags and inadequate rain parkas, found myself reluctant to get off our warm, dry bus. The Cailleach was not only
tramping her blankets, she'd put the world in the washing
machine. "I'm a good sailor," I'd blithely told Paddy when
crossing Clew Bay. But I'd not been at the northernmost tip of
Scotland then; I'd not been looking at waves of at least twenty
feet crashing up against the cement quay.

The channel between Scotland and the Orkney Islands, the
Pentland Firth, is considered one of the most dangerous
stretches of water in the world. Not because of the relatively
short passage through it—only seventeen miles from the North
Sea to the Atlantic, and at its narrowest point only about six and
a half miles wide. It is dangerous because of tides that sweep
through twice daily, from the Atlantic to the North Sea. These
tides, combined with the unpredictability of eddies and wave
patterns, caused by the churning back and forth of the currents
over reefs and around islands, can make the passage rough even
on a nice day, but very often it is not nice. In winter a force 8
gale, gusting between thirty-four and forty knots, blows seven
days a month, while a force 7, marginally less severe, is reckoned
to blow another fifteen days a month. In the summer months
seafarers contend with fog, when warm air from the southeast
meets the much colder water coming from the west. It's no
wonder the peoples of these northern coasts have as many
words for rain as the Inuit have for snow. In the Orkney dialect,
a day might be drivvy, ruggy, murry, hagery, roosty, eesky, friz-
zowy, muggery, rimy, or smuggery.

We rushed through a ragged wall of precipitation to get off
the bus and into the shelter afforded waiting passengers. This
rain and wind looked to me more like the beginning of a hurricane than a summer storm. It was clear now why captains and

ship owners in the past had preferred to make long detours north of Orkney or south via the English Channel, and why there were so many tales of ships going aground or sinking in the Firth. These days, the huge cargo ships and tankers moving through the strait hardly feel the surge and pull of the tides, but not all of the six thousand vessels passing through in a year are tankers. Some are small passenger ferries, for instance.

The teashop was closed but the gift shops were open. Today, their offerings seemed incongruous, but no doubt in summer flocks of tourists arriving here at the farthest point north on the British mainland bought a post card or an ice lolly, or perhaps one of the many tartan items for sale. I stood inside one of the gift shops, looking out the glass door at the heaving sea. Behind me, high on the wall, a promotional video flipped through the glories of the Highlands. It looked like another planet, and yet I recognized from the names that these were places not far from here, the lochs and glens through which I'd passed earlier today.

The Stewart tartan was here, too, in abundance. I'd always wondered why my father didn't change his name back to Stewart when he found out he was adopted. His ambivalence formed the basis of my own. "We're the Wilsons," he would always say when he was trying to cheer up my brother and me during the years of my mother's illness. "The Wilsons are all right. The Wilsons stick together." He would also often say, "Wilson, you know, that's not my real name."

Out the door of the gift shop I spied a tiny boat rocking dangerously off shore. It looked in terrible distress, trying to make for land. The women around me began to edge out the door and down in the direction of the quay. With some consternation I realized that this was our boat, the forty-five-minute passenger ferry across the Pentland Firth.

There is another sea cauldron or *coire* off this coast, the Swelchie, which comes from the Norse word for whirlpool, *svelgr.* The coastal current meets the firth's ebb and flow and creates a whiplash water maze, a boiling circle in the sea. There is a legend attached to the Swelchie, a story more influenced by Norse mythology than Celtic. Two giantesses, Finnie Grotti and Minnie Grotti, were enslaved by a Danish king called Frodi. He kept them endlessly at work turning a magic quernstone called Grotti, which had the power to grind out anything it was asked to grind. At first Finnie and Minnie whipped out a steady stream of peace and happiness, but then King Frodi demanded gold and more of it. Eventually Finnie and Minnie had enough and decided to grind out instead an army that would enable them to free themselves from Frodi's tyranny. There are two versions of what happened next, but both have the same result. In one the king was killed and Finnie and Minnie sailed off with a sea rover called Mysing. While sailing through the Pentland Firth, Mysing asked the giantesses to mill some salt. Since they were used to grinding in quantity, the salt soon overflowed the ship and sank it near the island of Stroma. The magic quernstone plummeted to the bottom and continued to churn. It created the whirlpool Swelchie, which is the source of all the salt in the sea. In an alternate version, it was the sea king Mysing who stole Grotti from Finnie and Minnie after Frodi was defeated in battle. He sailed off with it through the firth, and thought some salt would be a good idea. Unfortunately, he couldn't figure out how to turn the quernstone off, with the same result as above. The ship sank and Grotti kept grinding.

Long before the folktale was told in Orkney as "The Magic Quernstone" or "How the Sea Became Salt," the thirteenth-century Icelandic writer Snorri Sturluson, in the "Skald-skaparmal" section of the *Edda* (a guide meant to explain ancient metaphors, or *kenningar,* to writers of his time), describes a whirlpool: "'T'is said, sang Snaebjörn, that far out, off yonder ness, the Nine Maids of the Island Mill stir amain the host-cruel skerry-quern—they who in ages past ground Hamlet's meal." Snorri also tells the story of King Frohdi, the owner of a giant mill he couldn't turn, and two giant bondswomen Fenja and Menja from Sweden whom he found to work it for him. He drove them relentlessly, allowing only time for one of the giantesses to sing her song. Some scholars believe Menja's song to be the oldest surviving example of Old Norse literature. She tells her story, mourning her and her sister's fall from power to slavery:

Such were our deeds / In former days,
That we heroes brave / Were thought to be.
With spears sharp / Heroes we pierced,
So the gore did run / And our swords grew red.

Now we are come / To the house of the king,
No one us pities. / Bond-women are we.
Dirt eats our feet / Our limbs are cold,
The peace-giver we turn. / Hard it is at Frode's.

The story of the millstone appears also in Saxo Grammaticus's *History of the Danes* which drew on Icelandic literature. Here it is the Nine Daughters of Ægir, the ocean god, who grind out the meal of Prince Hamlet. "They set the ocean in motion as if a quern were turned round and they crushed out life between the stones. Far out, beyond the skirts of earth, the

Ships caught in the maelstrom off the Norwegian coast

Nine Maidens of the Island-Mill stir amain the most cruel
Skerry quern."

As far back as the *Odyssey* there have been stories of giantesses who turn a millstone under duress. Whirlpools were once
called the navels of the sea, and the drowning of the millstone
has been given a dozen mythic meanings. A less mythic but
equally poetic description of a whirlpool comes from the *Sailing
Directions for the Northwest and North Coasts of Norway,* as quoted
by Rachel Carson in *The Sea Around Us:*

> As the strength of the tide increases the sea becomes
> heavier and the current more irregular, forming extensive
> eddies . . . These whirlpools are cavities in the form of an
> inverted bell, wide and rounded at the mouth and narrower
> toward the bottom . . . Fishermen affirm that if they are
> aware of their approach to a whirlpool and have time to
> throw an oar or any other bulky body into it they will get
> over it safely; the reason is that when the continuity is
> broken and the whirling motion of the sea interrupted by

something thrown into it the water must rush suddenly in
on all sides and fill up the cavity.

O N   T H E   quay I had plenty of time to mull the mythology and
geometry of whirlpools as I watched the ferry make a pass at the
dock and then retreat. It seemed as if there was no way it could
find its way through the tall waves beating against the quay. If it
sank offshore, what a terrible sight that would be. Equally terrible was the prospect of the boat's disembarking its passengers
and collecting us for the return crossing.

"You're American, right?" a voice emanating from a dark
poncho said over my head. A new prospective passenger had
joined us. He hadn't been on the bus but had been hitchhiking.
His name was Matt and he was a rangy twenty-five-year-old
from the San Francisco Bay Area.

"This is something, isn't it?" he said admiringly. "You think
we'll make it? Where you going, anyway? I'm going to the
Orkney Islands and maybe I'll get to the Shetland Islands.
You're going there? Cool! You're going to the Faroe Islands?
Where are the Faroe Islands? Wow! I want to go! Can I come?"

His fresh-faced excitement was a distraction in any case.
The four or five ladies around me were a tight-lipped bunch. I
had earlier felt myself to be the only tourist except for a quiet
Englishwoman who was going to Stromness to take a painting
course. Now there was me and Matt, two Americans, and he was
so American that he infected me, and my gender became less
important than my nationality. All the ladies moved slightly
away from us and I could hear them thinking, So boisterous,
these Yanks.

But I noticed that Matt's appearance on the quay made me

feel more cheerful, and certainly more intrepid. "It is something, these waves. It's great," I said firmly. Underneath our streaming rain gear, Matt and I had the same hearts, beating with the desire for adventure on the high seas. He asked me more about my trip. "Wow, you're going to Iceland, and to Norway! You're going by boat all the way? That is so cool."

The ladies looked flabbergasted by the notion of all this sea travel. It was plenty for them to think of getting on this boat. "Ooooch, aaach," they'd been saying to each other. "And me with my stomach."

The ferry finally docked intact, and the passengers disembarked looking only slightly green. "Come on, ye," waved the crewmen to us. Their skin was soaked, and water gushed off their yellow slickers. "Get on, get on."

Matt dared me to go on the upper deck. Even tied to the quay the boat was rolling like a top. It was hard to even get up the stairs. When the ferry pulled away from the dock we were enveloped in a vicious mist. The wind carried off the rain droplets before they hit our faces, so it almost felt as if it weren't raining, but rather that water was attacking us from all sides like a manic, cold car wash. The roar of the boat and the wind was inconceivably loud. Around 325 B.C. the Greek explorer Pytheas wrote that the North was the sea-lung of the world. He wondered if the northern seas were the end of the earth, a place where sky and land no longer separated but surged together in endless chaos. I expect he wrote that description attempting to cross the Pentland Firth.

We went downstairs and peered out the fogged-up windows. I told Matt the story of Finnie and Minnie and the magic quernstone. I'd hoped to see the island of Stroma and the Swelchie, but they were lost in the mist. Storm cauldrons and millstones with holes through which all the waters of the world gush are all very well to read about, I suppose, but perhaps it was for the best that our route took us well away from them. I settled back to listen to Matt's travel soliloquy:

"So you can only go to the Faroe Islands once a week by boat well that wouldn't fit into my plans because I don't have that much money and it's probably expensive and then I have to work out how to get back to the Mediterranean I'm on a six-month trip and I'm actually hoping to get to India so if it took two weeks to get to the Faroes because you'd have to hit the days right and I didn't plan to spend so much time up here but I am sure interested in all these places . . ."

And I thought of Finnie and Minnie off in the mist, singing their songs of lost power and getting ready to chuck the millstone in the sea ("You want salt? We'll give you salt, Buddy.") and to move on with their own lives.

"What's your name, by the way?" Matt asked. He was really a nice guy, though a little bit too gee-whizzy.

Minnie? Finnie? Muileartach?

"Bonnie," I said, sticking out my hand. "Bonnie Stuart."

"Cool," said Matt.

CHAPTER IV

RAISING THE WIND

Kirkwall, the Orkney Islands

THE SCOTS, Orcadians, and Shetlanders have an extensive folklore about the sea, but there are more stories about sea witches than about sea goddesses. It's in cautionary tales for children that we find lingering traces of the whirlpool queens once so revered. These folktale witches are more malicious than terrifying; when they take to the sea, they use eggshells as boats. No ordinary eggshells will do, of course; they must have been emptied by good people, decent people, or else they wouldn't float. This was why children were taught to crush their eggshells carefully after they'd eaten the contents. Inattentive children and wicked children forgot this or purpose-fully disobeyed—that's the reason there were always plenty of eggshells about. A witch who wanted to set out to sea would secure her eggshell boat to a "lucky line" that attached to a rock on shore. If, by chance, the line broke, the witch had no means of returning to land.

"Lucky lines," clews, threads—especially red threads— these spider-spun strings turn up frequently in stories of sea witches. The Orcadian folklorist W.R. Mackintosh tells us that sorcerers have used colored clews since ancient times, and that the notion of the sacred thread comes originally from the Hindus. Threads are dangerous and powerful.

In windy transactions, a mariner would buy a thread or bit of rope from a witch. On the thread, the witch tied three knots, with a chant for each knot. The witch then told the mariner that if he wished for a light wind, he should undo the first knot. For a stronger breeze, he should undo the second. But on no account should he unloosen the third. Of course, that's exactly what many curious or impatient sailors did do—with the result that they created hurricanes, were blown off course, and all around the sea.

Besides threads, a sea witch might bang a wet rag wrapped around a piece of wood against a stone, saying twice over:

I knock this rag upon this stane
To raise the wind in the devil's name.
It shall not lie till I please again.

A witch might also fill a vessel with water and place a cup on its surface. Then she would stir the water with her finger until the cup sank. Alternately the witch might float a small wooden bowl on the surface of milk in a churn. She would then pronounce spells that so agitated the liquid that the bowl was flooded and sank. Many a ship went down, it's said, because a witch bore some malice against its captain. The Scottish witch Margaret Barclay was said to have sunk a ship by making a wax model of it and tossing it in the waves.

Going to sea was an activity fraught with superstition in most cultures, but the fishermen of the northeastern coast of Scotland and the archipelagoes of Orkney and Shetland seemed particularly prone to worry. It was unlucky to meet a red-haired person, or anyone who was flat-footed, or a dog, or a minister on the way to the boat. In some fishing villages asking a man where he was off to that morning was enough to make him turn around and head back home.

It was important to turn your boat in the direction of the sun; bad luck came to those who turned it widdershins. Once on board there were many words that could not be uttered: *minister, rabbit, salmon, pig, salt.* Many sailors believed that wind could be produced by whistling. No housewife would think to blow on her oatcakes after she took them from the oven. To do so meant a hurricane would surely arise at sea.

In the rough seas of the North, vessels contending with fog, wind, storms, and gales were constantly lost, and seafarers through the centuries prayed for safe sea passage to Celtic, Roman, and Christian goddesses at shrines on the coasts of the North Sea, the Baltic, and the Atlantic. At one time or another Isis, St. Gertrude, and the Virgin Mary were all invoked. One of the most enduring of the marine goddesses was the Celtic Nehalennia, whose sanctuaries have been found around the North Sea, and whose cult drew devotees with business interests across the waters, wine merchants and traders in fish and pottery, as well as sea captains. On some stone shrines she appears to be standing on a ship's prow, handling an oar or a rope; sometimes dolphins accompany her. Her name may mean "steerswoman."

SELLING THE WIND

A witch selling the wind to sailors

Nehalennia was a powerful deity, but over the centuries her popularity was replaced by images of Christian saints. Eventually the stern faith of Calvinist Scotland had no room for women at all except as scapegoats. The useful power of female sea goddesses lived on in folklore about the sellers of the wind, whose weather services could be purchased up until the early nineteenth century. More often the old connection between women and the sea was held to be evil. As memories of sea goddesses died away, rumors of sea witches who caused shipwrecks, storms, and drownings grew.

I WOKE my first morning in the Orkney capitol of Kirkwall to rain flying at the window and a slightly dismayed sense of having been transported back in time to the bedroom my new stepmother had designed for me when I was a young teenager. This room was pink, too, with twin beds, a chair, and tiny desk, prints of fluffy kittens hanging too high up on the walls. Draped over the chair was a thin paper rectangle announcing that it was a "Personal Bath Mat." These personal bath mats made an appearance everywhere I stayed in Orkney.

Mrs. Harris's bed-and-breakfast, arranged for me last night by the tourist bureau, seemed the very opposite of everything I'd expected to find in these northern isles. Photographs of stone circles and breathtaking cliffs hadn't prepared me for a view, when I tugged open the curtains, of wet washing on a line, and some rain-bedraggled geraniums in pots. My immediate thought was that I needed to find another place, but on the way back to the tourist office in the town center, I discovered an enchanted woods across the street from Mrs. Harris's ranch-style house, and this mysterious little forest made me decide to stay where I was.

A woods of any sort was unusual in Orkney, where the fierce Atlantic winds make forestry a difficult art. As I'd find on all the northern islands, trees often grew sideways, if at all.

Instead of a tree sheltering a house, it took a town with thick walls to shelter a few trees. The sycamores in this stand seemed to have been planted long ago. Most of them had their lower branches lopped off, so that the upper, leafed-out branches formed a canopy over the carpet of bluebells and grass beneath. Other trees had thick trunklike branches snaking out only a few feet from the ground, and those branches had a sinuous, gray-barked solidity.

It was always noisy in these woods, I found, morning, afternoon, or evening. The wind whooshed through continuously and the cawing of the rooks who lived there trumpeted through the wind's bass notes. The rooks had at least two dozen big, twiggy nests in the upper canopy. They rarely seemed to rest however; they careened away from the trees and swooped the fields, then returned to settle with a multitude of squabbling caws. I noticed that they pushed each other off the branches whenever they could, like black-suited gentlemen sidling up to each other on a bench and shoving. There was no fighting, just this endless positioning, nudging, and jostling. One rook would eventually topple off and soar noisily into a recuperative spin before returning again.

Although the rain stopped while I was in Kirkwall, the wind never did. It was a freight train of a wind, too, barreling over the land with a cargo of salt fresh from the Atlantic. It was a surgeon of a wind, poking a scalpel of ice into any uncovered sliver of skin. It could dry your eyes and take the words from your mouth. I'd expected to meet this wind farther north, in the Faroes and Iceland, but Orkney in these first days was where it became my constant companion. I put on the long underwear I'd been saving for Iceland, bought new woolen gloves and a tighter-fitting watch cap. My lips grew chapped; my ears ached from the howling. When I came into any enclosed, human-created space, I panted involuntarily, the way I saw others do, like a dog.

There was another guest at Mrs. Harris's, and he almost never went out. He sat in a big upholstered chair in the spacious living room in front of the electric flames of the fireplace and read steadily through the *Times,* the *Daily Telegraph,* the *Scotsman,* and the *Orcadian.* The living room had a big picture window and he would occasionally look up at the clouds being knocked about like billiard balls and say, "Wheew, I'm better off here, eh?" He was from Winnipeg. Every morning he ate an enormous breakfast. He was in his late sixties and had been traveling by bus through England and Scotland for about two months. He had a way of ducking his head and giggling like a preadolescent boy. Yet he had a life behind him. An unexpected trip to the ICU a few years ago—a feeling that he had been only a tiny step away from death, perhaps he *had* died and returned— had led him to give up everything and start traveling. His favorite place in Orkney was the Wireless Museum; he had been there twice, his only excursions from the house, and he was adamant I'd like it. Every time I came into the house, he asked if I'd been to the Wireless Museum yet, and then gave an embarrassed little chortle.

The town of Kirkwall stems from Norse times, but the history of the Orkney Islands begins much further back, in the Neolithic period. Burial cairns and stone circles date from 3500 to 3000 B.C., and the village of Skara Brae, miraculously preserved in sand until a ferocious storm in 1850, is one of the only ancient villages in Europe still intact after five thousand years. But you have to get out into the countryside to experience the sense of time, to one of sixteen inhabited low-lying islands, of which there are sixty-seven that make up the Orkney archipelago and offer vistas of huge skies and stone circles.

Kirkwall itself, while hardly modern, having in its midst the medieval St. Magnus Cathedral and the ruins of the Bishop's Palace, is distinctly buttoned-down and Calvinist in feel, with rows of granite-faced buildings along a stone-flagged narrow street. Once this kilometer-long street, variously called Broad, Albert, Bridge, Victoria, and Main, ran by the sea front; when the inner harbor was filled in and a new section of the town built closer to the new piers and jetties, the street became enclosed, a good thing, too, as the buildings on either side now offer protection against the wind. Kirkwall is a twee place, in spite of its long and often bloody history, less bohemian than Stromness on the other side of Mainland, more like a grayly genteel Victorian town on the east coast of Scotland. Shabby, too, with a number of shops closed along the main street.

Of course, I was there in late spring, before the proper beginning of the tourist season, and a cold wind and rain make it difficult to appreciate any place properly. I found myself spending most days in the public library, one of the oldest in Scotland, upstairs in the Orkney Room. There I sat cozily, while the wind rattled the small-paned windows and the rain lashed down, and I searched for stories in the glass-fronted bookcases about sea witches, those much maligned daughters of the Cailleach and the Mither o' the Sea.

I was particularly intrigued by tales of the sellers of the wind. According to some sources, it was the Finns and Lapps of the Far North who'd specialized in selling knotted rope to sailors, with the advice not to untie more than one or, at most, two of the knots. This advice was so rarely followed that it seems to bespeak an unconscious need to keep alive the mysteries of the storm goddesses. In a book on women pirates translated from

German, I'd come across the interesting note that a woman called Bessy Miller had been "the last European wind-seller," and that she had lived in the Orkney Islands. A little more research had turned up the fact that Sir Walter Scott had based one of his main characters in his novel *The Pirate* on this real woman, Bessie Millie, whom he'd met on a trip to Orkney and Shetland in 1814. The existence of Bessie Millie seemed to suggest a place and a time when the legendary powers of the storm goddess to control the wind and waves had intersected with the fortunes of a mortal woman who made her living off the association of women and the sea by convincing sailors that she could speed their return home. Was Bessie a witch or simply rather clever?

A friend in Edinburgh had given me a copy of *The Pirate*, and I planned to spend my evenings reading it. Meanwhile, I searched in the library for stories of sellers of the wind. I found none. What I did find were stories of witchcraft and witch trials, so many of which took place here in Kirkwall, especially in the early seventeenth century.

Although Scotland had prohibited witchcraft since 1563, the law hadn't been implemented extensively until James I of England (the son of Mary, Queen of Scots, and still, at that point James VI of Scotland) became personally involved in the trials of the North Berwick witches in 1590. It was said that witches had raised such storms that James's bride-to-be, Anne of Denmark, had been unable to cross the North Sea for their wedding in 1589. Three times the ships came near Scotland and three times they were turned back, until the captain made for Norway. The witches from North Berwick confessed—when tortured—to raising storms at sea when James and Anne were returning to Scotland from Scandinavia the following year. The earl of

Bothwell was named as the instigator of the plot, and treason became mixed with witchcraft. Fear of losing power through human disloyalty and supernatural forces seems to have led to James's obsession with witches, which culminated toward the end of a witch-hunting decade with his tract, *Daemonologie.*

Although some men were tried and executed as witches, there were fewer of them than there were women, and few as malicious and evil. "The reason is easie," wrote James, "for as that sexe is frailer then man is, so is it easier to be intrapped in these grosse snares of the Devill." The trial of the North Berwick witches took place while Grace O'Malley was still harrying ships off the coast of Ireland, but while Queen Elizabeth's Irish governors sparred and battled with the unwomanly Pirate Queen, no one had ever suggested anything "devilish" or "evile" in her behavior, or that she carried out daring feats at sea through supernatural means. But Elizabeth's heir was far more superstitious than she. Although James, when he crossed the border to become James I of England, soon had other things than witchcraft to worry about, the damage in Scotland was done, and the following sixty years saw over three thousand trials of witches, particularly in border areas around Edinburgh and in Orkney.

I KEPT busy in Kirkwall, but I can't say I liked it overmuch. In town I evaded the wind by doing imaginary errands in old-fashioned shops, and drinking endless cups of tea. "Don't think I'll go out today," the man from Winnipeg told me every morning as he settled into the easy chair with his newspapers. "If I did, I suppose I'd go back to the Wireless Museum. It is really something. You ought to go, you know."

In the evenings, in my pink bedroom with the scent of pot-pourri seeping under the door, I worked my way through *The Pirate* with its portrayal of the charlatan witch Norna, based on the real sea witch Bessie Millie. In the old edition of *The Pirate* I was reading, there was a note crediting Bessie Millie for the story that became the plot of the book. Scott describes her as "nearly one hundred years old, with light-blue eyes that gleamed with a lustre like that of insanity."

But in Scott's journals of his travels around Orkney and Shetland, in an entry made August 17, 1814, Scott describes making a climb into the hills above Stromness, in company with a sea captain paying a call on Bessie Millie:

> An old hag lives in a wretched cabin on this height, and subsists by selling winds. Each captain of a merchantman, between jest and earnest, gives the old woman sixpence, and she boils her kettle to procure a favourable gale. She was a little miserable figure; upwards of ninety, she told us, and dried up like a mummy. A sort of clay-coloured cloak, folded over her head, corresponded in colour to her corpse-like complexion. Fine light-blue eyes, and nose and chin that almost met, and a ghastly expression of cunning, gave her quite the effect of Hecate.

In *The Pirate* the compelling figure of Norna roams the cliffs at the southern end of the Shetland Islands, chanting runic nonsense that nevertheless strikes awe into everyone she meets, and declaring "Do not provoke Norna of Fitful-head!" Norna can see the future; she can control the weather, even create it. She moves in thunder, to the crashing of waves. Many fear her, yet her power is based on a willful act of self-creation, which is

Norna from *The Pirate*

more sand than solid earth; in the end her magic fragments to nothing, and she's revealed as a deranged impostor. It's a fascinating portrayal of a nineteenth-century man's ambivalence about female power. Scott recalls, romantically, with great gothic flourishes of description, an ancient reverence toward the winter hag and the storm goddess. At the same time, his awe has something of disgust and even fear in it; by the end of his novel, he's done all he can to demolish the old legends.

By the time Scott came to write the character of Norna of Fitful-head in *The Pirate*, pitiful, laughable Bessie Millie had become a towering figure of mystery, to exploit and then destroy. Scott's choice of Norna as a name for his weather witch and prophetess comes from the Norns of Scandinavian mythology, the three Weird Sisters, the Fates. The Norns are the northern version of the Greek *Moirai:* Clotho the Spinner, Lachesis the Measurer, Atropos the Cutter. The *Moirai,* in turn, are Western names for the earlier Triple Goddess from the East: Creator, Preserver, Destroyer. The Celts also had a tradition of tripling their goddesses, for instance Brigit, who made a smooth transition from pagan deity to St. Brigit, Catholic saint.

The *Edda* of Snorri Sturluson refers to the Norns as the "three mysterious beings." Because they write the book of destiny and know past and future, they're also called, in German, *die Schreiberinnen,* "women who write." Other names for them are Become, Becoming, and Shall-Be. Or Fate, Being, and Necessity—Urth, Verthandi, and Skuld. Skuld was the Norse death-Norn, who cut the thread of life. The Norns were associated with the giving of names; they were often present at the birth of a child and could foretell its destiny. In Norse mythology, fate is woven of separate threads that give each of us a cloth to wear. The Norns are weavers; they give us threads that lead us into mystery and out again. These threads are full of wind, tied in knots.

E ACH MORNING on my way to the library I passed through the woods and each afternoon returned under a hail of disdainful cawing.

"I hate those crows," said Mrs. Harris. "I wish we could kill them. They make such a racket, and a terrible mess." Mrs. Harris was a very tidy woman. The house, which, on closer inspection, had two decorating motifs—maps and mementos of the Falkland Islands, and ceramic and crystal swans—was spotless. Each morning I had a new personal bath mat.

I said I didn't think they were crows, known to be solitary, but rather rooks, ancient and sociable birds—at least social among themselves.

"Rooks, crows, they're nasty birds, here and all around St. Magnus Kirk, too. It's a shame we can't have a bit of woods without all those evil-looking birds."

I sometimes felt the same, that the rooks were rather sinister. Yet I also knew that their relative, the raven, was a sacred bird, revered among many northern peoples, particularly in my own Pacific Northwest, for its swift flight and intelligence. I was fascinated by these birds, too. Whenever I walked in their woods, I stared up at them until they grew annoyed and swooped at me and sometimes shat. In olden times a group of these birds was called a "parliament of rooks." They did indeed look like rows of irritable backbenchers, waiting for their day to shine.

Sunday morning I walked down to the town center to find all the tearooms and most of the shops closed. I gravitated to the cathedral, the only public building that was open, and sat through two services to keep out of the wind. St. Magnus is small as cathedrals go, very pleasingly faced with an alternating pattern of ochre and red sandstone. It is Romanesque, built over the course of three centuries, beginning in 1137, and dedicated to the peaceable Norse earl who was murdered for trying to carry out Christian principles in his leadership. Next to the medieval cathedral in Trondheim, Norway, St. Magnus is the finest surviving example of a Norse church building and evokes the many centuries of Norwegian rule in Orkney. The cathedral is still the natural center of the town; it sits on Kirk Green, next to the ruins of the Renaissance Earl's Palace and the twelfth-century Bishop's Palace. All these structures are grand, and quite overwhelm the next spate of construction, from the nineteenth century, when landowners, rich from potash production, put up townhouses. In the seventeenth century all the houses would have been smaller than those standing today. How the cathedral must have loomed above the market square then.

The Church of Scotland service was safe and kindly. A woman next to me took my hand when the minister asked us at the end to turn to our neighbor, and she welcomed me to Orkney and seemed pleased I was in church. But outside the cathedral I found the walks slippery with rook droppings, and their cries tore up the air in a haunting, angry refrain. Their beady downward looks of irritation were personal. They didn't wish me or any of my kind well.

The next day, back upstairs in the comfort of the library's Orkney Room, I thought about St. Magnus and the rookeries in the sycamores around its old stones as I began to read about Orkney's seventeenth-century witch trials, many of which had been conducted here in Kirkwall, in the cathedral. The Calvinist kirk in post-Reformation Scotland wasn't made up of kindly churchgoers like those I'd met the day before. The ruling order was composed of men of the church dedicated to rooting out sin wherever they might find it, which often seemed to be in women's bodies.

It was here in the library that I first came across the curious story of a woman seafarer whose very abilities were seen as evidence of witchcraft: Janet Forsyth, the "Storm Witch of Westray." In 1627, Janet was twenty, living with her father on the outer island of Westray. She loved a young man called Benjamin Garrioch, who put off to sea one morning with friends. Janet had begged him not to; she'd had a terrible dream the night before. Sure enough, although the day was cloudless at first, a fog soon came up and the boat and its crew vanished.

Weeks passed and Janet fell into melancholia. Soon after,

her father died. She took to putting out to sea in her father's boat, especially when the wind blew strongly. That she always came back safe and sound impressed no one. Instead, her neighbors started to call her the Storm Witch and to say that when she sang plaintive songs to herself at night (local boys knew this from peering into her poor, thatched house), she was calling the Storm King from his caverns deep in the sea. Her neighbors began to blame her for shipwrecks and drownings. One day, during a terrific gale at sea, a large ship was sighted offshore. The island folk stood waiting on shore, making no move to help the crew. They expected the ship to break up on the rocks, and were ready to scramble for the spoils.

Then Janet came down to the shore and set off in her small boat. In spite of the rough seas that obscured her craft from the onlookers' view at times, she managed to sail up to the foundering vessel and to board it. She took the helm, giving the crew a series of orders that brought the ship into harbor. The captain tried to reward her with a purse of money; the crew crowded around to thank her. But she hurried away, saying only that she wished that someone might have done the same for her poor Ben.

Probably her neighbors were angry that they'd missed the chance to scavenge; perhaps they were ashamed to have been shown up by a mere girl in front of the foreign crew. At any rate, instead of being rewarded, Janet's heroism at sea was taken as conclusive proof she was a witch. She was arrested and brought to trial in the Cathedral of St. Magnus in Kirkwall.

No place in Orkney is without a sea witch story or two, and in many of the tales the witch is killed without benefit of trial. On the Isle of Stronsay, my next stop after Kirkwall, there is a natural seat in a cliff overlooking Mill Bay, called the Maiden's Chair. This is where Scota Bess used to sit and predict the

weather at sea. One day the men of the local kirk decided she
was a witch who must be killed. Scota Bess was dragged from
her cliffside seat by Stronsay men and beaten with flails washed
in communion water. But the day after they buried her she rose
to the surface. After this happened twice more, in desperation
the men flung her body into the Muckle Water and then
brought boatloads of dirt out to cover her. In this way, it's said,
they created the sole island on the Muckle Water, and Scota
Bess stayed buried.

But Janet Forsyth did have a trial. Its record opens with her
crime:

> In the first ye the said Jonet ar indytit and accusit for airt
> and pairt of the abominable superstitioun and superstitious
> abusing and disceveing of the people within the said Isle
> and for practeising of the wicked and devilish pointis of
> witchcraft and devilrie done by yow.

Witnesses were brought forth to describe how they'd been
bewitched. In Janet's case, Robert Reid testified that he had
been taken ill at sea and had to be brought back by his mates to
land. He then sought Janet out and accused her of bringing his
"seiknes" upon him. For answer she seems to have thrown a
bucket of salt water on him—in irritation or in an attempt to
cure him, it's not recorded, though he did seem to feel well
enough the next day to return to the sea.

Janet Forsyth had numerous accusers. No one stood up for
her. At the end of the trial she was, unsurprisingly, found guilty.
Such was the fate of hundreds of women and a few men in
Orkney during the seventeenth century, at the height of witch-
hunting fever. Many were hanged or burnt because a cow

stopped giving milk, or a child fell ill; others for crimes to do with the sea, for selling the threads to raise the winds or causing storms or casting spells on ships offshore. Whatever respect and reverence women had been accorded in ancient times for their connection with the forces of life and for their abilities as healers were transformed to suspicion and murderous hatred within the Calvinist church.

Janet's recorded trial ends with the verdict that she must be "taine be the lockman and conveyit to the place of execution with her hands bund behind her back and worried at ane staik to the dead and brunt in assis."

In other words, she must be hung on Gallows Hill in Kirkwall and burnt to ashes.

There is another version of her trial, however, told in an old collection of nineteenth-century newspaper columns called *Around the Orkney Peat-Fires*. The story, "The Westray Storm Witch," has an unexpected conclusion, one I'd like to believe is true. In this story her trial took place in the cathedral before a crowd violently and noisily against her, but Janet defended herself bravely from all charges: "In saving the crew of the vessel referred to, I had no assistance but from God, with a powerful arm to guide the tiller of my boat, and a quick eye to avoid the breakers which surrounded me."

The judge nevertheless found her guilty and sentenced her the next day "to be fastened to a stake, to be worried to death by the hangman, and her body thereafter to be burnt to ashes."

As this sentence was being delivered, some sailors from the Royal Navy came into the court and cheered along with the crowd. Contemptuously Janet turned to face the crowd; she suddenly said, "Save me, Ben," and fainted. In a moment, one of the sailors was beside her. They pulled him off and took Janet to her cell. She would be hung the next day with great ceremony. The crowd assembled in Broad Street, and at ten in the morning the cathedral bell began to toll. Everyone awaited Janet's appearance. But when there was no sight of her or the hangman, the sheriff went to her cell. He found the door open and the hangman and guards dead drunk.

Some years later, when an Orkney man was passing through Manchester, England, he saw a shop sign with the Orkney name "Benjamin Garrioch." When he went inside, he found Janet Forsyth at the counter, looking years younger. She told him that her Ben and his companions had been picked up in the fog by a ship from the Royal Navy and press-ganged into service in the French wars. His appearance in Kirkwall the morning of the trial was his first return to Orkney in two years. He hadn't let her hang, but had spirited her away to the ship she'd saved from destruction a few weeks before. The captain gladly took her aboard and deposited her in Liverpool until Ben could join her. They never returned to Orkney—who could blame them?—but made a success of their business in Manchester, and lived there ever after.

On my last evening in Kirkwall I returned from the library through the woods as usual, and stood a while looking out over the hill that led down to town and the harbor. The wind, unquiet, muttered around my shoulders and tried to tease the scarf from my neck. You could sooner imagine someone making a living in Orkney calming the wind than raising it. Could I unloose the wind just by chanting an incantation? The rooks stood out like black candles on the strange, thickened gray branches of the sycamores.

"I am Norna of Fitful-head!" I shouted on impulse. "Double, double, toil and trouble!"

One of the birds flew up and headed toward me. The wind roared. Anybody watching would have thought I was mad. Or maybe just a witch.

CHAPTER V

HERRING LASSIES

Stronsay, the Orkney Islands

A CURIOUS old photograph hangs in the Scottish Fisheries Museum. In it several women carry men on their backs. The women, their full skirts tucked into waistbands, are knee-deep in sea water. They grip the men's booted legs firmly; the men clasp the women around the necks. These are wives hauling their husbands from shore out to their fishing boats, carrying them high above the water so their feet don't get wet. Apparently this was common practice on the east coast of Scotland around 150 years ago. In his book *Fishing Boats and Fisher Folk on the East Coast of Scotland*, Peter Anson describes the women of one village, Avoch:

> The women were as strong as the men. They could carry
> immense burdens without apparently feeling the strain. They
> thought nothing of a hundred pounds of fish in a creel on their
> backs. At that time there was no pier at Avoch. The shore is
> flat, and the boats had to lie some distance off, so the women
> used to carry out their husbands on their backs, "to keep the
> men's feet dry." In a like manner they brought in all the fish
> and tackle from the boats, never objecting to wading out into
> the sea, no matter what might be the weather or time of year.

Two weeks ago, my friends in Edinburgh had taken me

Women carrying their husbands out to the fishing boats

north of the city to the coastal village of Anstruther to see this photograph, and I was glad they had. For it was in the Scottish Fisheries Museum that I first began to glimpse the old, preindustrial world of fishing, when women and men worked together in the family and community. Before the advent of decked sailing smacks in the mid-nineteenth century and the steam drifters and trawlers that came into use around 1880, fishing tended to be done on a smaller scale, and few fishermen ventured out in their open skiffs more than a day's row from their coastal villages. In those days women's contribution to the home economy was prized. In many Scottish fishing villages, women kept their maiden names, and their initials were used to mark their husbands' fishing gear. In addition to keeping house and caring for the children, women mended the nets and baited the lines with shelled mussels and limpets. "White fishing" (for cod, halibut, and haddock) was line fishing; "full" or "great" lines had about twelve hundred hooks and could be two miles long; "small" lines were about three hundred feet. Women helped bring in the boats at day's end and prepared the catch for sale.

Toward the end of the nineteenth century, women and men came to do more sharply defined tasks; however, women were still active and important participants in the fishing life all around the Scottish coasts and the western and northern isles. The museum has a large room devoted to Scotland's once thriving herring industry. In addition to photographs on the walls, there is a group of male and female mannequins in nine-teenth-century dress displayed against a painted background of wharves and fishing boats. The women wear long, striped skirts and shawls over their hair; their fingers are wound with rags and string called "cloots" to prevent infection from knife cuts and fish guts. While the men put together barrels, the women stand in front of troughs of shining silver fish. These were the herring lassies, the gutter girls, an astonishing number of whom migrated like fish in their thousands up and down the Scottish and English coasts and islands, from Lerwick in the Shetland Islands to Great Yarmouth in England. In economic terms they were a migrant workforce that followed the fishing fleets and dealt with the catch. Some were fishing widows, but more were independent, often young, women who saw a chance to improve their lot and to support themselves. Their mothers and grand-mothers may have worked closely with their menfolk to bring in the catch in the villages, but the herring lassies forged commu-nities of their own.

ORKNEY IS made up of more than seventy islands, and I wanted to know more of the archipelago than just Mainland's Kirkwall, so I took a ferry to the village of Whitehall on the island of Stronsay. Whitehall was once a major fishing port for all of Orkney. Its harbor on Papa Sound faced the North Sea and was easily accessible to foreign vessels from the east. British ships, meanwhile, could dock on Stronsay without getting too close to the Pentland Firth. Most importantly, Stronsay was near the route the herring shoals took on their annual migration south. I'd come to Whitehall looking for traces of the strong-backed, no-nonsense herring lassies who had flocked here in such numbers—fifteen hundred each season—up through the 1930s.

It was a bleached-cold day, gusting heavily, and Whitehall looked bleak and abandoned as I walked off the ferry. Everything spoke of crushed dreams and straitened circumstances, yet the gray stone and pebble-dashed stucco buildings that lined the waterfront gave evidence of a once prosperous and thriving little town. It didn't help that the wind bent me double as I walked to the hotel.

The man who'd taken my two-night booking had made a pretense on the phone of checking to see that a room was available. It was clear from the absence of tourists on the ferry that, more nights than not, *all* the rooms were free. Mine had hideous yellow walls, a lumpy bed, and the ubiquitous personal bath mat. It looked out at the harbor and a street that was always empty except for the few cars that drove on or off the ferry three times a day. A hundred years ago, looking out at this same view, I would have seen the harbor filled with sailing craft and steam drifters, the summer herring fleet. Horse-drawn carts would have been taking herring to the many curing stations on the docks. The wharves would have been jammed with barrels, just made by a raft of coopers. The herring lassies, in long skirts and shawls and with cloots on their fingers, would have been standing at troughs of fish, gutting them with a quick flash of the knife and tossing them aside to a packer, who'd sort them into grades and layer them into barrels to be salted.

In the 1920s and '30s, the scene would have looked almost the same, except the "Zulu" sailboats and coal-fired steam drifters would have been replaced by diesel trawlers and large herring seiners. The women would no longer be wearing shawls, but oilskin aprons over overalls, and sweaters rolled up to show muscular arms. Their hair would be bobbed; many would sport jaunty round caps and berets. They'd be from all over Scotland, looking forward to freedom, fun, and the chance to make their own money. They roomed by the hundreds in close quarters across the harbor on the tiny island of Papa Stronsay, in dormitories that still stand, but are derelict now. All of it was abandoned now, on both sides of the bay: the wharves, the shops, the houses. In half an hour of looking out the window, I didn't see a single person go by.

Across from the hotel was a long low building called the Fish Mart. The brochures had made this sound like a bustling place: "And while in Stronsay, be sure to visit the Fish Mart, with its museum of herring culture and its teashop." *While in Stronsay* . . . There was actually not too much to do in Stronsay *except* visit the Fish Mart. After unpacking, I went over to take a look. Marion, the other owner of the hotel, had to let me in. She put on a brave front; like her husband, she seemed chagrined at the emptiness of the hotel and the entire village, but acted as though that would all change when summer finally came. It seemed to me it might take more than blue skies to get people to Stronsay, but I didn't want to argue with her determined optimism. Marion's dyed-red spiky hair and colorful leggings were the brightest things about Whitehall. She had a bevy of tiny yapping dogs and an intermittently vivacious manner.

The Fish Mart was a warren of thirty rooms where each

herring agent had kept a temporary office during the fishing season. Each office held a desk with a ledger book and a small safe. Back when Whitehall was a busy port, fishermen would bring a sample of their catch to the Fish Mart, and in their ledger books the agents would note how many tons of herring they bought, the price paid, and to which fisherman. Over the years the building had taken on the status of a quasi museum. One or two displays were properly exhibited, but other rooms were completely empty or held odd collections: One had nothing more than a baby's wooden cradle and five gramophones, each one with a Victrola trumpet like a large dusty brown flower.

Part of the Fish Mart had become a café with plastic-flowered tablecloths on round plastic tables; a vase of plastic flowers sat in the center of each. Various "hand-crafted" items were cheerily displayed on the windowsills and counters—painted dishes, a shawl, a tea cozy, none of them particularly well made, and all priced very high.

I asked Marion if there was a way I could get over to Papa Stronsay, to see the dormitories of the herring girls.

"Possibly. It's a bit complicated, you see," she said. "The island was just sold last week. It used to belong to some friends of ours who farmed it. But they decided to pack it in. A group of Catholic monks just bought it!" She considered. "I'll see what I can do. Bill Miller has a boat. He's a retired police inspector from the London CID."

Two hours later I found myself climbing down a slippery green set of stairs off the Stronsay pier into the *Nora* with Bill, his Irish wife, Breida, and Marion, who wore a green velvet jester's cap with a bell for the occasion.

Bill was a strongly built man in his fifties; it was easy to

imagine him as one of the stolid inspectors in a British police
thriller. I asked him if his detective work had been more like that
of Morse or Dalgliesh.

He laughed dismissively. "Not much like either," he said. "I
like John Thaw as Morse though."

"I have a soft spot for Sergeant Lewis," I said. "He's so put-
upon and decent. I like Helen Mirren in *Prime Suspect*. Is the
CID more like that?"

"Umm, a bit," he allowed.

The trip across the harbor was short. A thousand years ago,
there had been a church and a monastery on Papa Stronsay (the
word *papa*, found on islands from Orkney to Iceland, indicates
Irish monks once lived there). The order that had just bought
the 250-acre island was the Transalpine Redemptorist
Missioners. An offshoot of Redemptorists originally founded by
St. Alphonsus, this order was firm in its desire to live in solitude
and to hold to Latin for its services. The Stronsay people, who
no longer even had a church on their island, thought, cautiously,
that the monks might be a good thing for Papa Stronsay. At this
point, anything that might bring a few more people out to the
islands couldn't hurt.

Yet the sale was so recent that the monks hadn't yet moved
in, much less begun building a new monastery. The stone farmhouse had an old greenhouse attached to a south-facing room,
where a rosebush bloomed with clematis twining through. One
of the roses pressed its big satiny ivory-peach head of petals
right against the glass. It seemed as if the owners had just gone
away for the day, not abandoned their home to monks forever.

Bill and I went for a walk around the dormitories. Two long
ones were still standing. They had lately been used for pigs, and
smelled of it. Other dormitory buildings were gone except for

the foundations. The Stronsay herring industry was at its
height during the teens, twenties, and early thirties. In the
summer season, with all the fishermen, herring girls and
coopers, the population swelled to five thousand. There were at
least three curing stations on Papa Stronsay—the piers still
stood, with rail tracks embedded in the cement—but many of
the herring girls worked over in Whitehall and were ferried
back and forth by a motor launch named *Welcome Home*.

The Scottish girls were renowned for their speed and
agility with a sharp knife. They could gut a herring in a few seconds. Since they were paid a piecework price, by the barrel, it
was crucial to be quick. They worked in teams of three: two to
stand at the "farlin," or open trough, and one to pack the fish.
The first layer of herring was laid with the silver side down, and
the last layer silver side up. This ensured that no matter which
end of the barrel was opened, the "silver darlings" would gleam.
The packers kept the layers sprinkled with salt and put a lid on
the barrel when it was full. In ten days the herring would have
pickled; the coopers then drilled in a bunghole and drained out
some of the liquid. They pried open the lid and topped off the
barrel with another layer or two of fish. This method was called
the "Scotch cure." Most of the herring was sold to the Baltic
countries.

It was tough work. The herring lassies routinely stood on
their feet for twelve or fifteen hours a day, with few breaks. They
had to work at lightening speed or lose their place. Their
clothes were spattered with blood and guts; they could never
get the oily stench of fish out of their skin and hair. A cut to the
fingers could mean blood poisoning; at the very least their
hands were always raw, salt-stung, and unhealed. The weather
couldn't have been much different from today, which means that

Herring lassies gutting fish

even in summer it would have been chill with wind and wet. Only in later years did they work under any covering. Nor were their accommodations good. They slept in crowded rooms, on straw-filled mattresses. All they had to sit on were the clothes chests they carried with them from port to port.

No one, in writing about the herring fishermen, the coopers, or the haulers, bothers to tell us how cheerful and high-spirited they were, so I'm suspicious that these adjectives come up so frequently, with a hint of defensiveness, in describing the herring lassies and their working conditions. All the same, it's clear from photographs and oral history that the women not only worked hard and well, but thrived on the independence of a paycheck and the camaraderie of the wharves. Many herring girls started gutting at age fifteen or sixteen, and not a few continued to work into their sixties. Christina Jackman was a herring girl from the Shetland Islands, whose granddaughter, Susan Telford, transcribed an oral history of her life that is short on self-pity and long on laughter. Christina describes great friendship among the women, many of whom gutted herring together for years, even as they married and raised families. For some it was purely local work and only at the summer peak. Others, like Christina, worked a full season, traveling all the way down the coasts of Scotland and England to Great Yarmouth or Lowestoft, where the fishing ended in October. It was this camaraderie that enabled them to band together to demand better working conditions and wages. In the thirties, when catches began to decline and wages dropped, the women went on strike and won.

Bill and I were making our way slowly across the island to the remains of an old chapel, currently under excavation by archeologists. We saw Marion off in a field, apparently running after an errant sheep. With her bright red-and-yellow leggings, green jacket, and green jester's cap, she threw a festive splash against the somber gray sky and dull meadows. When we came to the shore, Bill pointed out a cantilevered reef that stretched out into the sea. It was the site of many a shipwreck off these coasts. He bent and picked up a religious medal, showed it to me, and replaced it carefully. He'd been here a few days ago and had found other medals. He believed the monks had made a circuit of the island's perimeter and dropped the medals at intervals in order to bless the land.

I had an instant's fantasy that Bill and I were on a CID case, looking for clues to a murder. I thought of mentioning to him that I had written some mysteries and had won a British Crime Writer's award. I had even done a reading once with P. D. James. But the fact was, I'd always been a bit of a fraud as a proper thriller writer. I never bothered to learn anything about poisons, weapons, or police procedures. As if to prove my utter ineptness as a detective, it was Bill who found all the medals.

Back at the pier, Bill and I stood waiting for Breida and Marion to catch up with us. Bill was a photographer and had restored many of the old photographs I'd seen this morning at the Fish Mart in a series of albums of Stronsay life. Years ago this bay had been so full of boats that it seemed you could walk from Papa to Whitehall. Now all you could see were a few shiny-wet seal heads, popping up from time to time to give us a curious look.

THE HOTEL pub filled up in the evening. I bought Bill and Breida a drink, had my dinner, and retired upstairs to continue reading Peter Anson's classic book about Scottish fishing life. The jacket said that he joined the Anglican Benedictine community on Caldey Island when he was twenty-one, in 1910. He cofounded the Apostleship of the Sea, which still provides Catholic chaplains for ships, about ten years later, and then left the order to concentrate on drawing and writing. First published in 1930, his book already has an elegiac tone. Due to a combination of declining catches and changes in the way fish were caught and sold, many of the fishing villages he describes had lost population. Young people moved away for better opportunities; boats lay rotting on the shore. The herring fisheries, in particular, would never again reach their pre–World War II

Three generations of New Haven fishwives

level; the industry would be finished by the 1960s, when the stocks dropped to unsustainable levels.

Yet the world Anson describes has its roots in an earlier time, when women's work was fully apparent, and partnerships between men and women still in living memory. In the coastal village of Buckie, for instance, in the late eighteenth century, Anson tells us: "[T]here was a maxim among the fisherfolk that 'no man can be a fisher and want a wife.' This was literally true: without a wife a fisherman at that period would have been quite unable to carry on his job."

An appreciation of women's important work in the fishing industry has declined precipitously since the 1700s—or even the 1930s, when Anson was describing the old ways. Anson himself saw no reason to disguise his admiration for the hardy fishwives of Newhaven and Fisherrow on the Firth of Forth near Edinburgh. These women would trek to the city several times a week, carrying on their backs heavy creels of freshly caught fish weighing from a hundred to two hundred pounds. Sometimes the women walked in relays, shifting the basket to each other every hundred yards.

> They did the work of men and had the manners of men, in addition to the strength of men. Their amusements too were masculine. They played golf long before it became the present-day fashionable sport of women. On Shrove Tuesday there was always a football match at Musselburgh between married and unmarried Fisherrow women, and it was the former who were nearly always victorious! The fishwives were famous for their rude eloquence.

There was a sound like hammers striking anvils, and the whole hotel seemed to stagger briefly. It was just the pipes. The noise downstairs in the pub went on for quite a long time, but the next morning the hotel was deserted as usual. I took a long walk along the shore in the biting wind. Arctic terns darted at the crown of my head, and sea gulls cried relentlessly. Forests of bladder wrack and tangle, like soaked shoe leather, seemed to have washed up overnight; down by the low-tide mark a rusty brown carpet of rockweed covered the stony shore. Long years ago, before the herring industry made Whitehall an Orkney boomtown, there had been a kelp factory on the island. In 1722 a local laird, James Fea, got the idea to harvest the seaweed here and burn it down to a glossy slag. Its high alkali content made the potash valuable for soap and glass manufacture. The kelp factory thrived for a hundred years, until 1830, and at its height employed three thousand workers and made a substantial profit

The Fisherlass

for James Fea and the lairds who followed him. Seaweed is free, after all, and the labor of crofters was almost free as well. A few days ago, in Kirkwall, I'd found a haunting post card of an old, sepia-tinted photograph showing three women burning kelp. They are wearing old-fashioned long skirts and shawls; the land is barren; the smoke half-obscures their faces and makes them seem like ghosts beginning to materialize.

I bought a little food for lunch at the local shop, which was open only sporadically, and around midafternoon went up past several large farms to the ridge that ran along Stronsay's back like a spine and gave stunning views on either side of sand-ringed bays. Marion had suggested I talk with an elderly couple who had a small farm up here, as they might be able to give me a sense of the old Stronsay way of life.

As soon as I walked into their parlor, I felt welcomed as I hadn't been since leaving my friends in Edinburgh. My hand was pressed, sherry was poured, homemade buttery shortbread appeared on a green glass plate. Edwin (Eddie) and Charlotte (Carrie) Cooper were in their late seventies, dignified and lively. They were remarkably good-looking people, who must have been stunners in their youth. Both had been born on the island, Eddie in this very house. Eddie's grandmother had worked as a herring girl at More's curing station; his father had worked at the fish-gutting factory. Carrie had been born right across from the Fish Mart, above what was then the post office and is now part of the Stronsay Hotel. Her first job was to take telegrams from the post office to the agents in their offices in the Fish Mart. She would dash across the busy street, avoiding boys rolling hoops and horse-drawn carts full of fish guts on their way to the factory. There were shops in every building then: sweet shops, barbers, chip shops, butchers, shooting galleries.

"In the summer," Carrie added with a smile, "there were five ice cream shops, three of them owned by Italians. The bar in the hotel was the largest north of Inverness. There was a cinema." That hotel burned down in 1939. Of the cinema there is no trace. "And on Sundays, oh, you can't imagine," said Carrie. "You would hear the sound of singing all over the island. At the Stronsay Kirk, at the Salvation Army, at the missions."

I'd read that Bible reading and churchgoing were big on Stronsay. Every summer the evangelist Harry Young would conduct "tent missions" just outside the village. It was part of the entertainment in a short summer where the work pace was fast and furious. The girls would come over on Sunday from Papa Stronsay, dressed in their finest, smelling of scent, lotion smoothed over their raw hands, carrying their Bibles. After services they would stroll and flirt, eat fish and chips, ice cream and sodas.

Carrie and Eddie plied me with more sherry. They brought out albums and scrapbooks. They had excellent memories. Carrie had kept a journal most of her life. She joked that after I left she would write down what we'd said so she'd remember it. We exchanged addresses, and then Eddie gave me a ride back to Whitehall village, taking a longer route so he could show me some of the farms. He'd left school at fourteen, and in addition to tending the small family farm, he'd delivered the island's post. Up to and all through the war he'd used a horse-drawn cart, but afterward he made his rounds by automobile. He said the fields used to be full of people working, the roads busy whatever the season. Now the island's economy was in worse shape than ever. The sons and daughters of the small farmers had moved away, the farms had been consolidated into larger concerns, and no one grew anything now but hay for the cattle. A European Union embargo on British beef had wreaked havoc on that, too. The population was down to only a few hundred. Most of the people he and Carrie had grown up with had left.

Eddie drove me slowly through Whitehall village. "There was a general shop there. And a barber there." A cold white light had fallen over the street, as if the whole village were an underexposed print with only ghostly images visible. The photographs that Bill had restored showed prosperous men in suits standing in front of the Fish Mart, and herring lassies and coopers crowding the wharves. If only it were so simple to redevelop the original negative and see the ghost shapes fill in and the village come to life again.

CHAPTER VI

A MAN'S WORLD

Stromness, the Orkney Islands

THE OFFICE of the Orkney Fudge factory in Stromness reminded me of one of the offices my father used to share with accountant friends in the 1950s and early '60s. Like those rooms, these offices had linoleum floors and plain metal or wood desks, straight-backed chairs, venetian blinds—everything solid, nothing flimsy, all of it looking vaguely army surplus, in drab brown, beige, and green. Not a computer or fax in sight, only an elderly adding machine and a few typewriters. Vanilla was in the air, and chocolate, and cigarettes, and the mustiness of old paper and leather.

At the largest desk sat a dapper gentleman in his late seventies with some fat ledger books bound in crumbling leather in front of him. He wore a tweed suit with a sweater vest. His eyes were very blue against ruddy skin. The ledgers didn't belong to the Orkney Fudge factory, but had come from his great-great-grandmother, Christian Robertson, a well-known merchant and whaling agent in Stromness in the early 1800s.

I'd seen cellophane-wrapped bars and gift boxes of Robertson's Orkney Fudge for sale in shops since arriving in these islands, but it never occurred to me to put the name together with the woman whose story I was seeking. Christian Robertson was another of those tantalizing names that had floated across the pages of a guidebook. "The Doubles is a large pair of houses built as a home by Mrs Christian Robertson with the proceeds of her shipping agency, which sent as many as eight hundred men on whaling expeditions in one year," said *The Rough Guide to Scotland*. I'd wanted to come to Stromness, of course—a history-rich seaport as well as the departure point for the ferry to the Shetland Islands—but the story of Christian Robertson was what drew me, that and the prospect of lively stories of maritime women. After my melancholy stay in Whitehall, ghosted by herring lassies, I was especially glad to find myself again in the bustle of a thriving town.

A chance encounter in Kirkwall had put me on to a relative of Christian, and it was Anne Robertson, a dark-haired, forceful-looking solicitor with an office on the main street of Stromness, who told me to call her uncle. "Uncle Jimmy is the family historian. He has her papers and everything in his office."

The papers were the ledger books detailing provisions ordered and paid for, and wages held and paid to seamen. There was also a letter book containing copies of the correspondence that went on between Christian and whaling ship owners in the northern English port of Hull. The bulky books were piled in a large trunk that had also belonged to her, rescued by her family from a moldering barn.

Jim Robertson had an engaging smile under a well-clipped white mustache, and a swing to his step. His girl, he said, making me a cup of tea, was at the dentist. Jim's responses to my questions about Christian were mixed in with stories of his own past. He had been a singer, had even been invited to audition for the newly formed Scottish National Opera. He had been a saxophonist with a swing band, and had played all over the islands. Once or twice a man in coveralls and a puffy blue paper cap poked his head in the door of the office, but at four or four-thirty

the faint noise from the factory stopped. The sun had come out
and filtered through the venetian blinds and the smoke of Jim
Robertson's cigarette.

"So, you're asking about Christian, are you? She's someone
we're very proud of. She made this family. Johnston was her
maiden name. She was born around 1780 on a large farm near
Birsay on Mainland. She was sent to a ladies' academy down
south, that is, on the Scottish mainland. She was well educated
for a woman of her time. Her brother had the family farm; he
went bankrupt and she got nothing. She married into the
Robertson family, who were merchants in Stromness. Her husband died young, in 1808, after a long illness. She was left with
five children and a great many debts." One of the earliest letters
the family has of Christian's mentions these debts. She writes to
her cousins William and Nicolas Leith:

> That I am much pinched owing to a deal of bad debt that is
> owing my late husband and whatever claim is against the
> family every person is calling on me, and I am paying every
> person off as quick as in my power to save the property as I
> hope in God I shall do it.

Within eighteen years, not only were the debts cleared but
Christian had built up business to such an extent that she was
able to leave a significant amount of property in her will. The
business that she took over and expanded was varied, but it was
built on provisioning the vessels that made a last stop in
Stromness before heading off across the Atlantic, either to
Canada or Greenland. Orkney at the beginning of the nineteenth century was a far different place from the Norse-
Scottish backwater of earlier times. Wars with France had

rendered the English Channel frequently unsafe for shipping through much of the eighteenth century, and the blockades, privateers, and trade embargoes of Napoleonic times had made even the ferocious Pentland Firth an attractive option. As ships made their way north around Scotland, the protected harbor of Stromness, with its alehouses and inns, its fresh water, produce, and meat, was discovered by traders.

Increasingly, too, Stromness had become a place to recruit men for work in Canada with the Hudson's Bay Company. The company first engaged Orcadians in 1702, thirty-two years after it was incorporated in London for the purpose of seeking a passage to the Pacific and engaging in whatever sort of profitable trade it could, which turned out to be trapping beaver and other fur-bearing animals. The profits from the fur trade sustained the company for over two centuries and gave it an economic monopoly and a quasi-political jurisdiction over a territory called Rupert's Land or the Nor' Wast, which began as the area around Hudson's Bay and came to encompass most of Canada. Orcadians were much in demand in the Nor' Wast for their "patience and perseverance, quiet disposition and industrious habits and power of endurance." By 1799 the men from Orkney made up four out of five workers on the company's payroll.

Robertson's had had its own pier out into the harbor, and its offices above the shop gave a good view of the activity on the wharves and main street below. The ledger I'd opened showed page after page, in the neatly flowing script of the time, now sepia with age, of orders for tea, ale, chicken, whiskey, blacking, timber. Robertson's made up provisions for ships heading out to sea, as well as for requests brought back from Orcadians in Canada on five- and ten-year contracts at the trading posts and settlements. Robertson's handled orders for clothing, books, musical instruments, biscuits, sweets, and spirits. Hudson's Bay ships brought the requests in the autumn; Robertson's compiled the orders over the winter, packed them in watertight wooden boxes and sent them out in early summer. Christian Robertson was also a temporary recruiting agent for Hudson's Bay when they were between company managers in Stromness, and more importantly as the years passed, for the whaling trade based in Hull. Owners of the whaling ships wrote to her asking for men to make up the crew; her letter book holds copies of correspondence with ship owners Gardiner and Joseph Egginton, twin brothers and Hull's biggest whale-ship owners, and with John Voase, the owner of the *Truelove*, which made over seventy trips to the Arctic. Christian hired local men, arranged for cash advances, and made financial arrangements for relatives at home. At one time there were eleven hundred men on her books.

The boom years of the Hull whaling trade were 1813 to 1820, when ships returned with casks of chopped-up blubber to be boiled down for oil, and whalebone or baleen for corsets and umbrellas. The ship owners prospered and with them Stromness. For after the hunting grounds around Spitsbergen to the north of Norway were depleted, the whaling ships headed for Greenland and the Davis Strait, destinations that made Orkney a more obvious port.

The 1820s were good years, too, and hundreds of Orcadians were taken on by the Hull whaling ships. Adept rowers, and accustomed to wet and cold, they were perfect for Arctic conditions and much in demand on whalers. But in 1830 expeditions began to encounter harsher weather than they'd ever known. Late that summer the ice advanced with terrifying rapidity in Melville Bay and floes were driven against the land ice, crushing the ships between them and grinding their hulls until they split apart. One observer wrote:

> At one fell swoop the *Baffin* was cut asunder; in the same
> dreadful spot the beautiful *Ville de Dieppe* and *Achilles* of
> Dundee were pressed to the water's edge; the *Ratler*, an old
> sloop of war, that, by her firmness and wedge-like form, had
> rode triumphant over the floes in 1821, was now projected
> from the surface and shivered in her fall.

Nineteen British ships and one French vessel were crushed that season; many more were barely able to drag themselves back across the Atlantic. Worse years were to come in terms of falling catches and more ship breakups; in 1835 many ships were trapped in the ice for most of the winter, leaving crews with dwindling provisions and almost no water. A relief expedition, finally sent in January 1836 by the British Admiralty to find eleven missing ships, was unable to cross the Atlantic and was driven back to Stromness. It was fortunate that the relief ship, the *Cove*, with its bedding, medication, and food, was in harbor, for soon two whaling ships staggered into port, carrying frostbitten, starving, scurvy-plagued survivors. The town became a hospital, and then a morgue. Many seamen never came back at all. It was almost as bad the next winter, in 1836.

Through it all, Christian Robertson kept Robertson's warehouses and agent services going. She drummed up business by writing ship owners:

> That you may have some idea of the rate of wages here last
> fishing season I shall hereto subjoin a note of the wages of

the ship *Alexander* of Aberdeen and *Cumbrian* of Hull from
which you will perceive that the wages are (I presume)
much lower than they are in your quarter.

She was clearly in charge. All letters came addressed to
"Mrs. Christian Robertson, Stromness."

I paged through the ledgers and letter books, a bit overwhelmed by the steady brown script, and was distracted by
other stories Mr. Robertson wanted to tell me. Stories about the
sinking of the German fleet at the end of World War I, and
much more about his own life. He had gotten into confectionery
by chance. He'd been working in a café and playing sax at night
here in Stromness, when he and a friend decided to start a
bakery. This was right after the war, when rationing was still in
effect. Jim Robertson's friend could decorate a cake like an artist
paints a painting; they had a dozen ideas for fillings for buns and
tarts, but there was an apparent bakery mafia in Stromness. The
mafia had sewn supplies up tight, and there were no flour, no
eggs, no butter to be found. All the two friends could get was
sugar and chocolate, so they decided to try candy making
instead. They made something that in Orkney was called
"tablet," a rather granular, hard bar of flavored sugar, without a
hint of cream or butter. Visitors called it "Orkney fudge," and
the name stuck. "I expanded, had a factory in Edinburgh. Now
it's small again, winding down. It's hard to get good help," Mr.
Robertson said. "Engineers, I mean. People who can fix the
machines. They can make more money abroad, or at the oil terminal on Flotta. Business used to be much stronger, in the
eighties. I had lots of important visitors then."

I noticed he had a photograph of himself and a kilted Prince
Charles on the wall, and next to it, one of himself and Margaret

Thatcher. "Margaret and I got on very well," he said. I asked if I could take his photograph, and he turned, posing so I could get his profile. A lifelong bachelor, he still played the sax.

Before I left, Mr. Robertson gave me a tour. The factory was deserted, and its machines strange and wonderful. They were heavy and foreign-looking; some had been built in Poland and France, others looked as if they'd been constructed in Hollywood in the 1950s for films about interstellar or under-water travel. The milk condenser was a giant ball of shiny steel, pale enamel green with complicated levers and gauges and bolted portholes that appeared to have been designed according to instructions by Jules Verne. Others were painted, cast-iron machines, decorated with buttons and knobs of unknown use, now pushed to the side of the cavernous warehouse. "We did fancier chocolates, once, truffles and so on. But no one knows how to run some of the machines now. We used to have fifty people here. The old ones retired, the engineers went to work for the oil companies, the young ones leave Orkney. The techniques are lost."

Over everything hung the scent of chocolate, vanilla, and sugar with a flicker of rum, a rumble of whiskey. One of the specialty fudges was called "Stag's Breath." Mr. Robertson loaded me with boxes of fudge and I walked out of the factory to find welcome sunshine. Even the weather seemed more cheerful here than in Whitehall. I left the fudge at the Ferry Inn, where I was staying, and began to stroll along the narrow main street, so unified between the gray flagstone pavement below and the gray sandstone houses on either side. What might Stromness have looked like in the late 1700s or early 1800s?

I imagined the salt-crusted timbers of the wharves stacked with water butts and rum casks, hogsheads of wine, barrels of

salt pork and ship's biscuits, with coils of rope and folded sail-
cloth, and waterproof boxes. Two three-masted ships are
anchored out in the harbor; in deeper water, barks and cutters
are tight alongside the wharves, with seamen heaving boxes on
and off the vessels, to rattling oaths and songs. The main street
is lined with the workshops of carpenters, sail makers, rope
makers, with ship chandlers, tailors, barbers, and drapers, with
inns and alehouses. Here, where the post office now stands, are
the premises of Robertson's, shelves stocked with goods, ledgers
neatly acknowledging orders requested and filled. The sharp
smells of salt fish, tobacco, coffee, and pickles permeate the
walls, spill out into the street, mingle with the sour-sweet reek
of peat fires and damp, dung-infested narrow alleys and closes.
Pigs and cows are being driven over these gray flagstones, and
chickens in coops squawk down on the wharves. Horses pull
carts of hay and fodder for the animals being taken aboard. And
the squealing and lowing, the clucking and the calling out,
"Cockles, fresh cockles," and "Look sharp, mate!" are the background to singing on the wharves:

> O, 'twas in the year of ninety-four,
> And of June the second day,
> That our gallant ship her anchor weighed,
> And from Stromness bore away, brave boys!
> And from Stromness bore away!

On a clear evening like tonight Christian Robertson is at a
window in her upstairs office, looking up from her correspondence and her ledger books with interest at the progress of the
loading, hardly aware of the commotion and noise in the street,
it being so familiar. Taking her pen, she dips it in ink and writes:

G & J Egginton, Esqs.,

Gentlemen,

Your ship *Leviathan* arrived here the 7th, with 15 fish, all
well and sailed the 9th at 4 A.M., and I hope has arrived safe.
Enclosed you have the Certificate & copy of my acct. Which
I trust you will find correct. I only sent 2 oxen by Capt. K as
I could not ship any more without detaining the vessel, it
being Sunday. —There is a ship in sight which I hope is the
Kiero . . .

THE HOUSES on this main street were built in the eighteenth
and nineteenth centuries by sea captains and merchants, and
from the outside they seemed hardly changed, tucked together
tight and tall. Few cross streets, but many steeply squeezed
lanes, sporting fanciful names like Khyber Pass or Hellihole
Road, wound up into the hills above the town. It was easy to
imagine the parlors of these elegant graystone houses still decorated with shells from the South Pacific, paintings of barks and
schooners, carved teak furniture, Chinese vases, stuffed parrots.
Gardens were squeezed in wherever there was a bit of space, a
single sycamore or lilac spreading low, with ivory and teal
hostas beneath, or an intensely worked paradise of bold yellow
Welsh poppies, airy columbines, and dark-blue irises. I followed
one pinched alleyway down to the water's edge to admire a lush
garden tucked next to a boathouse draped with nets, a rusty
spar, a crumbling rowboat. Stromness met my inexact criteria
for favorite places: Could I live here? Yes.

Standing by the boathouse and the garden, I saw the tide
was out, and the two green hillocks across from the inward
curve along which the town was built were once again revealed

as the higher ground of a small peninsula. You could walk over the mud flats and sand to reach them; occasionally, from my room at the Ferry Inn, I'd seen a truck driving across the sand bar, for the smaller of the two hills had a farm atop it. When the tide was in, the only way to approach was by boat, for the hillocks became islets, or holms. The Inner Holm and the Outer Holm they were called on my nautical map of Orkney, and I hadn't yet invented new names for them. Since leaving Ireland, I'd sometimes given names to islands on my voyage: Papa Stronsay was, to me, the Isle of the Herring Lassies, for instance.

Holm was a word I knew from Norwegian; it meant small island. Although you didn't hear it much in American English, the word was everywhere along these Celtic-Norse coasts. Its meaning was islet, from which I extrapolated that a holm, unlike a sea rock, was always visible, just not in its entirety. The tides could claim it and lap it and hide most of it, and then, six hours later, expose it again. This natural rhythm of conceal and reveal was pleasing to me somehow.

Walking through Stromness this evening, I came to a halt in front of Login's Well. No one drank from it now, but it was still preserved as a watering hole, with a plaque that recalled several important expeditions that had made use of it when provisioning in Orkney. Captain Cook and Captain Bligh had both set forth from Stromness, as had the Franklin Expedition, which later came to grief in the Canadian Arctic and never returned. Across from the well was Login's Inn, which had flourished as a hostelry for ships' officers and passengers in the early 1800s.

Margaret Login, like Christian Robertson, was a widow with children to support. She was the daughter of a merchant who had traded to the West Indies from London, and had later retired to Orkney. Margaret's husband, John Login, had been in the merchant navy, too, but settled in Stromness to become a ship owner and agent. His death was followed by a string of other losses, including the wrecks of several vessels in which he had been part owner. Margaret took over his shipping and whaling interests and ran them from an office down on the pier. She turned her home into a hotel, and Login's Inn became known for its genteel hospitality.

On an evening like tonight, with many officers and their families in town, one might have heard music from the spinet through the open windows of the inn and glimpsed women in low-bosomed, sprigged chintz dresses and lace caps flitting by the windows. Candles later, when it was dark, and glasses of claret raised in toasts, perhaps some whist, and conversation sprinkled with Jane Austen niceties of speech. Not far away, of course, would have been many more inns and alehouses run by widows who entertained a different clientele in an atmosphere of tallow and peat, tobacco smoke and whiskey. In June of 1817 the Town Council decided to enroll the "respectable inhabitants" of the town as a police force "against . . . the outrageous and turbulent proceedings of seaman and others who frequent the harbour." The "others" may well have been prostitutes, for as a port town, Stromness would have attracted young women who had no other means of income.

The sea has spawned a thousand livelihoods over the centuries; maritime work is not always seafaring. In Stromness, certainly, it's difficult to think of women doing anything not connected with the sea. Anne Robertson had said to me, "It was a man's world, of course, but in Scotland there doesn't seem to have been such a prejudice against women in business. They started schools, ran inns and shops. They inherited businesses from their husbands and ran them profitably." Some prospered greatly, like Christian Robertson, whose two huge houses I was passing now. The Doubles were constructed gable-end to the water. She had lived in one and let out the other. Now each house is divided into three, and only the flats on the end face the harbor. Christian Robertson was an exception, of course, as was Margaret Login. But one suspects that they were less exceptional than later historians might find them. It may have been a man's world, but it was a world that had room for them, and that they helped create.

I HAD arrived by now at the outskirts of Stromness and was following a road that led alongside the channel separating Mainland from the small island of Graemsay and the much larger island of Hoy rising behind it. If I were to follow this road several miles into the face of the wind, I would come to a point where it could properly be said that I was on the shores of the Atlantic. But even from here it was quite possible to look west and see nothing on the horizon but a reflection from the sun. It was easy to imagine a convoy of three-masted ships bearing for Stromness, the pilot boats competing to be the first to escort them around the point, the excitement growing back in the town. In days gone past young women gave their sweethearts a garland of silk, knotted for as many whales as they hoped they'd catch. These young women would have been waiting at the wharves to catch sight of their beloveds.

Not all women stayed at home waiting. On many sailing ships in the nineteenth century, it was common for wives to follow their captain or officer husbands to sea, and to take their

families with them. Christian Robertson's daughter had married
a captain and voyaged with him. In the Stromness bookshop I'd
found a delightful memoir by Elizabeth Linklater, the mother of
a well-known Orcadian writer, Eric Linklater. Her book, *A Child
Under Sail*, recounts growing up at sea in the late nineteenth
century on voyages with her mother and captain father across
the Atlantic, around Cape Horn to New Zealand and Cape of
Good Hope to India. Some passages reminded me of Pippi
Longstocking's adventures. Linklater recounts:

> When we got home from the Boston voyage I had to go to
> school. This was hard on one who had acquired the lovely
> importance of a child at sea. I had become, I suppose, a
> most objectionable little girl. I had been taught songs of all
> kinds, and stories such as no nicely brought-up child would
> ever have been allowed to repeat. One such anecdote, I
> remember, was punctuated by frequent *hics*, which I did so
> well as always to elicit rounds of applause—from the
> sailors, that is. Others were in broad Scots, with an occa-
> sional snore, also well done, I think. But this impropriety
> soon yielded to treatment when my mother got full control
> of me again. It was not by her will that my education had
> begun on these lines.

I could see why the young Elizabeth had loved the salty
vigor of shipboard life, especially compared to the way girls
were raised in those days. Hardly seedy any longer, yet still
tinged with the raffish, Stromness made me remember how
port towns had always thrilled me. Was it from spending stolen
time as a child at the Pike in Long Beach, where sailors from
around the world strolled smoking and joking past curio shops,

tattoo parlors, and sideshows, where the air smelled of fish, smoke, cotton candy, and the sharp tang of illicit excitement. During my mother's illness, when I was eleven and twelve, my father, who had an office downtown on Atlantic Boulevard, would take us to the Pacific Coast Club for our swimming lessons. We had strict instructions not to leave the fortress of the club; as soon as the lessons were over, however, I took my younger brother by the hand and set out for the Pike, the seaside amusement park that had descended into seediness. What did I want? Danger, pleasure, the chance simply to look and sniff and imagine. Port towns have a pungent density of smells and sights; yet they are open, too, one whole wall removed and exposed to the sea, a place of comings and goings, dreams hatched and dreams dashed. Downtown Long Beach was not a place for a young girl, and yet in the Pike I found everything to stir my imagination, to feed my wanderlust.

How was a woman of an earlier time to experience adventure and autonomy in the world? The sea, for so many of the women I'd come across in Scotland and Orkney, had been work or trade, not the high road to independence. The women were coastal folk for the most part—fishers and fishwives, kelp gatherers and herring lassies—who stayed close to loved ones on shore. Within the bounds of their society, widow entrepreneurs like Christian Robertson and Margaret Login were successful and emancipated, far more so, in fact, than the scruffy whalers and drunken seamen of the port towns. Yet in our collective imagination, freedom belongs to the sailor, the one who leaves friends and family behind for the wind and the waves.

The Stromness captain's wife with the most remarkable story was Eliza Fraser, who left her three children here under the care of a pastor and sailed off to Australia on the *Stirling*

Castle, a merchant brig, with her husband in 1835. After a long voyage from London to Buenos Aires to Cape Town to Sydney, Captain Fraser unloaded his cargo, and received instructions to sail to Singapore and load up goods for England. Eliza was by this time heavily pregnant with their fourth child, and the only woman on the ship. Unfortunately her husband was in poor health (one reason Eliza had accompanied him), and in Sydney most of his crew jumped ship. The new recruits were in some cases less able, and certainly less experienced. In stormy weather the ship went aground on a reef north of what is now Brisbane, and the crew was forced to abandon the vessel in two smaller craft, a pinnace and a longboat, which immediately began leaking. Eliza, in the almost swamped longboat, went into contractions and delivered a baby, which drowned immediately. She said later that she was hardly conscious of having given birth at all.

The two boats finally put in at Great Sandy Island, and there their troubles began in earnest. The island was inhabited by aborigines. We don't have the aborigines' account, only the white survivors, of course, but their story goes that the two boats were separated while they were trying to escape. Eliza spent almost two months as a captive. She was starved, exhibited, beaten, and had her legs burned. She was most likely raped. She watched her husband speared through, and others of the crew die horrible deaths. Finally, in a daring rescue by an Irish convict backed up by soldiers from Brisbane, Eliza was saved, and taken back to Sydney. There her story becomes less certain, a bit ludicrous, and rather sad. Although she was said to have been strong-willed and capable of command during the first days of abandoning the ship and reaching land, two months of degradation and physical misery had troubled, if not unhinged,

Mrs. Fraser fought over by rival claimants

her mind. She fell under the sway of a Captain Greene, who seems to have seen in her a good possibility for making money. After an appeal for funds in Sydney for Eliza, they sailed to Liverpool, and made their way to London. Further appeals for money were investigated and exposed, reducing Eliza to humiliation, especially after Captain Greene decided to exhibit her as the only survivor of the *Stirling Castle.*

Most of the women who went to sea had more fortunate, if sometimes equally exciting, experiences, particularly in the eighteenth and early nineteenth centuries, when as wives of seamen in the Royal Navy, they found themselves under attack by the French. Wives of gunners played a great role in naval battles by carrying up gunpowder from the hold and repacking the cannons. Surgeon's wives as well as other women acted as nurses and even surgeons themselves if the doctor became incapacitated. In a battle, everyone's help was needed. As Suzanne Stark points out in her book about women aboard ship in the age of sail, *Female Tars*, it wasn't that women didn't live and work aboard sailing vessels, it was that they were in general invisible and unpaid. But there were also women, and Stark tells numerous stories of them, who disguised themselves as men and joined the ranks of seafarers, particularly in the Royal Navy, where sailors were greatly needed due to the wars with France.

Although the ballads that tell the stories of these women invariably hint at lovelorn girls who longed to be with their sweethearts, it's probably more accurate to say that these male impersonators longed mainly for a sweetheart's wages or a sweetheart's life of adventure. There was no single reason that a woman might join the navy or become a sailor; the life of a woman on shore was so restricted and impoverished that even life before the mast could seem vastly preferable. But economics are never as tuneful as romance. In songs like "The Handsome Cabin Boy," the only reason for a girl to come aboard ship is love.

Stromness has at least one story of a woman disguising herself as a man aboard ship. She was Isobel Gunn, who called herself John Fubbister when she signed on with the Hudson's Bay Company. The year was 1806 and young Orcadians were flocking to the town of Stromness to set sail for Canada, with its unknown hardships and secure wages. Perhaps John Fubbister was following a sweetheart, perhaps not. What's certain is that she looked and acted enough like a strong young man to be taken by the Hudson's Bay Company as a laborer. Arriving in the town of Moose Factory on the shores of Hudson's Bay, she seems to have worked as hard as any man, giving no cause for complaint. It was not until about a year later that her sex was discovered (by her superiors; it's likely her fellow Orcadians knew and supported her).

With others from the company, she had canoed eighteen hundred miles along the Red River in 1807, to spend the winter

A woman dressed as a sailor

there at a fur-trading post. A group of HBC men were celebrating Christmas dinner when she asked to lie down, as she
was feeling unwell. "I was surprised at the fellow's demand;
however, I told him to sit down and warm himself," wrote
Alexander Henry, the householder where the celebration was
taking place. A short while later Henry went into the room
where Fubbister was and, as he later wrote:

> . . . was much surprised to find him extended on the hearth,
> uttering dreadful lamentations; he stretched out his hands
> toward me, and in piteous tones begged me to be kind to a
> poor, helpless, abandoned wretch, who was not of the sex I
> had supposed but an unfortunate Orkney girl, pregnant and
> actually in childbirth. . . . In about an hour she was safely
> delivered of a fine boy.

Isobel Gunn traveled the following spring with her child to Albany, New York. She managed to stay almost another two years in Canada, although instead of packing furs and canoeing she was put to laundering for her former co-workers. She was in no hurry to return to Orkney, which is reasonable since when she did return, with her astonishing story and her illegitimate son, she was a social outcast. She made a poor living back home knitting stockings and died a vagrant in 1861. The story of her adventures survived her, but as the years passed, any mention of her stamina and courage was left out. Her later years as an outcast took on particularly witchlike characteristics in the telling. It was said of her, without any factual basis at all, that she was the daughter of Bessie Millie, and that she survived by selling charms and love philters to young farmers and maidens.

So often, when we imagine ourselves in the past, we give ourselves permission to have been among the bravest and most fortunate. Perhaps I couldn't have been Grace O'Malley, but why not the mate of a gunner carrying gunpowder from the hold and repacking the cannons, or the spouse of the ship surgeon, taking over when he was crushed under a falling spar? Surely I might have been the captain's wife who navigated the ship back to civilization after he was eaten by savages, or the daughter whose genial father allowed her the run of the ship. I saw myself as "The Handsome Cabin Boy" in the old ballad, disguised as a sailor to see the world. Would I have had the nerve, the opportunity, the courage to change my clothes and my sex? Or would I have been a fishmonger's daughter, an alehouse waitress, a sailor's whore, a sea witch? No, in imagination I was always on deck, waving at those who stayed behind.

Our gallant ship her anchor weighed,
And from Stromness bore away, brave . . . girls!
And from Stromness bore away!

Tonight I'd have dinner and a half-pint of bitter, and take another evening stroll if it stayed fine. There would be Robertson's Orkney Fudge for dessert, of course. I'd return to gaze out my window and, since it was light so late, finish off a small watercolor of the Inner Holm at high tide. The Island of Isobel Gunn, I might call it. I had finally figured out a use for my personal bath mat, delivered daily like a newspaper. It made an excellent blotting paper on which to lay my watercolor brushes out to dry.

CHAPTER VII

ENCHANTMENT

From the Orkney Islands to the Shetland Islands

IT WAS ten in the evening when the P & O ship, the *St. Sunniva*, departed Stromness for the Shetland Islands. The sun still hung in the sky, though the town, protected by a rounded arm of hills against the Atlantic winds, was in shadow. A line of gold fire ran along the top of Brinkie's Brae, and a peach glow filtered gently along the paths leading down to the harbor. Standing on the top deck of the ferry I was high above the dock and eye level with the upper houses and trees of Stromness. I seemed to stand in daylight, while the town below turned to thoughts of sleep.

The heavy ropes that bound us to the dock were unloosed and winched up. We moved off with a blast from the horn. There was rain in the air, more a fine mist through which the sun sparkled. The harbor waters were gold, overlaid with a scalloped pattern of frost and dark green. I was sorry I didn't have my camera with me and debated for an instant whether it was worth threading my way back down to my berth to retrieve it. Years ago, feeling the heart-swell of *How beautiful*, travelers might have quoted Wordsworth or Browning to themselves or each other. We moderns had come to rely almost entirely on photography to respond to the divine in nature. To want to take a picture was to want to perform some act of reverence. How else to explain the fact that so many photographs we snap we never look at again?

But I didn't dash down to my cabin after my camera, or even go below deck, for as I turned away from the last sight of Stromness, and we began to round the Point of Ness, I found myself looking at a rainbow at least a mile high, whose perfect arch created a gate. The arch had a foot on the island of Graemsay and one on Mainland, with a channel leading to Scapa Flow underneath. Between the portals of the gate was a lighthouse that looked like a candle. I had never seen a rainbow so very tall nor so very close. It must have been the combination of the setting sun and the salt mist that gave it such crystalline radiance. All the colors were present; yet it wasn't the brightest rainbow I'd ever seen. It was almost more white than multicolored, with glinting filaments of emerald, ruby, and sapphire.

My knees went weak to see this phenomenon in all its perfection, and I was astonished that the people near me didn't stop their conversations and fall down and begin worshipping it.

"Look—the rainbow," I said softly to the woman nearest me.

She was English, and hardly paused her conversation. She and her husband were discussing which boarding schools would be better for their grandson. "Yes, it's very pretty," she said.

Was I the only one to see this unearthly spectacle? Now I really wanted to rush below deck for my camera, to prove it somehow, but I couldn't bear to take my eyes from the sight. Already its colors were fading slightly. We'd come out into Hoy Sound, and the island of Hoy rose majestically to our left. The sun was dropping fast over the western horizon and a strong cold wind met the prow of the ship head on. Passengers were deserting the top deck now, and the rainbow was behind us. I watched it until it vanished completely, and even then I still seemed to see it, a gateway to another country of the imagination.

The Orcadians have long held a myth about an enchanted

world called Hilda-land. This was a place rarely seen, for it was almost always hidden by heavy fogs and mists. Only when the light was absolutely right, when the atmospheric refraction of clouds and sea turned into solid earth, could you look upon the rich green fields and river valleys of Hilda-land. As for getting there, you'd need a guide, a guide perhaps like Annie Norn.

Annie was a young woman on one of the Orkney isles who went to the shore one evening and never returned. Three or four years later a ship was returning to Orkney from Norway in the autumn of the year, and on that vessel was a cousin of Annie, called Willie Norn. Storms and tempests kept the ship whirling around the North Sea, and then, even worse, a thick fog came and the wind abated, leaving them directionless and their ship becalmed.

It was then they heard the splash of oars and became aware of someone or something coming toward them through the fog. When they could finally see, it appeared to be a small boat rowed by a woman. Was she a Fin Wife? If so, it was more trouble for them. She approached the side of the ship and before they could stop her, leaped aboard. Once she was on deck, Willie Norn recognized her as his cousin Annie.

Turning to the crew, quoth she to them, "Ye muckle feuls! why stand ye gaping an' glowering at me as gin I war a warlock? Gae veer your vessel aboot," and then she put the helm to lee, brought the vessel in the wind, and sang out her orders to the men, as if she had been a born skipper.

When the fog lifted they found themselves in a bay as calm and bright as a lake, with beautiful hills and valleys all around. The men thought they were dreaming, but Annie brought the ship to anchor and led them to shore. She took them to a magnificent house that was her home, and gave them meat and drink. Then she showed them to their beds, where they slept a very long time. When they awoke, another lavish meal had been prepared for them, to which the neighbors all arrived riding on sea horses. Annie's husband sat on the high seat next to her and welcomed the sailors to Hilda-land. When the feasting was over, Annie bade them all go back to their ship. Willie asked Annie to return with him, but she told him she was well off where she was with her husband and would not think of leaving. She did tell Willie to give all the folk at home loving messages, and to tell her mother she had three "bonny bairns."

Hilda-land was the summer home of the Finfolk, who otherwise lived at the bottom of the sea in Finfolkaheem. Anyone lucky enough to visit Finfolkaheem would find palaces of crystal and coral illuminated by phosphorescence. The dancing halls had curtains made of the aurora borealis. The sand was gold, and the gardens of the great houses were full of waving seaweed, richly colored. The Fin Men hunted on sea horses; otters and seals were their dogs. If you were invited to a banquet in Finfolkaheem, you could count on whale, otter, and seal—fried, roasted, or boiled—with tureens of whale soup, thickened with cod roe, accompanied by seaweed stewed in seal fat, and washed down with conches of blood-red wine.

How did you get to Hilda-land or Finfolkaheem? You had to be lost or in love to find those lands of harmony and abundance, so much wealthier than the barren, stony islands that lay above. But sometimes, if the sun hit the clouds just right, in the rainbow mist you could see the outlines of Hilda-land, with its green pastures and bubbling brooks.

◉   ◉   ◉

I T WAS long after eleven when I finally went below deck to my cabin. As on all my night voyages in northern summer seas, where it didn't get very dark, I found it a dilemma whether to sleep or to stay up and explore the ship and watch for the first sight of land. Boarding the *St. Sunniva* I'd had the sense that only now, after several weeks of travel, had my own seafaring begun. Clare Island, Stronsay, and Papa Stronsay—they were all islands, certainly, and I had reached all of them by boat, but only now did I feel well and truly launched out into the vast Atlantic, onward to places that were far away and less known, floating in the mists.

I was tired, as I'd spent the day hiking around the island of Hoy before returning to Stromness to catch my boat, but I wasn't sleepy. I slipped between the clean white sheets of my narrow berth and surveyed my small overnight domain with pleasure. The *St. Sunniva* was west of Orkney now and the current pulsed upward and the waves knocked sideways and the ship pitched and undulated so that my pack fell over and the porthole curtains swung like a girl tossing her hair. I know many people who do not enjoy this kind of motion, not one bit, but I do, very much. On nights like these in cubbyhole cabins at sea, I feel deeply cozy. The rolling of the sea is restful to me. I can sleep well and remember my dreams. Now I wanted to rock and to dream, but not quite to sleep yet. I wanted to feel where I was, feel myself at sea.

Earth is a misnomer; we live on a water planet. Some of our earliest myths are of the watery deep, the dark liquid abyss, the oceanic womb of formlessness. Since organic life began in the water, it's not strange that we would feel at home there, nor that the depths could cause us anxiety as well as reverence. At the beginning of human history it was the Goddess who divided the waters and her names became legend. She was Nammu in Sumeria, Tiamat in Babylon, Temu in Egypt, Thalassa in Greece, Yemaya in Yoruba. Aphrodite, "she who rises from the waves," sometimes called Marina or Mari, was a sea goddess and so was the Virgin Mary, whose name in Latin, Maria, means "the seas." St. Jerome gave the name of Stella Maris, Star of the Sea, to Mary. Her symbols were a blue robe and a pearl necklace, sea and sea foam. In the North, where I was traveling, there was the Mither o' the Sea, and Ilmatar, from the Finnish epic, the *Kalevala*. Its opening pages tell a creation myth.

> Ilmatar, the daughter of the wind, lived long ages in sacred
> loneliness in the smooth and endless gardens of the air. At
> last she grew tired of her life in boundless space, and
> stepped down to the waves on the broad back of the open
> sea.
>
> At once there came a great blast of an angry east wind,
> which raised the sea into a foam of white-capped waves.
> The winds rocked Ilmatar, the frothing waves cradled her,
> until wind and wave had wakened life within her womb.

Pregnant for seven hundred years, she floated around in the sea until a sea bird lit on her knee and laid its eggs and brooded them. When the eggs broke open, the lower half became the earth, the upper half the sky. Nine years later,

> [Ilmatar] lifted her head from the waters, and in the throes
> of birthgiving began her creations on the wide back of the

sea. Where she turned her hand, she made the headlands. Where she touched her feet, there sank the fish holes, and wherever she splashed bubbles came the depths of oceans.

More ages passed, but still her child, who was to become the hero Väinämöinen, was not born. "Then Ilmatar swam farther from the land. She stopped upon the endless waters, creating seas, and planting hidden reefs where ships are shattered and where seamen meet their deaths." Finally her son had to free himself, by moving "the bony lock of his chamber with his forefinger." Once he was out, he had to swim in the sea for eight years before reaching land.

I remember reading the story of the Finnish world maker in a book of northern myths and tales as a child. It reminded me of my own knees sticking up from the water in the bathtub, or my mother's, between whose legs I'd splashed as a baby, whose arms and knees and feet, with red-enameled toes, were the holms and headlands of an early water world.

My mother was no great swimmer, but she was at home in the water. Born in Brooklyn, raised in the Midwest, she'd taken easily to the pools and beaches of Southern California, and I have many memories of being with her, skin to skin, in varied waters, from the backyard wading pool with its silky sides to the salt-soft lapping waves of the shallow bay at Belmont Shores. It was my mother who gave me my first swimming lesson, who took me to an indoor pool one evening when I was five. The water had a greeny-white glow; the sides were white tile; everything was chlorine wet. My mother's arms were white and slightly freckled; her head looked small in the tight cap, because her hair was usually so fluffy and dark. I splashed around, centered in the hole of a pink plastic tube.

"Kick," my mother told me, and demonstrated in a flurry of scissoring water. She was with me, surrounding me, showing me, and then, suddenly, she was at a distance. She had slipped away so I would come to her. Her arms reached out to me, but there was a vast expanse of water to cross, water that was pale green, jam-thick and hard to move through. "Do the same thing you did before; just kick. That's all you have to do, kick and come to me." The force of her eyes held me; she was smiling, laughing. She was an island rippled round with rings of aqua light; she rose firm from the invisible floor of the pool on mysterious tall white legs. I kicked, and I arrived back in her arms. "Strong girl," she said; "brave girl," she said. "Now, try it again."

I LAY on my narrow berth on the *St. Sunniva,* as the ship rolled and rumbled under me and around me, reading Walter Traill Dennison's book of Orkney folklore about the sea. The story of Annie Norn intrigued me; she was so lively and real in the midst of the fairy tale, an accomplished sailor who rescued men at sea, much like Janet Forsyth. Her tart rebuke to the crew of the becalmed ship, "Ye muckle feuls! why stand ye gaping an' glowering at me as gin I war a warlock? Gae veer your vessel aboot," is something that it's easy to imagine Grace O'Malley shouting as well. Yet Annie's last name of "Norn" connects her with the Three Fates, or Norns, and with Norna of Fitful-head. She was a Fin Wife, and thus something of a sorceress.

In Orkney lore, it was wedlock that turned a mermaid into a haggard witch. Dennison tells us, "During the first seven years of married life she gradually lost her exquisite loveliness; during the second seven years she was no fairer than women on earth; and in the third seven years of married life the mermaid became ugly and repulsive." The Fin Wife, after losing her youth and beauty, "was often sent on shore to collect white money [silver] by the practice of witchcraft among men."

Although a mermaid is one of the most ancient of images—some of the earliest goddesses are Semitic moon deities with fishy tails—she has become sadly reduced in the last hundred or so years, first through Hans Christian Andersen's tale "The Little Mermaid" and then by the Disney version of the same, to a pathetic, silent love martyr wearing a bikini top. In ancient cultures the fish tail was a symbol of the Goddess's power, not an impediment to dancing; the mirror is a symbol of the sea, not a sign of the mermaid's golden-haired vanity.

Along the shores of Scotland and Orkney there are many old tales of sightings of mermaids on the rocks and skerries. Sometimes she's called Maid-of-the-Wave. She is always lovely, and alluring. She's the kind of woman you don't mind following below the ocean's surface. The songs she sings will make you forget everything you ever knew and wanted. The tales evoke the longing for beauty and intimacy with some other creature, perhaps with the unconscious, the mother as giver of both life and death, the all encompassing, the irrational, the beloved.

Like tales of mermaids who take off their scaly nether parts and walk on land, the better to lure unwitting men to their watery kingdoms, transformative stories of the seal folk abound in the northern islands. But seals embody an old animism, when animals were regarded as powerful and numinous, and when humans would mimic them and wear their skins to take on their power. So many stories of the seal folk, *selkie* or *silkie* in the local tongue, seem to be about humans trying to capture the spirit of the selkie. One common version begins when a man spies a group of girls sunbathing naked on a beach or rocky shore.

Seal folk listening to a mermaid's song

When he approaches, most of the girls get away, but one
doesn't, for he steals her spotted skin and hides it somewhere
secret in his house. He takes her home, and she tries to be a good
wife to him. But always in the story comes the time when she
finds, or one of her children tells her where to find, the box or
the chest with the skin inside. As soon as she finds it, she's gone.
Although the tales often seem to be about love, they are never
about renunciation. The choice of Andersen's Little Mermaid,
to become human and to suffer, is not for the selkie wife. No,

she's tricked into living in a human body for a time, but she always escapes back to her true element at the end.

The many stories of seal folk aren't all about capturing seals for wives. Some are about seal men seducing women (an explanation for out-of-wedlock pregnancy, perhaps) and about crossing a boundary between human and animal, about understanding the connection across species. Sometimes men who are great hunters of seals are taken below and shown the wounds of their prey, after which the hunters hunt no more. But many of the stories are about shape shifting, about changing from animal to human and back. The appeal of the selkie, and indeed the seal, is its amphibious nature. That possibility of living in both worlds is what humans hold to, especially seafarers, fishers, coast dwellers. What if drowning were only a dream from which you woke into a beautiful marine world filled with lavish meals and luxurious houses? What if the fathers and brothers who never came back from fishing were safe and sound under the waves? What if the large gray seal lifting his curious head from the sea to look at you were a relative? How comforting that would be.

An intriguing book I picked up in Stromness, *Seal-Folk and Ocean Paddlers* by John MacAulay, proposes that old and recurring tales of selkies and mermaids might have some historical truth. Lapps from northern Scandinavia, sometimes called Finns, may have accidentally or deliberately come south in sealskin-covered kayaks, he says. From shore, it may have looked as if the body sticking out of the water were half-person, half-fish. From the outer islands of the Hebrides, as well as from Orkney, come stories of families who claim to be descended from seals. *Sliochd nan ròn*, "the race of seals," they're called. They were known for dark liquid eyes with a touch of pathos, for their love of music, and sometimes for particularly horny feet with a little webbing between the toes. For MacAulay this identification with seals would make most sense if the islanders had intermarried with the amphibious men, or women, who arrived by kayak.

Folktales about the seal people seem, to me, to be more haunting than those of mermaids and Finfolk, but all of them speak of loss and rebirth, transformation, and love beyond death. More importantly, they offer a rich and imaginative way to cope with drowning, so frequent in these rough seas. Throughout history the sea has been divided in two: the surface and the deep. Very often sailors and captains, mostly men and a few women, have seen the sea as road, as a watery thoroughfare between ports of arrival and departure. In these stories of sea as road, we hear of exploration, navigation, settlement—of battles and trade. But there's another, vaster marine world, and since the beginning of our collective memory of it, it has been populated by dangerous beasts and monsters, Sea Trows, Finfolk, mermaids, and seal folk, as well as underwater goddesses like Sedna, the Inuit seawoman of the deep, or Ran of Norse legend. When praying to Aphrodite or the Virgin Mary doesn't work, when our ships founder and sink, we humans have needed to rely on some deeper wisdom, that the sea will return us to our origins, that the sea means, as *Mer* does in the old Egyptian, both "waters" and "mother-love."

WHEN I dream about my mother—when I allow myself to remember those dreams—I dream, not so much that she is dead, but that she's across the water. She's on a ferry that is just departing (there's still time to step aboard); she is on a raft in the river, a raft that has just gone downstream ahead of me. Or

I dream that she's swimming or flying, somehow moving around me, a liquid shifting presence, not close, but near. She doesn't always look like herself, but I know her in my body, in every molecule.

Sometimes she calls to me. She wants me to follow. But I don't follow. What would happen if I went toward her?

Once, during a dream in which she was leaving on a big car ferry, I knew I had to get hold of her. I ran to a phone booth on the dock, frantic with anxiety, and flipped through the phone book. I paged and paged but I couldn't find Wilson, nor could I recall the street where our family lived. It was night in this dream, and there were hot white beams spotlighting the ferry. I heard engines roar, the water churn hugely as the ferry pushed away from the dock. I stood there in the lit phone booth and I knew she had a different name now than what I remembered, and a different address, too.

It has been dreams of parting that have haunted me, not dreams of drowning. I was quite a young child when I had my first dream of drowning. How well I recall the first moment of panic, followed by the knowledge that here, underwater, I could breathe.

Now, on the *St. Sunniva*, I fell asleep to the seesaw of the ship, and I had a dream, darker in color than the light aqua nightmares of childhood, of falling off the ship and down through the ocean. I would have many drowning dreams on this trip. This was the first, but all it was, was falling. I fell a long time and it was cold and leaden.

WHEN I awoke it was dim in my cabin; outside, through the porthole, spattered with rain, I saw misty cliffs and raw, rocky shores. This must be the Shetland Islands, I thought, and was afraid for a moment. How dark everything looked out there, how gray and wet and inhospitable. I'd read that in olden times the Shetlanders would not rescue a drowning person, even when it was safe and easy. For they believed that the sea demanded a sacrifice. If you took away the sea's victim, someone else, perhaps you yourself, would be taken instead.

I curled back into sleep, held to the beating heart of the ship and rocked by the waves. Now I was enveloped and safe and warm in my berth, in my cabin. When I next woke up, the *St. Sunniva* was docking in Lerwick. The magic eggshell had broken, with earth at the bottom and sky at the top. Sun shone into the space between. The thick gray mist was lifting and for an instant Shetland, green and bright, looked like Hilda-land. I rushed to pack my things and disembark.

CHAPTER VIII

THE LONELY VOYAGE
OF BETTY MOUAT

Sumburgh Head, the Shetland Islands

It was a bitter cold day at the end of January 1886, when Betty Mouat took passage on a ship bound for Lerwick. Some might wonder why Betty didn't just walk the twenty-four miles from her home at the southernmost tip of the Shetland Islands to the capitol. Walking was common at a time when the roads were bad and few had money for horse travel. It was winter, after all, and the seas were notoriously rough. But Betty Mouat didn't walk. She'd been born with one leg shorter than the other. She was also, by the standards of the day, old and rather frail. She was fifty-nine.

Betty Mouat had traveled to Lerwick by ship many times before, carrying shawls and other knitting to sell in town. The morning she embarked on the *Columbine*, she had a bundle of forty shawls, as well as a bottle of milk and two halfpenny biscuits for sustenance on the journey. The voyage was expected to last two or three hours, and Betty was the only passenger.

Eight days later the *Columbine* smashed into the Norwegian coast, three hundred miles to the northeast. Betty was still the only passenger; she was also the only person on the ship.

In order to find the house where Betty Mouat had lived, I'd come by bus from Lerwick down to Sumburgh Head, a journey

127

Betty Mouat on the *Columbine*

that now takes about half an hour. Sumburgh is the longer of
two pincher-shaped peninsulas that seem to reach out after Fair
Isle, which can just be seen on the horizon. Sumburgh is the site
of the Bronze and Iron Age ruins of Jarlshof and the Victorian
hotel that was once the home of the Laird of Sumburgh. In
Betty's day the land was inhabited by crofters, tenants of the
laird, who fished and farmed in a limited way. Now much of it is
home to Shetland's main airport. Betty lived with her half-
brother and his family in a small stone house on the shorter of
the two pinchers, known as Scatness.

One of the many things I liked about Shetland was the place
names: Spiggie, Bigton, Brig o' Waas, Busta, Symbister, Quarff,
Mid Yell, Gloup, Funzie, Muckle Flugga. Fitful Head was
another. You could see the massive headland of Fitful Head from
Sumburgh. It was the fictional home of Norna, the prophetess
in Sir Walter Scott's novel *The Pirate*, and as I looked at its bulky

outline across the bay, I could almost hear Norna's runic incantations and her weird cry, "Do not provoke Norna of Fitfulhead!" Many of the Shetland place names are of Norse origin as, from sometime in the ninth century, Shetland had been a Norwegian province. Only in 1469 were the islands forfeited to Scotland in lieu of an unpaid royal dowry.

I had lunch at the Sumburgh Hotel and strolled through dunes covered in marram grass to a glittering white beach. The sky was a very pale blue and the clouds moved fast, in long wispy streamers, as if they were being sucked in the direction of Fair Isle twenty-five miles to the south. Behind me, to the north, thunderclouds were stacked like giant bundles of indigo and black velvet with gold piping. Earlier, in Lerwick this morning, it had been raining; now, on the beach, between Sumburgh and Scatness, the light was clear, almost silvery. From time to time there was the sound of a small jet landing or departing, and then silence, punctuated by the cries of oystercatchers and gulls. I had my bird book with me and was trying to identify the gulls. I thought a black-backed gull sounded like a dog snarfling in a dream. The bird book called it an angry *kuk-kuk-kuk*. The common gull was meant to have a more "benign" expression than the herring gull, but so far I had only distinguished them by the color of their legs: yellow and pink.

East was a blue sky; west was trouble. You often saw the two weather systems collide over Shetland; it was what made the weather change so swiftly here. Situated over one hundred miles out into the Atlantic, the islands had been shaped by wind and waves into a landscape of dramatic bluffs and barren ridges. Except for a few pockets of stunted trees in Lerwick, and some battered shrubbery and flowers around individual houses, much of the vegetation was grasses and wildflowers. I'd noticed earlier, in Orkney, which was a traditionally agricultural land, there was a great deal of talk, mainly moaning and complaining, about the wet spring and the slow start of summer. But in Shetland the weather as a topic hardly came up at all. The constant massing and dispersing of the clouds, the restless coming and going of the sunshine and the rain were quite normal here.

W HEN BETTY Mouat set off in the *Columbine*, the day was cold and clear, but the wind came up offshore and the sea quickly grew heavy. The skipper, James Jamieson, and his two crewmen, regularly sailed up and down the Shetland coast, but that day luck wasn't with him. In resetting the sail for the stronger wind, he and his first mate were swept off the ship. The mate managed to claw his way back onboard, but to his great distress he saw Captain Jamieson, of whom he was very fond, still flailing in the sea. The mate and the other crewman immediately launched a boat to save the captain, but they were too late. The captain's head had disappeared. Worse, when they turned back to the *Columbine*, they found that the ship had already tacked off to the northeast. It was all they could do to get themselves through heavy surf to shore.

When the voyage began, Betty Mouat had settled herself below deck with her quart bottle of milk and two biscuits. The ship soon began to roll so much that when she heard shouting, she wasn't able to climb up to the open hatchway to take a look. She heard "Get away the boat," and then nothing except the wind. When she finally managed to get up the stairs, she found the boom swinging wildly in the gale, the mainsail flapping, and all three crewmen gone. Waves were breaking over the bow; the sky had darkened; a terrible storm was taking shape around her.

◎　◎　◎

By the time I went looking for Betty Mouat's croft house in Scatness, I'd been in Shetland about a week, asking my usual questions about women and the sea. My bed-and-breakfast host in Lerwick, Mr. Gifford, first told me about two girls from an island in the north of Shetland who drifted to Norway in a boat. Later I read about these two servant girls from the small island of Uyea, south of Unst, who had rowed over to the even smaller islet of Haaf Gruney to milk cows kept there for grazing. On the return trip they ran into a gale and were carried across the sea to the Norwegian coast. It's said they married Norwegians. At any rate they never returned. A surprising number of girls were blown over the northern seas, as it turned out. Some were from England, a couple from Holland, the majority from Scotland. Although some were blown south, more drifted to the Norwegian coast, the result, no doubt, of the Gulf Stream's north-flowing current.

It was of interest to me that almost all the men I asked in Shetland about women and the sea immediately began to tell me the story of Betty Mouat and the other women and girls who drifted to Norway in boats. The greatest drifter of them all, of course, was St. Sunniva, whose name now adorns the ship that brought me to Lerwick. St. Sunniva was a tenth-century Christian princess from Ireland who, in escaping from her Viking persecutors, jumped into a ship with her companions and pushed off without benefit of oars, rudders, or sails, because she trusted in God to save them. Although St. Sunniva bypassed Shetland to land in Norway, the remains of a chapel once dedicated to her can be found on the small isle of Balta off Unst.

No one knows how long it took St. Sunniva to reach

Betty Mouat rescued by Norwegians

Norway, but it took Betty Mouat and the *Columbine* more than a week. For all that time she had no idea where she was and no way of ascertaining. The storm battered the ship for four days before there was a respite and some sun, and then another storm blew up. Betty Mouat had nothing to eat but her milk and biscuits; she spent most of her time holding on to a rope and bracing herself against the rolling of the ship. Only at the end did she see land and shortly afterward feel the shock of the *Columbine* going aground. By some miracle the *Columbine* had missed the reefs off an island north of Ålesund and had lodged itself firmly on the rocks. Betty climbed on deck and found two boys on shore staring at her. They shouted to each other in their own language, and then the boys ran off for help. Fishermen not far away had been watching the lurching of the boat and its crash into the rocks; they were astonished to find an elderly woman onboard, alone.

The image of women drifting helplessly in the sea and being rescued after a harrowing voyage seemed to be an appealing one to my male informants. But Mr. Gifford was able to tell me a few other stories when I persisted. He had once been a lighthouse keeper on one of the rocky isles of the Out Skerries, a group of islands northeast of Lerwick. Mr. Gifford recalled that, because the Out Skerries had no peat, women would row in open boats over to the island of Whalsay to cut the peat in spring and collect it in autumn after the bricks were dry.

"These women must have been very strong," I said, after looking at a map. It was no little distance from the Out Skerries to Whalsay. It looked at least ten miles, over a rough stretch of water.

"Oh aye," said Mr. Gifford. "They would be strong, to row that far and back."

Douglas Sinclair, the chief librarian at the Lerwick library, agreed. "The women of Trondra were also well known for their rowing abilities," he told me. Trondra is one of several islands tucked next to the west coast of Shetland's mainland.

"They would row out for peats, and out fishing, and to take the sheep back and forth to new grazing places. The men would be away at the fishing and the women would do everything. That's why they were such strong rowers. Once, early this century, the men of the Royal Navy in Scalloway challenged the Trondra women to a regatta. And the women won! There should be a photo of the Trondra women upstairs in the museum. You ask up there; they'll find you the photos."

I'd been upstairs already and had found a typical maritime museum: wide-planked, dark-stained floors and glass cases full of sextants, barometers, and nautical curiosities—from scrimshaw boxes to carved coconuts to peg legs, with nary a

The women of Trondra were famed for their boatmanship

trace of women in all the exhibits. But now, emboldened by Douglas's enthusiasm, I rang the bell and told the curator that I'd like to look in the archives for pictures of women and the sea.

"Women and the sea?" He drew his eyebrows together. "Women didn't go to the fishing," he explained politely. "No, they didn't go to the fishing. They stayed at home; they did everything else: the animals, the food, and clothing, the children, the farming . . . but they didn't go to the sea; they didn't go to the fishing. Only men did that. Women and the sea, you say? There was Betty Mouat, of course."

I said that the librarian downstairs had told me that the women of Trondra were renowned as rowers, that they'd beaten the Royal Navy in a regatta.

"Yes, well, yes . . ." he said, and pulled out a couple of stacks of photographs. "You can look . . . I don't know if you'll find anything though."

It was with a small flash of triumph that I came across two old photographs, one of women from Trondra rowing a boat, and the other of women in Edwardian dress who may have been the winners of the regatta. There was also an illustration of Betty Mouat, going hand over hand on a rope stretched from the wrecked *Columbine* to the Norwegian rocks.

The publicity surrounding Betty Mouat's voyage was extraordinary and international. While she recuperated in Norway from her ordeal, a journalist from Edinburgh made a special trip to interview her, and the resulting story appeared around the world, including in the *New York Herald*. Betty Mouat's fantastic voyage inspired ballads in her honor and a number of illustrations, most of them dramatic, but incorrect. For instance, weeks after I left Shetland and was up on a remote island in Norway's Lofoten chain, I ran across a colored rotogravure print on my way to the restroom in a small hotel. The illustration on the wall showed a terrified young Betty with long blond tendrils waving in the wind, cowering on the open deck of a storm-tossed ship. I suddenly had a jolt of recognition. The plate of the ship read the *Columbine.*

The museum curator unbent a little when I showed him the photographs I'd found and asked if I could Xerox them. He even admitted that he'd heard something about the women rowers of Trondra. "You might ask . . ." he paused. "I'm sorry, I don't remember her name, but she's the wife of Tommy Isbister, a boat builder who lives on Trondra. She's a rower, I seem to recall. . . ."

I'd heard of Tommy Isbister when I'd been on the northern island of Unst a few days before. I'd decided to go up to Haroldswick, to a small museum called the Unst Boat Haven. It was a glorious day when I set off from Uyeasound, where I was staying at the youth hostel. First I hitchhiked to Baltasound (the first time I'd hitchhiked in about twenty-five years), and then walked along the highway a few kilometers. Although I was to go much farther north on my trip, there was something about Shetland, particularly Unst, that made me feel as though I were on top of the world. It seemed there was nothing to look at but the wild sky and the sea that changed from cobalt to purple in an instant. With the wind at my back, the very earth seemed insubstantial. Out in the sea was a small craft of some sort, with a white sail, scudding like a top.

Was it a white sail, or was it a sheep? I found myself considering the whole question of getting one sheep, much less two or three, into an open boat, and then rowing that sheep or those sheep from island to island in search of fresh pasturage. Sheep were big, sheep were smelly, shit-smeared, scared. How did the women get them into the boats, and out of the boats? How did everyone keep their balance in a boat in the middle of the sea with the wind and the waves and the sheep bleating and terrified?

THE UNST Boat Haven in Haroldswick was a barn of a place with lots of boats—sixareens, traditional yoles, Faroese eight-man-oared fishing boats with a coat of black tar. They had been lovingly restored, in many cases by Tommy Isbister.

A tall man came up to me, introducing himself as Robert, the volunteer curator. He was full of goodwill ("Where are you from? Seattle! That's a long way."), which changed to suspicion when I said I was interested in women and the sea.

"There was a woman who drifted to Norway in a boat," he said finally. "Betty Mouat was her name. She drifted all the way from Shetland to Norway . . ."

"I know the story," I interrupted. "What else about women and boats?"

"They didn't go to the fishing," he told me sternly. "Only men went to the fishing. The women stayed home. Of course, women did a great many things. They raised the children, made the clothes, took care of the animals, grew the food. No, they certainly weren't idle . . . but they didn't go to the fishing."

His reverent tone was backed up by the sacrosanct tools, craft and fishing paraphernalia around me: the beautifully preserved boats, the nets on the walls, the hooks and baskets and buoys, the photographs, none of which showed a woman's face.

"I've heard they rowed from the Out Skerries to Whalsay to collect the peat," I said doggedly. "So they must have had some familiarity with boats."

"They may have known how to row," he said, after a minute. "After all, a boat was how you got places in those days. And while the men were at the fishing, the women would have to keep things going—taking the sheep to different pastures to graze, gathering seaweed, catching a few fish for dinner."

"So the women *did* fish," I said eagerly, too eagerly.

"They may have caught a few fish," he conceded. "But they didn't go to the fishing."

I decided to ring Tommy Isbister's wife, who turned out to be a lovely woman named Mary. Like many Shetlanders, she was friendly and modest and seemed surprised I would be interested in her story. She had grown up in Scalloway in the fifties. "Oh, yes, we all rowed, we girls, growing up. My father taught me to row when I was seven. It was important to him that I be able to manage a boat correctly. He was severe about technique."

Mary and Tommy Isbister lived on Trondra now. She ran the croft and her husband built traditional Shetland yoles, many of them for the new racing teams that had started up in the last few years. She told me that the Trondra women had always been strong rowers. They had rowed to Scalloway for provisions, about half a mile away from the island. Until 1970 there was no bridge to Trondra. A few women still commuted by boat. "As for the boats," said Mary, "they were the small, flat-bottomed ones we used to row in, a bit less safe than yoles. The yoles were used for collecting peats, and taking lambs off one of the smaller islands for weaning."

"And did you fish at all?"

"Oh yes, we all fished." She again seemed surprised at my question. "It was just one of the things we did then. Part of life on the croft when the men were out at sea. You might call it pleasure fishing, but it was a necessary thing."

"What about the Royal Navy and the women of Trondra?"

"It was about 1912, at any rate before the First World War. A Royal Navy ship's crew challenged the men of Scalloway to a rowing competition. The women turned up instead and beat them!"

I told her that the evening before I'd seen a group of women rowing across the Lerwick Harbor.

"Oh yes, racing has become quite big again. Lots of women are taking it up. I've seen them myself, rowing around the harbor."

We talked a little more about women and boats, the whole question of getting sheep on and off a boat. She didn't mention Betty Mouat.

It took me a long time to find Betty Mouat's croft house. In the photograph it had looked very charming, whitewashed stone with green trim. It had apparently been turned into a "camping bod," a small dormitory-like hostel, and I'd toyed with the notion of staying there a night. Yet something about the emptiness of this far end of Shetland made me uneasy, and I found myself eager to take the bus back to the bustle of Lerwick. The sun was shining here, but the wind was picking up. My eyes smarted and my ears were beginning to ache.

I wandered up a hill and down another, over to the edge of the sea and then back in the direction of the fields skirting the airstrip. I crawled through a gap in a barbed-wire fence, and avoided sheep droppings. In the distance I saw a few sheep and pondered whether I could ever get even one of them into a boat and row it around. Finally I saw two cottages just off the runway, and headed for them to ask directions. Who could possibly live next to a runway? It's not that Shetland is a major destination for most of the rest of the world, but the islanders themselves come and go pretty frequently, and living practically in the middle of an airport can't be very restful. In the open door of the more rundown of the two cottages I spied a man in his undershirt eating directly from a can of beans.

"I'm looking for Betty Mouat's cottage," I said. "I seem to have gotten turned around and ended up at the airport."

"No, you're in the right place," he said, still eating. "It's the other house. Though they just tore the original one down because they're digging up some ruins underneath. They built a new one, for the campers. That rubble over there, under the black tarpaulin? That's Betty Mouat's old croft."

I thanked him and walked over to the cottage. There were two rooms of bunk beds and a kitchen with running water. At the archeological site was a large hole in the ground, with the stones of a house piled next to it, under a black sheet of plastic.

A small sign said they were excavating Old Scatness Broch, an Iron Age fort. A small jet began its ascent only a few hundred feet away. I covered my ears against the air-sucking roar. I actually felt a little disoriented, between the Iron Age and the Space Age, with a replica croft house (now including indoor plumbing) behind me. It was mind numbing to think that in our day Betty could have flown directly from her little stone house to Norway in about half an hour.

Betty Mouat's astonishing voyage seems to have the hand of either God or Lady Luck in it. Yet it's her quiet heroism that in the end impresses me. Except for an initial wail of horror when she discovered she was all alone on a ship rapidly heading out of sight of land, she seems throughout to have been composed and alert, though rather unhappy with the whole business. Fame did not unhinge her or bring on a fit of bragging. When she finally returned to Shetland, to a rousing welcome, she went back to her croft house and her knitting. She lived a good many years longer, until she was ninety-three. I haven't been able to find out, however, whether she ever traveled by ship again.

CHAPTER IX

SEAGOING CHARM SCHOOL

Unst and Yell, the Shetland Islands

"YOU ASK," wrote Margaret Fuller, in 1845, "what use will she make of liberty, when she has so long been sustained and restrained? . . . if you ask me what offices they may fill, I reply— any. I do not care what case you put; let them be sea-captains, if you will."

That women had *not* been sea captains in the past was all too clear; otherwise this American feminist author wouldn't have reached for such an audacious metaphor. Certainly, all through the great Age of Sail there had been, as we know now, women passing as cabin boys and marines, as well as acting as navigators and helmswomen to their husband-captains on the clipper ships that sailed back and forth across the Atlantic and around Cape Horn to Australia and San Francisco. On more than a few documented occasions, when one of those husbands fell ill or died, it was his wife who took control of the ship and the crew. One of the most extraordinary stories is that of Mary Patten, the nineteen-year-old wife of Captain Joshua Patten, who in 1856 took the helm when he developed a brain fever en route from New York to California in the magnificent clipper *Neptune's Car*. For two months she was at the helm, finally bringing the cargo safely into San Francisco, to the great relief of the insurance company and the applause of the crowd.

But taking control in a crisis was not the same as being the captain. The striking thing about Grace O'Malley was not just her seamanship, but her role as commander at sea. Her circumstances were unusual: encouragement from her father and clan, and unsettled times in Ireland, along with obviously charismatic powers of leadership. One had to look far back in history, to stories of the exploits of Queen Tomyris, who in 529 B.C. battled Cyrus the Great off the Caspian Sea, and Queen Artemesia, who led five ships into battle with Xerxes of Persia in 480 B.C., to find comparisons to Grace.

All through my travels I'd been keeping an eye out for stories of women captains and commanders. Here in Shetland I'd encountered mainly doubt as to whether women had even gone to sea at all, except to drift. Drifting was, of course, the very antithesis of commanding. Shetland was no different than most maritime countries. I found no hidden histories, hard as I looked, of sea captains who were women. Yet in a curious way I did come closer to understanding how the dreams of girls who longed to run away to sea were converted into more traditional and respectable roles.

"I'VE BEEN up all night! I've been writing poetry!"

It was about seven in the morning and I was having a solitary cup of coffee in a glass room off the main body of the youth hostel at Uyeasound on Unst, the northernmost island of Shetland. This warm, slightly steamy little conservatory with its shabby chintz armchairs and ivy trailing up the inner glass walls was my secret. I'd found it a perfect place to sketch and write, snug when it rained and brilliant when the sun burst out. Since these two phenomena alternated on Shetland at ten-minute intervals, the glass room was also a watertight refuge.

"I couldn't sleep! I'm in a state of grace. I'm in love with life!" A vigorous woman of sixty suddenly materialized before me, wearing bright red-and-blue floral leggings and a red sweater tunic. She had a matching floral scarf tied gypsylike around her head, with the ends falling over her shoulders. A large rhinestone cross rested on her ample bosom, and a tattoo of a swallowtail butterfly decorated her inner forearm.

She had a pack of cigarettes in one hand and a pen in the other. She grabbed a pad of paper from one of the armchairs. "Sometimes poetry is the only way to say what you feel, isn't it?" she called back as she left the room.

A few moments later I could hear her having an animated conversation with someone on the phone in the hallway. I walked past her to get another cup of coffee from the kitchen, and asked Bob who she was. Bob was retired from the merchant navy and running a leadership retreat for boys here at the hostel.

"Dorothy Thomson? She's the sister-in-law of the warden," he said. "She used to live up here on Unst—divorced now. She was in the merchant navy, too."

"The merchant navy! What did she do?" I asked excitedly.

"She worked on one of the ships that went back and forth to New Zealand. After the war, in the fifties and sixties, a good many people decided to leave Britain for the colonies. I believe she was a child minder, or some such thing."

Dorothy vanished before I could talk to her, but the next morning, as I was setting my backpack out by the bus stop, the hostel warden appeared and right behind her, Dorothy, again wearing bright red, with a scarf tied dashingly around her short, streaked blond hair, and a great deal of gold jewelry. Her pumps were big and white and her manicured fingernails long and red. She was driving back to Lerwick today, she said. She didn't live there, but she had some errands. She'd be glad to take me, no, she *insisted*; the company would be grand, and she could show me more of Shetland. I had to excuse her for yesterday— she'd been in such a state of bliss. She'd just been substitute teaching on the remote island of Foula, off the west coast, and felt transformed. The children in her class—all two of them— the people on the island, getting to and from the island, especially when the weather was so terrible, then driving up to Unst to see her son's soccer team, oh, all of it made her heart so full that poetry was her only response!

She laughed and lit a cigarette, and opened the door for me. "Don't worry, I won't quote you any on the drive. Though I may sing you a song or two."

THERE ARE lots of jokes about the name of the island of Yell, which so easily rhymes with hell. It has no trees and not much of a population. But on an intermittently sunny day, as this turned out to be, one could almost be south as well as north, in Baja California or some other barren landscape that is mostly rock and water. Yell isn't as green as some of the other islands. It's brown and soft like a long cat that continually changes position; a cold bright wind blows over the hills. A hundred inlets, or *voes*, invite the sea into the island. The clouds billow and unfurl and pile on top of each other like sumo wrestlers. Every turn in the road is a different vista, the Atlantic one way, the North Sea the other.

The *Northern Star* had been Dorothy's ship, she told me, as we careened around the narrow roads that cut around the hills of Yell. It was the newer of two sister ships built in the fifties by the British Shaw Savill line. The *Northern Star* and the *Southern*

Cross were, at the time, the very model of comfortable postwar ocean travel. They carried no cargo, so they were always on schedule, and without a hold, the engines could be placed aft, creating more room for cabins and decks. They sailed from Southampton to Wellington, New Zealand, and back, about seventy-five days round trip.

Dorothy first went aboard the *Northern Star* in May of 1968, when she was twenty-seven. She was one of only fifteen women out of a crew of five hundred; five of the women were officers—two "nursing sisters," the assistant purserette, the social hostess, and the children's hostess. "Yes, I was a chili ho," said Dorothy, "for three years on the *Northern Star*. I went around the world nine times, and once to Japan and Hong Kong on the Cherry Blossom Tour." Dorothy's father had been a ship's engineer. She was born in Orkney, and after finishing at the University of Edinburgh, she married her childhood sweetheart. He was going to be a captain and she would be his wife and travel the world with him. He drowned three months after they were married. "I had a strong Orkney accent," she said. "They claimed they hired me because of that. Because there were so many Orcadians on board, going to the colonies, they wanted someone to make the children feel at home. You had to have a teaching certificate to be a children's hostess, and be at least twenty-four."

The *Northern Star* carried fourteen hundred passengers, of which about two hundred were children. Dorothy had two assistants to help her keep them amused. There were also a few hairdressers and stewardesses on the ship and two laundresses, nicknamed "steam queens." Their quarters were variously called Fluff Alley or Quality Street. The children's hostess and social hostess were on call seven days a week; their only free time came

when they were in port. The women who worked onboard were
expected to act like ladies and represent the ship. "I took a
course called Seagoing Charm School," said Dorothy. "It was all
about deportment, manners, manicures. They gave me a certificate. I remembered the manicure lessons anyway." She laughed
and waggled her long red fingernails. "Our wages were very
low. They held them back until the end of the voyage, but you
had an account. Sometimes at the end, you had nothing."

As she drove, she waved at people we passed, and told me a
story about each of them. He'd divorced. She had a cranky
mother. Dorothy had worked with him as a teacher. I kept
returning to her sailing days, however. "You're really interested
in all this ship business?" she asked.

"I worked on a ship, too, the summer I was twenty-two. It
was the *Kong Olav*, one of the coastal steamers, in Norway. I
loved it, though not the work. I was a dishwasher, at the very
bottom of the heap."

"Then you know all about the social stratification of a ship,"
Dorothy said. "The captain at the top, descending all the way
down. Oh, we did have fun though. We weren't supposed to frat-
ernize with the crew, but of course we did. The engineers traditionally did not get on with the mates. Oil and water don't mix,
we always heard. That never bothered me. A lot of the stewards
were gay. Management liked them because they were so neat.
Every voyage they'd put on a drag show for the crew called 'The
Sod's Opera.' Do you like to sing?"

"Yes, but I can't hold a tune."

"I love to sing. I'm in a singing group and we're going to
Norway next week on an exchange. Look, there's a little church
down that road, a Methodist one. Let's stop and I'll sing you
some songs on the organ."

We pulled alongside the tiny white church. Its door was open and it was neat as a pin inside, with children's artwork on the bulletin board. There were about ten pews and a dazzling view of the water. Dorothy flung open the small organ and played me a funny song about being seasick on the Pentland Firth. Then a religious tune or two. By the end she was wiping away tears. "Are you religious at all?"

"I had a religious childhood," I said.

"I'm a believer," she said, fingering her rhinestone cross. "God saved my life. My second husband was an alcoholic. I've had such tough times, such up-and-down times that I couldn't have survived without my faith."

We got back in the car and Dorothy sang some more. "Now I hope you're not in a hurry," she said. "It's not raining and I want to show you something else."

She set off again, down a winding road. "I haven't been here in a long time, but I know it's here. 'The White Lady,' it's called."

We parked by a farm and started a steep descent through sheepy pastures. The wind was frisky. I had on my hiking boots, but Dorothy was wearing big boatlike white pumps that didn't make the descent easy. "It's somewhere. It's somewhere . . ."

Then, lower on the slope, we saw it. A woman's figure, painted white, slanted to fit the prow of a ship with the long skirt sweeping behind and her chest proudly angled forward. She wasn't a bare-breasted beauty, but a sedate, high-collared matron with a book clasped in her hands over her heart. The White Lady came from a German clipper that was wrecked off this point last century. A farmer had rescued her and planted her here, forever looking out to sea. She was twice as big as Dorothy, but there was something of the same attitude in them as they faced each other on the promontory.

We climbed back up the hill, negotiating marshy bits and a fence with barbed wire that had popped out of nowhere. It was bright, very bright, but the wind took your breath away. We threw ourselves back inside the car and panted.

"I guess I'm still giddy from Foula," said Dorothy. "Or the sunshine. I feel like I could just wander around Shetland all day."

This worried me slightly. "Eventually I have to get to Lerwick," I said. "I have some more work to do at the library."

"We'll go by my house first," decided Dorothy. "I haven't been home for over a week. I need to check my mail and messages, take a bath. Then we'll drive straight on to Lerwick. You'll be there by lunchtime!"

Since it was already noon, I suspected not, but a delay of an hour or two couldn't hurt. The landscape grew more and more beautiful to me. We passed signs that said Hill of Vatsie, Ness of Queyon, Otterswick, Saddle of Swarister. We came to the ferry landing at Ulsta and crossed to Toft. We drove another twenty minutes or so to Brae, where Dorothy lived in a terrace house that, she told me, had been hastily constructed when the workers were building the oil terminal and airport at Sullom Voe, not far away.

"Just be a tick," she said. "Make yourself at home. Have a cup of tea, a biscuit. Wander around. See my collection of Japanese dolls upstairs. I'm just going to ring a friend, then I'll have a bath." I sat at the kitchen table and had a cup of tea and toast. By a strange coincidence Dorothy's Seaman's Record Book and Certificate of Discharge were sitting on the table among piles of paper. An authority had declared that "the person to whom this Discharge Book relates has satisfied me that he (she) is a seaman. . . ." There was a photograph of Dorothy Cogle, as she was called then, in the faded blue book.

She already had the blue swallowtail butterfly on her arm.

I heard Dorothy animatedly talking on the phone, while the water ran into the tub across the hall. She came downstairs with a book, a newspaper clip, and a sheaf of notebook paper. "I wondered if you might be interested in some notes that one of the social hostesses gave me. We had a get-together a while back." She rushed into the bath to turn off the water and soon was splashing noisily. She'd brought her phone in with her and was talking as she bathed: "You'll never guess! I have a writer here with me. I found her in Unst when I was up visiting my son. Now she's at my kitchen table. She's writing a book and I'm telling her about the *Northern Star.* Yes, my old ship."

I read the newspaper clipping first. It was an interview with Dorothy in a q-and-a format in the *Shetland Times.* One of the questions was "What's your greatest ambition?"

"I'd like to be the first female Pope," Dorothy had responded. "Just to be called el Mama."

The book Dorothy had handed me was *Splendid Sisters,* a history of the *Southern Cross* and the *Northern Star,* published in 1966. The fourteen pages of handwritten notes were a copy of "Instructions to Hostesses," originally compiled by one of the *Northern Star*'s first social hostesses, a woman named Jeanne. At the top of the first page, in caps, was written: KEEP YOUR SENSE OF HUMOUR AT ALL TIMES.

The writer of the instructions obviously had, because her detailing of what was expected of the hostess—bridge, Woman's Hour, cocktail parties, the Children's Fancy Dress Ball, and organizing PR for the important passengers in different ports— was laced with wit: "Never say no to any (reasonable) passenger request—i.e. for a 'jugglers' get-together,' or 'discussion into psychic research,' etc."

The *Northern Star* sailed from Southampton to Las Palmas and down the African coast to Cape Town and Durban, and from there to Perth in Western Australia. There was a week in Melbourne and Sydney, then it was over to Wellington, where the ship was completely cleaned, and all the passengers, except those few who were round-the-world voyagers, finally disembarked. Some of the passengers were emigrating to South Africa, Australia, or New Zealand, about to begin new lives; some were returning home for visits. The return journey crossed the Pacific to Fiji and Tahiti, then passed through the Panama Canal to Curaçao and Trinidad (Note to hostesses: "Get to a Caribbean nightclub!"), before returning to Southampton.

READING ABOUT the voyages, I felt my old, seafaring wanderlust. I had imagined, after the summer on the *Kong Olav*, that I'd try to find a job on another ship, perhaps one going around the world. I had my Norwegian seaman's papers and a work permit. I could have even tried to go to a maritime academy. Instead, I'd used the money I'd earned to make my way to Seattle. Although I'd still fantasized, from time to time, of going to San Francisco and sitting in the Scandinavian hiring hall, within a year I was working at an alternative newspaper and soon after that started a publishing company. Why had I given it up? I wondered. I could have seen Japan; I could have seen the Caribbean.

Dorothy came out of the bathroom, wearing nothing but a big towel.

"Can I get a copy of these notes?"

"Of course. You'll need that for your research, won't you? We'll go to the high school where I used to teach; they have a copy machine."

But first the post arrived, and the postman, who was something of a writer himself, came in and was introduced; the post must be read and more calls made, and then Dorothy had to put on her face. As I read again through the notes, I began to recall a television comedy I saw as a child in the late fifties, *The Gale Storm Show: Oh! Susanna*. Gale Storm, a former B-movie actress who had become one of television's first sitcom stars in *My Little Margie*, played Susanna Pomeroy, the social director of a cruise ship. Her roommate on the USS *Ocean Queen* was the dithery ship's beautician, Esmerelda Nugent, "Nugey," played by sixty-year-old ZaSu Pitts. The script called for the sort of madcap antics and zany impersonations that Lucy and Ethel, and Margie herself, had engaged in so successfully. I remember lots of heads popping through portholes. To capitalize on Gale Storm's singing career, every third episode featured a big production number, as part of the ship's entertainment.

I loved Gale Storm's impersonations of duchesses and southern belles, the "doubling" acts she carried off so well, but it was the notion of a woman working at sea that left its mark on my imagination. She seemed to go her own way on the ship, getting around authority figures and constantly cooking up mischief with the scatterbrained Nugey. I never thought of her as Susanna, but always as Gale Storm, and to my young mind, it seemed a strange and magnificent coincidence that a woman aboard a ship would be called Gale Storm. In reality, someone at RKO studios thought up the name first, then handed it to the young Texas girl named Josephine Cottle who won their contest to go to Hollywood.

I hadn't thought of Gale Storm for years; yet now, at Dorothy's cluttered kitchen table, I marveled at how the imagination of a young girl subverts what it is given. To me, Gale

Storm and Nugey ran the ship, and were the most important people on it.

"I'm ready, I'm dressed, let's go!" said Dorothy, and we hopped into her car again. It was about two in the afternoon. We swung by the high school so I could use their copier, and were there for over an hour while Dorothy visited with friends and ex-colleagues. She introduced me all around as a writer who was interested in her seagoing life and was going to write about her. Back in the car, Dorothy sang me a song or two and told me more stories, but it was hard by now to keep her on the track of the *Northern Star*. Everything reminded her of something else. I was learning her whole life story. Love, divorce, love, and so on. "Men—they're hopeless, but you've got to love them. Some of them, anyway. Don't you?" She'd ascertained from my ringless left hand that I wasn't married, and no doubt assumed that I was of the same persuasion: divorced and looking.

"I'm more interested in women," I told her after a minute.

She glanced at me curiously and I wondered if she were trying to understand how a normal-looking woman like me could have made *that* choice. "Still have your teeth?" she asked instead. "That's good. I've had masses of dental work."

It was getting on four in the afternoon and I still hadn't had lunch. Though we'd finally arrived in town, I began to get the feeling that Dorothy might not let me go so easily. She did some errands, picked up film, dropped off shoes to be repaired. When we finally pulled up in front of the Queens Hotel, I thought she might be getting ready to come in with me. She hinted that its bar had once been a favorite haunt of hers when she'd had an intense affair with a Norwegian sailor.

I had to be firm. I'd chosen the Queens, a big pile of Victorian stone, right at the waterfront, for my return to

Lerwick precisely because I was so worn out with bed-and-breakfasts and youth hostels and all those fascinating, wonderful, talkative Shetlanders. If we went into the bar, we would never come out. I excused myself weakly, saying I had to do more research. It's true, I did have to go back to the library, and I wanted to read the book she'd given me, *Splendid Sisters*. But even more, I just wanted to get a sandwich and a pot of tea, and wash my underwear and socks in a bathroom attached to my room, and later watch something on the BBC, one of those odd shows, about gardening or cooking, that never gets picked up by public television in America.

All the same, when Dorothy and I hugged goodbye, I found myself sorry to part from her. It was like stepping off a carousel. My legs wobbled and I missed the whirl. I clutched my papers and waved as she drove off; then I walked to the reception desk.

"A room," I said expansively to the clerk. "With a view of the harbor."

"Certainly. Your name please?"

"Storm," I answered, knowing that meant I'd have to pay with cash. "Miss G. Storm."

"Just yourself, Miss Storm?"

"Just myself."

THE NEXT morning, lounging luxuriously in bed, with the drapes open to a view of Lerwick Harbor, I opened *Splendid Sisters*. There were a number of chapters about the history of the owners and engineers of the Shaw Savill line, and about building the two ships, the *Northern Star* and the *Southern Cross*. But then came a chapter on the women officers, all five, with the revealing title "You Need Stamina."

The author writes briskly:

> Their motives are the normal ones—a desire to travel, to
> see the world, get away from home, to change jobs and rou-
> tine, and possibly find a husband. It is a romantic potential,
> but the work is no sinecure, hours are often long—particu-
> larly before sailing and arriving—and shore leave at the
> various ports not automatic. They all seem to enjoy it.

He then goes on to describe the various duties of the
nursing sisters, assistant purserettes, and social hostesses. In
this book I found the story of Jeanne Pratt, who must surely be
the Jeanne who wrote Dorothy's "Instructions to Hostesses."

> Mrs Crawley was succeeded in *Northern Star* by Miss
> Jeanne Pratt, whose father worked in Shaw Savill's head
> office until retiring, and whose mother's family had bred
> sailors since the days of Drake. By the time she was eight
> Jeanne announced that at some time in the indefinite future
> she would go to Norway and take her master's certificate.
> Even though Reigate, in the heart of Surrey, was the
> nearest she could get to the sea, she made herself a cabin in
> the garage loft, furnished it with an uncle's old sea-chest,
> spent hours drawing and painting sailing-ships, and put up
> a notice to indicate whether "the captain" was in or out. She
> did, however, go aboard the *Pamir* and, when she was
> eleven, *Dominion Monarch*, where, with a number of small
> boys, she clambered up a mast.
> It was several years later before she saw *Dominion
> Monarch* again, and this time she went to sea in her as a

purserette. She was in *Northern Star* for the maiden voyage.
From purserette to hostess was a short step.

How many girls who clambered up masts or drew sailing
ships in these maritime countries had to put these dreams
behind them either to marry or to take the few seagoing jobs
available to them? I thought about my own work on the *Kong
Olav*. The captain had been immeasurably far above me, and I'd
never thought for an instant that I could do anything like stand
on the bridge and pilot the steamer up and down the coast.

Miss Jeanne Pratt's mother's family "had bred sailors since
the days of Drake," and at eight years old, the height of girlish
confidence, Jeanne knew her direction in life and saw no obstacles; she had a cabin in the garage loft, a sea chest, and a notice
to let people know whether she, the captain, was in or out. But
by the time Jeanne actually managed to get aboard a ship, the
option of captain was out. When I was a girl, I imagined everything was possible. I read *Pippi Longstocking* and saw Gale
Storm as the main character on the USS *Ocean Queen*. But by the
time I came to work on the *Kong Olav*, in 1973, I'd forgotten my
dreams, or bowed to reality. It was enough to go to sea, and if
that meant being a dishwasher, so be it.

In Jeanne's "Instructions," she stoutly urges her sister hostesses to be proud of their work and not put up with any jibes
from the crew and officers.

> Don't let junior officers tell you that your job is unneces-
> sary and that women should not be at sea! Yours is a senior
> officer's position, despite paucity of paypackets. Keep your
> dignity and deal firmly with junior officers. Keep well in
> with the seniors as equals.

Don't be depressed if the Captain does not make a fuss
of you. As I say, the job is yours. It *is* important—you are
literally the shop window of the company, even if they don't
realise it, and as long as you are pleasant at all times, the
battle is won.

GRACE O'MALLEY would have understood the message
about never letting anyone tell her she couldn't go to sea, but
it's likely she would have thumbed her nose at the instruction to
be pleasant at all times. Pippi Longstocking, the perpetual
eight-year-old and strongest girl on the planet, who didn't even
go to school, much less charm school, would certainly have
laughed it off completely. Captain a ship? Why of course!

"'A better seaman than my daughter has never sailed on the
seven seas,' Captain Longstocking would often say. And he was
right. Pippi guided the *Hoptoad* with a sure hand past the most
perilous underwater reefs and the worst breakers."

CHAPTER X

HALIBUT WOMAN

The Faroe Islands

My knees shook. My stomach lurched. The uneasiness that came over me at my first sight of the Faroe Islands, pin points of unnecessary punctuation in a vast uncaring sea, would creep up on me again and again during my time there. It seemed as if they could not really be anchored to the ocean floor; it seemed as if they might break loose and float off into the widening mid-Atlantic rift, helpless to hold on in spite of their Danish infrastructure of highways, bridges, and tunnels, in spite of the imported weight of petrol stations, supermarkets, and cultural centers.

I'd boarded the Faroese-owned car ferry, the *Norröna*, at two-thirty in the morning in Lerwick. Only a handful of passengers embarked with me, and as the ship glided slowly past the city's stately granite buildings, the tallest windows shimmering gold with the first rays of sunrise, it was easy to believe I was still among Scottish friends. To wake groggily six hours later was to wake into a different country. The cafeteria of the *St. Sunniva* had served oatmeal and eggs and bacon, marmalade and cold toast; suddenly I was in line for Scandinavian *smørbrod*—open-faced sandwiches decorated with single curls of cheese or roast beef dotted with semicolons of mayonnaise and shrimp. Danish money was required, and a new language. All around me were large families with blond, bored children,

157

en route from Norway or Denmark to a holiday in Iceland. If they'd started from Denmark they'd already been onboard two days. There was a weary, competitive jostle in the cafeteria line, and a mingled smell of dark-roasted coffee and yogurt-scented vomit.

On deck the air was as fresh as a salty mountaintop though, with only sea in sight. I cheered up and strolled fore and aft, imagining myself one of those boldly adventurous women travelers of a hundred years ago, voyaging to the Far North when it was considered one of the more remote and daring of destinations. Nowadays Scandinavia seems to many people synonymous with bland prosperity, and every self-respecting woman in search of risk is trekking across Australia, rafting the Boh in Borneo, or finagling a flight to Antarctica. But in the eighteenth and nineteenth centuries, the North pulled voyagers like a magnet, curious visitors as well as polar explorers. Mary Wollstonecraft was one of the first literary figures to try her hand at describing the exotic North: Her travel book, in letters *A Short Residence in Sweden, Norway, and Denmark,* first published in 1796, is often credited with starting the craze for icy adventures among the English (poet Robert Southey wrote to a friend: "She has made me in love with a cold climate, and frost and snow, with a northern moonlight."). Wollstonecraft made her journey alone with a very young daughter; she used the trip as a way to reflect on nature, society, and her own fragile existence. The *terra incognita* she explored was herself.

Many travelers bound for Iceland went through the Faroe Islands, but few left a record. Only American-born Elizabeth Taylor, who first visited in 1895 and spent more than ten years of her life in the Faroes, seemed to have made a specialty of this archipelago. Taylor was one of those doughty lady travelers we find turning up in old photographs and on library shelves, their names appended to books titled *On Sledge and Horseback to Outcast Siberian Lepers* or *An Overland Trek from India by Sidesaddle, Camel, and Rail.* They are clothed in long skirts, stout boots, traveling cloaks, and Tyrolean hats, when they are not wearing bear furs or reindeer skins. Their arms are free; a retinue of natives is in the background, hauling portmanteaus and trunks. But they are far from weak. They can go without food, and almost without sleep. They take for granted conditions we would find appalling. Their cheerfulness can be unnerving. After tramping her way through the Faroes, Taylor wrote:

> The way up Stóra Dímun is neither easy nor safe. In many
> places a fall means certain death, and no one subject to
> dizziness should attempt it. But the difficulties have been
> exaggerated. Anyone of ordinary activity, who is able to
> keep a cool head, can make the ascent if he wears Faroe
> footgear, has a good helper behind, and takes thought for
> each footstep.

Like her Victorian cohorts traveling in Africa and the Himalayas, Elizabeth Taylor was made of stern stuff. Long before she settled in the Faroes for an extended stay in her forties, she'd traveled by horseback through much of Canada, had been to Alaska, and had accompanied an expedition twenty-three hundred miles along the Athabasca River and Great Slave Lake to the Mackenzie River before it poured into the Polar Sea. She had traveled by foot and horse cart over the remote Hardangervidda in Norway, and spent ten weeks in Iceland, where she studied the eider duck and visited lava fields and archeological remains. Like many of the women who traveled without male companionship or chaperon, but who had no real work to occupy them, she took notes constantly, gathered specimens, especially of plants, and sketched. Part of this was meant as self-improvement; part was to look busy in a world that had no use for unmarried women without professions. Like many of the other ladies traveling in the North, Taylor meant to write a book and prove her knowledge and her worth; yet, though she published articles in periodicals from the *Atlantic Monthly* to *Forest and Stream*, she never managed to pull her essays together into chapters. Recently, her letters and uncollected papers were gathered into a paperback with the irresistible title *The Far Islands and Other Cold Places*. It was this book that had first put the Faroes on the map for me.

ELIZABETH TAYLOR'S initial impression of the Faroes was so positive that I was chagrined to find that, in spite of good intentions, I felt almost immediately at a loss in the islands. My room at the guesthouse had a splendid view of the sea, and the modern prints and blond furniture made a nice change from the frilly clutter of the average bed-and-breakfast in the Scottish Isles, but my landlady, far from being a warm and chatty Shetlander, was gruff and cool. She spoke no English, only Faroese and Danish; we settled on Norwegian, but she was also practically deaf, so that any question I put to her was initially answered with a loud, cranky "HVA?" (WHAT?). She was elderly, thick-bodied, her face like a vanilla pudding with whiskers. Every step was obviously painful; she mostly sat in the foyer at a table with a telephone, papers, and several full ashtrays under a sign that said "No Smoking."

My first afternoon in Tórshavn foreshadowed the rest of

my stay. I went to the post office first, eager to claim the package containing my Lonely Planet guide to Iceland and the Faroe Islands, which I'd cleverly sent to myself *poste restante*. It wasn't there, there was no sign of it, and the woman at the counter made only the most cursory of searches before announcing, "I'm not surprised." Coming out of the post office, I looked down to see what time it was and found that my trusty Timex had popped off my wrist, leaving only a faint indentation on the skin. The young man at the tourist office thought the only place I might find a watch was the shopping center, a twenty-minute walk away. "But you'd better hurry—they close soon."

I took the opportunity to ask about a Laundromat. He seemed bemused. "To wash your clothes yourself?" He engaged in a long conversation with a colleague while I perused the official Faroese tourist guide, which assured me, in exalted language, that the Faroe Islands were not about mass tourism, but about individual connections. "Each visitor is treated as an honored guest!" He passed me a slip of paper with an address on it. "This woman sometimes does laundry for tourists."

Sometimes? The watch shop was closed when I got there. I mooned around the supermarket and wondered at some of the food displayed. One refrigerated case had a shelf of a dairy product in cartons called Cheasy 0.1%, and a second shelf of Barbie yogurt in containers that displayed Barbie's pink-and-blond charms. I would not be disgruntled, I vowed. I would not sneer and get all curmudgeonly and Paul Therouxish. I would buck up and go to a concert at the Nordic House, rumored to be the most beautiful building in the Faroes. The man at the tourist office had told me that the Nordic House had a cafeteria. I'd have dinner there and write in my journal until the concert began.

As soon as I set off for the Nordic House, the overcast sky

let loose, and my walk, disappointingly along an unpicturesque highway with views of petrol stations, auto repair shops, and a soccer stadium, was a wet, cold one. The cafeteria served only cake and coffee, as it turned out. I opened my journal and wrote chirpily: *The Nordic House is stunning. It combines the traditional farmhouse architecture of the turf roof that seems to blend into the hillside with the glass and polished wood expansiveness of modern Scandinavian design. Even though it's raining, it feels warm, light, and spacious inside.* . . . And so on, down to the description of the cake on my plate with a drawing of it. My heart wasn't in it. I was filling time as I filled pages. Thus does a writer struggle to shape her disappointment and loneliness.

"WELL, IT's beautiful of course. But I couldn't *live* here," said the Danish woman in a blue anorak, with frizzy blond hair like a ruff around her anxious face. "I can't imagine *living* in such an isolated place. Without . . .without . . ." She gestured in the direction of civilization: of Denmark, of Europe.

We were standing midway up a grassy slope whose arc was broken on the other side by what I knew to be a sheer cliff dropping down to the Atlantic breakers. I couldn't seem to proceed any farther up the slope, even though it looked deceptively like the gently rising greensward of a fabulous golf course. Others from the tour bus had strolled up to what looked to me like the edge. From my vantage point below, they seemed to be obliviously chatting on the way to a fatal plunge. The soles of my feet, tender in hiking boots, quivered like fish.

"Could *you* live here? Could you?" she asked me. Behind us was the village of Gjógv (pronounced something like Jack). Around us the steep yet rounded hills were the softest green. A cleft in the cliff had made a natural narrow harbor for fishing boats, though the boats had to be winched up hundreds of feet to the level of the village. The houses here were the color of bitter chocolate with candy-red doors and windows trimmed in white. Some roofs were grass, with bright yellow marsh marigolds and forget-me-nots; others were corrugated metal painted a silvery blue-green.

If Greek villages are defined by the dazzle of white against cobalt blue, Faroese villages empty the light of the world by their negative, dense black on leaf green. Originally the split timbers of the houses were tarred shiny-thick against the winds and rain coming straight over the cliffs; now it's paint that keeps them dark fudge. Ever since arriving in Tórshavn, I'd noticed post cards of paintings by Steffan Danielsen; his scenes of black houses with angled roofs of blue, orange and the powdery verdi-gris of weathered copper could have come straight from Gjógv.

The Danish woman was on the same tour I was, a daylong trip to the northern part of Eysturoy, the large island lying par-allel to Streymoy, where Tórshavn is located. Aside from two Germans on the tour and me, almost everyone else was Danish or Norwegian. Our guide spoke to us in a combination of English and what she called "Scandinavian." The Faroes were settled, like Orkney, Shetland, and Iceland, by the seagoing Norse, and remained under the crown of Norway until the end of the fourteenth century, when Norway itself fell under the control of Denmark for the next four hundred years. Since 1948 the Faroe Islands have been a self-governing, autonomous region of the Kingdom of Denmark. In the past the Faroes were exploited by the Danes, who controlled their local economy through trade monopolies; now the Danes complain of losing money on the Faroes. The Danish government contributed heavily to constructing the Faroese infrastructure of highways and tunnels, and it has provided credit when fishing revenues have fallen. The Faroese proclaim their autonomy at every opportunity however, and often show a great coolness toward Danish visitors, a fact that my companion acknowledged.

"I came for curiosity's sake," she said. "But I am having trouble liking it. In Denmark we were having a nice hot summer when I left last week. Here I've been cold every day, all the time. There's not very much to do. The people are not very friendly."

THAT WAS not Elizabeth Taylor's experience during her first extended stay in the Faroes, from 1900 to 1905. Elizabeth Taylor liked the Faroese very much. Even on her brief visit half a decade earlier she had noticed the men, describing them as "ruddy blond with thick half-curling hair and very thick soft beards." They put her in mind of the old Vikings in the sagas. Five years later, she was back to stay. "I am going up to the Faroes, & even to think of it gives me a feeling of strength & enthusiasm," she wrote to a friend. She was forty-four then, a self-taught botanist, ornithologist, and ethnologist. She planned to draw, to take notes, to gather specimens for the British Museum, the Smithsonian, for collections at Harvard and Oxford. "In order to secure material, I must see different islands and have certain experiences. . . . I must write about trout fishing, bird cliffs, whales, etc."

Elizabeth had grown up in St. Paul, Minnesota; her father was appointed the American consul to Winnipeg when she was fourteen. She was close to him and made visits over the years to Canada; he encouraged her explorations. Middle-class women rarely went to college in those days. Most professions were closed to them. If they didn't immediately marry, their choices were few. They could be nurses or teachers. They could live with their families. For many women, of course, a life with such prospects was stultifying. Elizabeth first sought an identity as an artist. She studied at the Art Students League in New York for several summers; she went to Paris and took lessons at Colarossi and Académie Julian. She spent a winter in Venice. Like many Americans, she found that a small income went further in Europe. She did not think she was particularly talented as an artist; she turned instead to writing. Yet even though she published many articles, she felt undereducated. She did not want to be an amateur; she thought that if she settled in one place and thoroughly investigated it, the book that resulted would make a contribution to world knowledge. The Faroes appealed to her for their remoteness, and for the fact that no one else seemed to have written much about them.

She tramped, she painted, she botanized and collected specimens; she was rowed about by eight strong men in a boat.

So I climbed down and waited on the rocks for a lull, while the men kept the boat in a quiet spot under some cliffs across the inlet. "Now!" cried a man who was watching the sea. The boat shot forward to where I stood, I tumbled in anyhow, waved a farewell to those on shore, and in an instant we were tossing high in a whirl of white water between the reefs, cutting through masses of foam, and reaching the open sea just before the next big wave broke. There we were safe; there was little wind, and the great waves swept shoreward in unbroken lines. We could easily climb them and race down their outer slopes. It was a glorious day.

Pastor Peter Lorentz Heilmann and wife Flora are joined by Elizabeth Taylor (wrapped in a blanket) in 1901

In spite of the effervescence in many of her descriptions, Elizabeth's time in the Faroes was not completely euphoric. Dependent on her writing for income, she was forced to be the guest of various Faroese. The winter she spent with the governor of Tórshavn was long and difficult. There were nine children, five of them babies; they suffered that winter from whooping cough, chicken pox, and meningitis. The youngest baby died. The servants were "disorganized." Another winter found her with a pastor's family on the northernmost island. Although she buoyed herself with thoughts that here were the essentials: salt-of-the-earth peasantry, lots of fresh air, and the opportunity for good walking ("As to society, who wants it? I don't."), her spirits understandably flagged. "The surf is so bad that in winter no visitors can come. . . . There are but two shops & all the people except one shopkeeper & the schoolmaster are peasant fisherman." But soon she chided herself, "Do not look melancholy about the cold & make folks regret you are in the house."

She made friends, but not many were women. Educated, Danish-speaking men—the schoolteachers, governors, consuls, and pastors of the island—were her preferred companions. Elizabeth had wished to be a boy when growing up; all her life she envied male freedom. Like many Victorian women travelers, she achieved a kind of genderless authority by coming to a new country in the persona of an independent adventurer. Her foreignness made freedom possible; her announced occupation, to gather as much material on the Faroes as possible in order to write a book, gave her a reason for living in a remote island archipelago in the Atlantic.

She found romance in wondering, "Am I or am I not a *Kalvakona?*"

That means a halibut woman, one who possesses mysterious powers that can charm a big halibut to the hook of a
fisherman. But the fisherman must have promised her ver-
bally, or in his thoughts at sea, the beita—a choice bit cut
from the fish between the forefins. . . . Last week, a man on
the fishing bank promised me the beita, and a few minutes

Faroese women grading cod on the docks

later he was having a sharp fight with a halibut that
weighed almost two hundred pounds. . . . Two days later,
another man promised me the beita, and caught nothing. So
what is one to think?

Old photographs of the Faroes show dozens of women
working in the fishing industry, as they worked all over the
North Atlantic, particularly in Iceland and Norway, laying the
split cod out to dry on the rocks and gathering them up if rain
threatened. The women wear shawls and long dresses in the
photographs; they stand next to great piles of dried cod, which
were sold primarily in the Mediterranean for *baccalao*. But these
women were invisible to Taylor; she did not describe them in
her writing. She would rather be at a remove from everyday
working life; she would rather be an outsider, a traveler, a halibut woman.

◉ ◉ ◉

"WHAT ABOUT you?" asked my Danish companion. She had just taken a photo of me (months later the photograph would be held by a magnet to my refrigerator at home: I'm wearing the perpetual green rain jacket; my hair is flying. I look staunch and farseeing rather than very cheerful), and we were strolling back through the little village. "Why would you come to the Faroes? Do you like it here?"

I wasn't sure how to answer. Back in Tórshavn, things were not going well. My landlady seemed to have taken a dislike to me. Two months earlier I'd faxed a request to stay three days; once here, I'd asked to change it to five, which she'd agreed to—I thought. Then last night, the evening of my third day, she'd knocked forcefully on my door and demanded to know how long I thought I was staying. "Two more nights," I said. "We agreed."

"HVA?!?"

"TWO MORE DAYS."

"Impossible. I have other people coming. You must leave."

"I'm not leaving. We agreed."

"HVA?"

Yesterday morning I'd taken my clothes to the woman who was said to do laundry, and nearly had a tussle with her when she attempted to put them into a large bag full of other people's clothes. I said in both English and Norwegian, "How will you tell my clothes from anybody else's?" Finally her son came to the rescue and explained that his mother thought I was the same lady from England who had been by earlier and dropped off some clothes.

I bought a new watch, at a vastly inflated price. I went to the tourist office to arrange this trip to Eysturoy, and found my young friend in a puzzled mood. He had been an exchange student in America, he confided, and although he had asked his friends to come visit him, nobody would ever come to the Faroes. Why was that? I was American, could I tell him? I went to the post office several times looking for my Lonely Planet guide, to no avail. I collected quite a few stamps that showed an unfriendly sheep's head.

Back on the bus, leaving Gjógv for Eidi, another remote village in the north of Eysturoy, where Elizabeth Taylor had spent five years, our tour guide came back and sat by me to practice her English. She pointed out the "cheeps" on the hillside, and rehearsed what to say about the pilot whale hunting, the famous *grindadráp*. She thought the two Germans might disapprove and wanted to explain that it was a long tradition in the Faroes. The people waited months for the pilot whales to blunder into shore. The resultant killing supplied the natives with necessary nourishment.

"What is the word for whale fat in English?"

"Blubber," I said.

"It's not *spekk*?"

"No, that's Norwegian."

"Blubber," she sounded it out. "Blubber, blubber, blubber. Are you in Greenpeace?"

I changed the subject. "Eidi," I said. "Isn't that where Elizabeth Taylor, the American traveler, had to live throughout the First World War?"

"I do not know her."

Elizabeth Taylor left the Faroes in 1906, after spending six years gathering information and specimens. She lived for a while in England, then returned to the U.S. but did not progress with her book, though she did manage to place a few articles and

organize illustrated talks on the Faroes. She continued her restless ways, settling nowhere in America, visiting Europe again,
living a time in Scotland. She made another appearance in the
Faroes in 1913, and again, unluckily, in 1914. The First World
War broke out and few ships came into or out of the Tórshavn
harbor from abroad for five years. What was it like for her,
without mail, on short rations, a perpetual guest? She was in her
sixties by then; her vigorous cheerfulness must have been fading
slightly. She discovered she did not like the cold, after all.
Botanizing, painting, birding seemed less important. She pot-
tered stoically in a borrowed garden, taught a local boy to paint.
It would have been a good time to work on her book, perhaps to
finish it. Instead, she brooded over her perfectionism, her pro-
crastination. "Everyone seems to be dreadfully clever nowadays
and the public wants things that are striking, and a trifle sensa-
tional and picturesque, and I fear that is all beyond me." She
published only two articles from this second long stay. One is
called wearily, "Five Years in a Faroe Attic."

I wouldn't have liked to be stuck in Eidi for five years.
Taylor called it a "dirty disagreeable little village." It was not as
picturesque as Gjógv, though it was larger, ranged along two
roads overlooking a beautiful wide bay, just the sort of bay an
unlucky pod of pilot whales might mistakenly swim into. On a
windy viewpoint where we stopped to use the toilets, our guide
gave us an enthusiastic talk in English and Scandinavian about
the *grindadráp*. The Germans, contrary to expectations, were
not Green at all, but seemed very respectful of the need of the
Faroese for all that blubber. The Norwegians, longtime whale
hunters, also remained composed. Only the Danes seemed
grossed out. The Danish woman asked me to take a picture of
her. "I really don't want to hear what these people do to the poor

whales," she said, gesturing me away from the group. She smiled into the camera, bravely, I thought. She'd said she was a school-teacher. This wasn't her first trip away from Denmark, but it was the first time she'd traveled alone. "I return to Denmark tomorrow," she said. "I can hardly wait."

BACK IN Tórshavn, I sneaked into the guesthouse while the landlady was in the kitchen. I had half-expected my room to have been cleaned out while I was gone, but everything was as I'd left it. In fact, she hadn't dusted a single day since I'd been here. What was I so desperately hanging on to? Some futile desire for control in a foreign place. My own things, arranged my own way, my own place, if even for a few nights.

But travel is about letting go; there's no other way to experience it. I knew that it's only when you let go that the best things happen. That's why I traveled, and why I found it so hard sometimes.

I was about seven years old when I first realized that a girl, a woman, could go off by herself to see the world. One day my mother and some friends took me along to the Port of Los Angeles. From the dock we went up the gangplank of an ocean liner and down the corridor to a small stateroom. The voyager, my mother's friend, was a middle-aged lady whose name I don't remember, a teacher who had the summer off. She was going by ship around the whole world, and she took me on her knee and said, "I'll send you some post cards," which she later did, of Japan, and India, and Paris. Then there was a warning blast, and we all rushed off. We stood on the dock while colored streamers flew out and over the sides of the ship. The lady looked very small up there at the railing, wearing a hat and a corsage pinned to her jacket. "Goodbye!" she called. "Goodbye," we called back. "Don't forget to write!"

The idea of her sea voyage was enormous to me, and all the way home in the car I thought about it, and laid my plans. My first trip around the world would have to be via the cardboard globe, which I spun and spun, letting my finger touch the countries under it. "I'm in Japan now," I announced to my brother. He spun the globe and ended in the Pacific. "I'm drowned," he said. I organized a game in the backyard of me on the picnic table throwing down some colored streamers to the mystified dog. I waved to my mother at the window: "Goodbye! Goodbye!"

"Goodbye!" she waved back from the kitchen. "Don't forget to write!"

I lay on my bed in Tórshavn and thought about women traveling, about all those ladies without proper professions who wrote books. I was hardly any different from them. I'd come to the Faroe Islands because they sounded adventurous, because they were wildly remote, because no one I knew had ever been here. I was a lady who had sailed off on a boat and had come to an island in the middle of nowhere precisely to write about it. Elizabeth Taylor and her failure to finish her book haunted me. Who has the right to say another person's life is futile? Yet I mourned for women of the past, whose wildest adventures, most passionate and courageous acts had been reduced to anecdotes about "intrepid Victorian lady travelers." *Intrepid:* Well, that was one word I refused to use, about myself or any other unfortunate soul who found herself far away from home, having to depend on strangers.

I was so tired that I didn't eat dinner. I read a mystery and listened to a tape on compassion by Buddhist teacher Pema Chödrön, kept in my bag for just such self-pitying moods. I waited for the whiskery landlady to bang on my door and demand I leave instantly, but she didn't. Gradually I grew more peaceful; all the same, I fell asleep in my clothes, afraid of a nocturnal rousting.

The next morning I found I'd had a change of heart. Travel is the state of being homeless; we should welcome the opportunity it gives us to live nowhere. I wrote a note to the landlady in Norwegian, saying that I had thought about it, and that I would be leaving this morning.

She looked astonished, and then grateful, when I handed the slip of paper to her. She said, smiling somewhat ruefully, "I believe we had a misunderstanding. I am a little deaf, you know. Where will you go?"

"I don't know."

"I will call the Seaman's Hotel. They have reasonable rooms. I will drive you there."

Perhaps she just wanted to make sure I was really leaving. She called and there was a room at the Seaman's Hotel. I packed up quickly, suddenly lighthearted. I let her drive me the few short blocks; on the way we talked about the weather, whether it would rain or not today. We parted cordially. She apologized again, and I marveled that I had ever been afraid of her.

CHAPTER XI

AUD THE DEEP-MINDED

From the Faroe Islands to Iceland

I AWOKE one morning in Tórshavn to find the red-and-black wooden houses wrapped in fog, green turf roofs dripping. In the harbor, masts poked out of the mist like knitting needles from white cotton batting. The gulls swooped over the glassy water and perched watchfully on boats. Leaving the Seaman's Hotel after breakfast, I could feel the cobblestones of the old town under my feet, but I couldn't see my legs. I imagined that the islands might well have drifted overnight even farther away from the rest of the world.

That morning I left Tórshavn by bus for the island of Sandoy to the south. I'd decided to visit the village of Húsavík overnight and to see the ruins of a medieval farm once owned by the "Lady of Húsavík." Gudrún Sjúrdardóttir, a ship owner and merchant, was once counted as one of the wealthiest women of the North. She was born in Bergen, Norway, in the mid-fourteenth century; her father was Sjurdur Hjalt, Hjalt meaning that he came from Shetland. When he died, Gudrún inherited his considerable wealth and property: many houses in Bergen and some twenty farms along the west coast of Norway, as well as land in Shetland. She came to Húsavík with her husband, Arnbjørn Gudleiksson, who persuaded her to return to his home in the Faroes to rebuild the farm after the Black Death carried away much of the valley's population. She moved to the

Faroes and still maintained ties with Bergen and Shetland
through trading interests. How many ships she had, we don't
know, but one of them went down in the North Sea in 1403 with
her husband on it.

In medieval times, strangely, the Faroes would have seemed
no more remote than most places in the maritime countries of
the north. These islands may even have seemed more accessible
than Ireland or England, which were still forested and populated by hidden, hostile inhabitants. The Norse who settled the
northern isles were seafaring folk. Shetland was two days' sail
from Norway, the Faroes another two or three from Shetland.
Nowadays, when we get into our cars to go from place to place,
cities seem close and islands distant. Yet, until a century or two
ago, traveling overland was far more onerous and dangerous
than a sea voyage. Especially important to the Vikings and their
descendents was the fact that you could see your enemies
coming out at sea.

Hanus undir Leitinum, a schoolteacher and native of
Húsavík, was my guide. Growing up, he was one of five other
Hanuses in the village, so instead of being called by his last
name, Sorensen, he was called after his family's house. He'd been
the teacher in Húsavík for nine years; before that he taught at the
secondary school in Sandur, Sandoy's main village. I walked to
meet him at the schoolhouse. The evening sun was in the west,
coming over the hills, and laying down ribbons of lemon-silver
light along the ridges and hummocks. The black-painted houses
gleamed. Not all of them had turf roofs; some were constructed
of rippled, galvanized metal, and painted floury aqua, dusty rose.
Many had red doors and red trim. The dark-blue sea beat upon
the shore. Everything was colorful, quiet, and very cold.

We were meeting at the schoolhouse to get out of the wind

and to find a history book or two that mentioned Gudrún. It was a single room, with six tiny desks, a chalk blackboard, and posters of bears, seals, and whales. There was a library of picture books, novels, and information, a small, shiny black piano, and a brand-new computer, which had just arrived last month. The children, all three of them, already knew how to use it. Hanus told me he hadn't touched it yet.

The population of Húsavík is ninety-five today, about what it was in Gudrún's time and less than half of what it was when Hanus was growing up here fifty years ago. After elementary school the children go to the middle school in Sandur and then to Tórshavn to study. Few who study in Tórshavn or Copenhagen return to Húsavík. Every year more people move away. "You don't notice it so much in the summer," Hanus said. "People still keep their houses, and they come back for holidays. But in the winter, when you take a walk and so many houses are dark, then you notice it."

Hanus began to tell me about Gudrún, and to translate patiently from a Faroese history book that showed diagrams of how the houses at her farm once looked. He was tall and powerfully built, with a calmness and ease about him. He wore a darned wool sweater and a shirt whose cuffs were frayed: well-used clothes.

He explained that so much is known about Gudrún because six letters have been preserved from 1405. These documents concern the settlement of her estate. Gudrún not only outlived her husband but her two children as well; her estate went to relatives in Bergen and Shetland. The letters enumerate her properties and the rents she derived from them, as well as her possessions in Húsavík: silver platters, jewelry of gold and silver, fine clothes and headdresses, the house and the farm, horses and sheep.

By the fourteenth century, the Viking age was long over, and farming and trade were what mattered. Gudrún's ships would have traveled regularly between the Norwegian mainland and the Faroes, and perhaps farther afield, to England, Spain, and Constantinople. She was no Grace O'Malley; it's unlikely she captained her ships. But like Grace, she was a trader, amassing wealth by sea. I imagined Gudrún, like Christian Robertson, keeping a firm handle on her business. She would have had a grasp of geography much different from my own, and an understanding of weather as something to be reckoned with, not just ignored.

It was pleasantly sunny in the schoolhouse, and we sat for a long time and talked before venturing out into the chill so Hanus could show me what remained of Gudrún's estate, now part of the village. Around a large courtyard was a longhouse where Gudrún and her family had lived; across from the house were kitchens and storehouses for food. Still standing, too, were the foundations of a hayloft and a barn, and several outbuildings, probably once a washing house, a bakery, stables. Gone was the arch over the entrance to the courtyard, under which Gudrún would have ridden her horse to church. The church was only a few hundred feet away, but highborn women always rode. The church that now stood was the third church in that spot. It was wood not stone, painted white, with a steeple. Gudrún's bones lay beneath.

Not far away was a group of magical little boathouses built of drystone boulders. Each had a heavy green hat of turf pulled down over a weather-polished wooden door and large stone lintel. The doors had beautiful wooden latches and locks. Beyond the boathouses, the gray silk breakers rolled rhythmically onto a smooth sand beach. A band of twenty black-and-white oyster-catchers stood in lines, all facing the ocean, as if they were a tuxedoed concert audience waiting for the symphony to begin.

The fog had mostly receded, rolling up and back over the mountains like soft white sheets being taken off green armchairs. The bay was clear of large rocks, and the wide sand beach would have been a welcoming place to pull up a broad-beamed, shallow-draughted sailing ship, loaded with timbers and goods. The valley was marvelously green and flat, with a river running right through it. Before the Black Death the population had lived on one side of the river; afterward they built homes on the other side. The mountains closed in the valley, but unlike other parts of the Faroes where the peaks were often sharp black basalt, these were flattened on top. The mountains looked like green anvils hammered down by weather.

After leaving Hanus, I walked up and down the beach, imagining one of Gudrún's merchant ships appearing on the horizon and coming into shore. In autumn the ships were rolled up on logs into shelter for the winter, to be repaired and retarred. In the spring they would set off again with sheepskin, dried meat, and grain. It's believed that in those days the climate was somewhat drier and warmer; fodder could be grown to overwinter animals indoors. Gently sloped, treeless, bright green mountains surround the valley. At least two dozen waterfalls, some short and trickly, some much grander, leak out of the hillsides. I could see sheep. From this angle, there was no depth perspective: Two big white lambs seemed to be standing directly on top of their mother. Baaing and bleating, suddenly they rushed down to her, as if falling from a green sky, and buried themselves in her coat.

The sun was still high at this northern latitude. It was not a blaze of sun; it diffused through the sea mists as if silver and gold were being gently churned from the waterfalls and sprayed into the air. The combination of colors was electrifying: the jade green hills, the silvery gold light, the black houses with green grass roofs. There were no sounds but the round roll of the surf on the shore and the squashed-ducky cries of the oyster catchers. Back in Gudrún's day there would almost always have been ships and longboats out to sea; I strained my eyes to see one on the horizon. I imagined her standing on the shore, waiting day after day for her husband to return. Then, I had another vision, a woman rowing.

All over Tórshavn hung posters for a film called *Barbara* that showed a woman pulling the oars of a small boat in the direction of a merchantman sailing off into the fog. The film came from a classic Faroese novel about a captivating heroine who enchanted, then betrayed, a pastor sent from Copenhagen. The novel, in turn, was based on the real story of a woman called Beinta, who'd had a habit of marrying clergymen in the eighteenth century. Although the poster was misleading—Barbara/Beinta was not a seafarer—there had been a famous Barbara in Faroese myth, a sea sorceress.

The southernmost island of Suduroy was where this mythical Barbara of Sumba had lived. She'd been tried as a witch, but the judge dismissed the case on the grounds that she was too beautiful to be tarred. According to legend she once had a contest with the sorcerer Guttorm to see whose spells were stronger. Barbara raised such a storm while Guttorm and his sons were at sea that the waves turned blood red. When Guttorm reached shore, he found Barbara sitting on a hillside by a stream, her long yellow hair loose on her shoulders. Guttorm cut off her hair, and thus vanquished much of her power. He bound her to a chair, put it on the roof, and called up a storm from the northeast. When she was finally let go the next day, her spirit was broken. That's pretty much the message of the novel and film, too, though the film is more ambiguous about Barbara's punishment. She's allowed to row off endlessly into the sea after her lover instead of returning, humiliated, to Tórshavn.

I had to admit that it was a fine thing to walk around Tórshavn and see my name emblazoned everywhere. Barbara as a name had fallen out of favor in the United States, as dated now as Gertrude or Hazel of my mother's generation. Barbaras have been around all century, but the bulk of them were conceived in the forties and fifties. In the United States I've noticed that people rarely call me by my full name; it's too much of a mouthful. They want to call me Barb. Some of my friends call me just B. In Spain my name sounds lovely, with the *r*'s rolling through it like thunder—no accident that St. Barbara is the patron saint of artillery. My younger brother, of course, always pointed out that one of the meanings of my name is *stranger*. *Foreigner* is how I prefer to think of it, not *barbarian*.

I stood on the shore in this lonely place, thinking about the Barbaras of old, and about Hanus undir Leitinum. I was thinking about names and naming, about being so firmly attached to a place that you took its name, that you were of it. Two of my grandparents, immigrants from Ireland and Sweden, came from a peasantry that was once part of the land, and they put down roots in the Midwest. But my parents moved west for new opportunities, and my brother and I never considered staying in Long Beach. I was more rooted in the Pacific Northwest than I'd ever been in Southern California.

Yet if I could take the name of my family home, I would choose one of the wonderful street names that some fanciful developer had given to my childhood neighborhood: Monlaco, Gondar, Faust, Senasac.

Barbara of Gondar, that had a nice ring.

F IVE HUNDRED years before Gudrún sent her ships far and wide from Húsavík, another powerful woman traveled through the Faroes and stayed some time before sailing on to Iceland. Her name was Audur djúpúdga, Aud the Deep-Minded. Her father was Ketil Flat-Nose; one of her sisters was called Jorunn Wisdom-Slope. Aud's story is told in the two primary sources of Icelandic history, Ari the Wise's twelfth-century *Book of the Icelanders* and the *Book of Settlements*, compiled during the thirteenth to fifteenth centuries, where she's remembered as one of the four most important settlers in the new country.

We also know of Aud from the *Laxdæla Saga*, where she's called Unn. According to the saga, Ketil Flat-Nose was a powerful lord in Norway, who decided to leave the country, like many well-born provincial chieftains, rather than submit to King Harald Fine-Hair, who was trying to unite Norway by destroying other seats of power. Ketil's two sons, Bjorn and Helgi, set off for Iceland to make their fortunes, while Ketil took the rest of his kinsmen and women to Scotland. Aud married Olaf the White, a Norse-Irish king. He was killed in battle, as was her son, Thorstein the Red. An early chapter in the *Laxdæla Saga* describes her decision to abandon Scotland and join her brothers in Iceland:

> When she learned that her son had been killed she realized
> that she had no further prospects there, now that her father,
> too, was dead. So she had a ship built secretly in a forest,
> and when it was completed she loaded it with valuables and
> prepared it for a voyage. She took with her all her surviving
> kinsfolk; and it is generally thought that it would be hard to

find another example of a woman escaping from such haz-
ards with so much wealth and such a large retinue. From
this it can be seen what a paragon amongst women she was.

The ship constructed for Aud's voyage to Orkney and the
Faroes and her transatlantic voyage to Iceland was a *knarr* or
hafskip—an ocean ship. These were seagoing trading vessels,
smaller versions of the *langskips*, the great sailing galleys with
which the Vikings harried and plundered Europe from the
eighth century to the twelfth. These trading vessels were
clinker-built and broader in the beam than longships; they were
usually about fifty feet long, and had a curved prow, without the
dragon head of the fighting longships. They carried one large
square sail of hide or thickly woven cloth, and were steered by a
side rudder. The tackle and anchor were made of walrus hide.
The cargo was stored in an open hold and covered with ox
hides. There were few oars, as the ocean ship wasn't made for
battle; it was a load-bearing sailing vessel, capable of carrying
from forty to fifty people, as well as livestock and supplies. Each
voyager had something called a *hudvat*, a hammock in which
they carried their possessions and which offered shelter when
emptied. No fires could be set at sea; those onboard ate dried
fish and meat and drank sour milk and beer. It was with this
ship that the Norse people colonized Iceland, one of the largest
planned migrations of medieval times.

I STOOD on the deck of the *Norröna* as we sailed out of
Tórshavn's harbor on a bright evening. There were dark
maroon clouds to the north, but from deck the town looked
charming with its grassy-roofed houses of red, black, and blue.

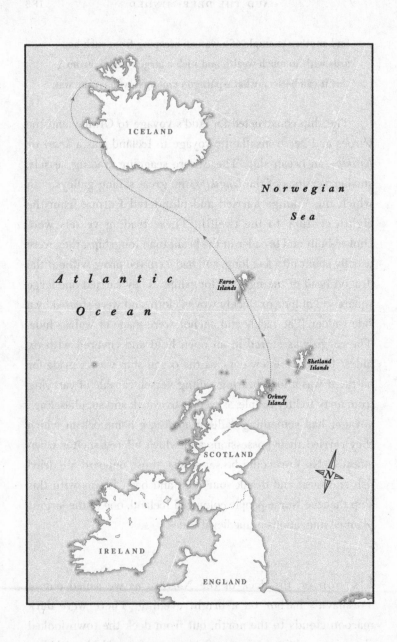

The journey of Aud the Deep-Minded

I wasn't sorry to be leaving; I was eager to move on to Iceland, a crossing of about fifteen hours. The *Norröna* was carrying a by-now thoroughly weary assembly of a thousand or so passengers, a number of whom had started their voyage in Denmark days ago. The ship was powered by huge engines and navigated using GPS and computers. There is always romance in crossing the sea; no matter how large the ship, it is always so very much smaller than the ocean. Yet for most of the voyage passengers are encouraged to turn their minds to other things than looking at the horizon and contemplating the vastness of the deep. The *Norröna* lacked the amenities of a first-class cruise ship, but it had a bar and a video parlor, both of which were heavily in use.

I'd already investigated my cabin and found it lacked a certain mystery with another person occupying the bottom bunk. She was Norwegian. She said she'd been on the ship from Bergen, or about twenty-five hours by now, and just wanted it to be over. The cabin smelled of her toiletries and some packaged fish cakes that she must have brought from Norway.

The wind grew stronger as we sailed north alongside and through the Faroes, and the rain began to spill like shards of stained glass from the gilt-lined maroon and indigo storm clouds. For a while the view was glorious, and the dedicated photographers were on hand with expensive equipment to capture the dramatic chiaroscuro effects. The clouds crashed together in brass-edged cymbals of purple and rust, and the mountains, vivid green below and black above, seemed to rise straight out of the sea. But after being lashed with freezing rain for half an hour, I was too numb to properly appreciate the splendor of the ongoing, ever-darkening sunset, and had to retreat to the cafeteria.

In Viking days, of course, I wouldn't have had that option.

Transatlantic voyages took place mainly in the summer months, but as I'd come to realize, summer in the North couldn't always be depended on. The *Laxdæla Saga* tells us that Aud's journey went well, though when they made land in the south of Iceland, their ship was wrecked. Most of the crossings from Norway or the Faroes to Iceland and back again were successful. Yet the sagas report enough stories of disaster and shipwreck to remind us what a hazardous journey it could be. I considered this as I sat at a table in the cafeteria with a bowl of soup before me. Outside rain slashed and slammed against the windows, and a murky purple dimness surrounded our ship. The jagged peaks of the Faroes began to recede until we were out of sight of land.

The flexible *hafskip* rarely swamped or foundered, for the simple reason that the sailors kept the prow to the waves. When a fair wind was blowing, the ship could make good time, but when the fair wind stopped or was replaced by squalls and contrary winds, or worse, thick fog, a ship might drift for weeks in the open sea. Sailors who lost their bearings were said to be in a state of *hafvilla*. As the *Laxdæla Saga* tells us in the story of another voyage: "They met with bad weather that summer. There was much fog, and the winds were light and unfavorable, what there were of them. They drifted far and wide on the high sea. Most of those on board completely lost their reckoning."

Dead reckoning was one of the main methods of Norse navigation. Over a long sea voyage, sailors were able to keep a remarkably good record of where they were and how far they had come. With a fair wind they could travel 144 nautical miles a day. In summer they used the sun to give them their latitudinal bearings, and in spring and fall, the pole star. When in sight of land they were careful to note distinctive landmarks and commit them to memory. They also noticed varieties of sea birds and whales to give them a sense of how far north they were. Icebergs, unwelcome as they were, oriented them as well.

Still, what would it have been like to be on a wooden ship with a single sail in the midst of a North Atlantic storm? Especially a ship loaded with people, farm animals, timber for building, goods for trading? A few long kayaking trips in Puget Sound and along the east and west coasts of Vancouver Island had made me appreciate the strength of currents and the power of the wind to stir up waves. A kayak is a flexible boat, low in the water, difficult to capsize, but it is still not reassuring to see a regiment of dark-gray waves approaching. My Canadian friend Nancy and I had once made an ill-fated expedition to one of the northern Gulf Islands from the mainland of British Columbia. Midway across the channel a thirty-five-knot gale rose suddenly. A passing water taxi had his window blown out by the force of the wind. It was this fortuitous loss that enabled the boat's captain, Mike, to see our two kayaks battling through ever-increasing and ever-higher waves. He persuaded us, meeting little resistance, to let him pull our kayaks onboard. At the time, we experienced it as an ignominious failure. In retrospect we realized we were lucky to have been spotted by Mike (who was tremendously pleased to write in his logbook, "Saved two female kayakers").

In the North Atlantic, in the Middle Ages, there would have been no passing water taxi. There would have been no weather radio, no GPS. You could call "Mayday" all you wanted, but no one would come. Of course, this made the Norse much better sailors than we are now.

I finished my soup and wandered about the ship for a while, before returning to the cabin. My bunkmate was already tucked away and the room smelled of night cream and fish cakes. I climbed up to my bunk and put on my headphones. What better time than now to listen again to a cassette of Shaun Davey's *The Brendan Voyage*, an orchestral suite for uilleann pipes that I'd found in a music shop in Westport, on Clew Bay? Centuries ago one of my Irish ancestors could have been traveling (far less comfortably) on a *hafskip* as the slave of a Norse master or mistress. The great settlement of Iceland took place over the course of sixty years, from 870 to 930. As many as twenty thousand colonists took all the arable land, cut down all the trees and formed themselves into a culture that valued law but not central authority. Although this decentralized form of rule eventually led to family feuding among the medieval Icelanders, it was a noble experiment, and one that echoes, in all its idealism and tragedy, through the sagas.

Aud was one of the early arrivals. She went first to her brother Helgi. But not meeting with as much hospitality as she had hoped, she left his household and sailed north and into the wide mouth of the Breidafjord to her other brother, Bjorn, who greeted her warmly and didn't seem at all put off by the number of companions she had with her. Here she spent the winter. The following spring she went land hunting, and a thousand years later, there are still names that recall the places where Aud stopped and surveyed. The name of one headland can be translated as "Breakfast-ness"; another, where she dropped her hair comb, is "Comb-ness."

She "took possession of as much land as she pleased," built a home and became the matriarch of a large family. As she approached old age, she began to free some of her slaves and to give land grants to her younger relatives. She put on a huge wedding feast for the youngest of her grandsons, and made a speech, leaving everything she owned to him.

Thereupon she rose to her feet and said that she was now
retiring to her bed-chamber; she urged them all to enjoy
themselves in whatever way each thought best, and ordered
ale to be served to the whole company. It is said that Unn
was tall and stoutly-built. She walked briskly down the
length of the hall, and those present remarked on how
stately she still was.

    There was drinking all that evening until it was
thought time to go to bed. Next morning Olaf Feilan went
to his grandmother's bedroom. When he entered, Unn was
sitting propped up against the pillows; she was dead. Olaf
went back into the hall and announced the news; everyone
thought it most impressive how Unn had kept her dignity to
her dying day.

The wedding celebration became a funeral as well, and on
the last day of the feast, Aud was buried, fittingly, inside a ship,
and the ship laid in a mound with a treasure trove, and closed.

    The pagan Norwegians weren't the only ones to colonize
Iceland. First- and second-generation Norse born of marauders
who had stayed to settle Orkney, the Hebrides, and Ireland also
came. They brought with them Celtic thralls, Christians with a
mythic history and oral literature far different from the Norse.
The Celtic influence, many say, is why Iceland isn't like the rest
of Scandinavia, and why the preoccupation of the sagas with
great deeds and revenge has an Irish flavor.

    Some believe that Iceland was first settled by Irish monks,
who fled when the Vikings arrived. It's the voyage of St.
Brendan, the wandering monk, that Shaun Davey's musical suite
commemorates. I listened to the achingly sweet pipes floating on
the swell of oceanic orchestration until I fell asleep. I awoke very

early, around five. Wrapping up as warmly as I could, I went out
on deck. We were about four hours from landing at
Seydisfjördur, on the east coast of Iceland. But everything was so
fog-curdled it was impossible to see beyond the railing.

Hafvilla. Somewhere out there I seemed to hear the wet
flapping of a woven wadmal sail, the eerie creak of a wooden
ship on a glass sea. Everyone except the helmsman was asleep;
they dreamed of forests they would never see again, and families
who counted them as dead. Their skin was caked with salt; it
thickened their hair, flaked into their eyes, roughened their
breathing. They didn't know it but they were close to the
longed-for yet fearsome sound of waves slapping around half-
submerged rocks, to breakers smashing on the rough Icelandic
coast. Getting into shore was the true test of seamanship and
luck. Many a ship had crossed the Atlantic only to break up in
sight of land.

Hafvilla. Had I lost my bearings on this trip or was I merely
shifting direction? Perhaps I could never be Barbara the Deep-
Minded or Barbara Wisdom-Slope, but it came to me, with a jolt
of recognition, as I stood in the chill white mist with the vast
bulk of unknown Iceland somewhere off the port bow, that an
unexpected transformation had begun to work in me on this
journey. More like a reverberation in my body than an actual
voice, but with all the authority of a spoken annunciation, I now
heard clearly what had been rumbling, in a joking way, for weeks.

I wanted to change my name.

Doubts would come later. This morning I felt as if I held a
compass in my hand.

CHAPTER XII

CAUGHT IN THE NET

Reykjavík and the Westmann Islands, Iceland

AT THIRTY, she was a mother of a young child, living on the island of Heimaey off the south coast of Iceland, when the Algerian pirate ship appeared offshore. Like the other islanders, she lived in a sod house, smoky and dark, with earthen floors and only one exterior door. Heimaey was volcanic and farming was poor; the only water the islanders had came from rain. It was a bare and unforgiving landscape in a country fallen on hard times. Seventeenth-century Iceland was a colony of Denmark, and as with the Faroes, Denmark sent governors and pastors, but supplied little defense. The climate had turned colder since the 1500s, and the golden age of the Vikings in Iceland was long past. But the fishing around Heimaey had always been the best in Iceland; that's what sustained the small population of the Westmann Islands.

That morning Gudríd Símonardottír had said goodbye to her husband as he set out to sea. He may have seen the foreign ship set anchor in Heimaey's bay, and known with a sinking heart that it wasn't Danish. He may have seen the corsairs, in striped pantaloons and turbans, spilling from the rowboats onto shore, may have heard the screams of the women and children as they tried to flee. But if he had, he didn't return and Gudríd never saw him again. She and her two-year-old son were hunted down that day in 1627 and kidnapped, along with 242 of the island's population of five hundred, to be sold as slaves in the market of Algiers. Like the others, Gudríd ran, holding her child close. Some found shelter in caves; others were murdered on the spot. The island has no trees, and they had no ships in which to flee. Other Icelanders were kidnapped that week off the mainland—there were five corsair ships in all—and in Icelandic history the event has the same status as a cataclysmic volcanic eruption. The Turkish Raid, it's usually called, because the Algerians lived under the Ottoman Empire, governed from Istanbul.

Nine years later a handful of the captives found their way back to Iceland, ransomed through a combination of their own savings, collections from the Icelandic people, and a gift from the King of Denmark. Many died in captivity, others converted to Islam, but some managed to hold on to their Christian faith and hopes of being rescued.

For all that I was enchanted by Grace O'Malley's long career as a pirate queen, my blood ran cold to think of being hunted down outside my home and carried off in a ship to a distant land, the fearsome Barbary Coast. That was the other side of piracy. As a woman, it's more likely I would have been the victim of a pirate than a pirate myself. Unlike Grace, though, the Algerian corsairs were less interested in plunder than in people. They attacked ships, but most of their prey came from villages along the Mediterranean and the Atlantic coasts (Grace O'Malley fought off Algerians herself in the memorable battle just after giving birth to her son). They killed all who resisted and subdued and kidnapped the rest to sell as slaves or hold for ransom. Jesuit priests often acted as the intermediaries; sometimes governments collected money and sent emissaries to buy the freedom of their citizens. These corsairs weren't all

Algerians; in some cases, the pirate ships had foreign captains, renegade Christians. The captain of the ship that took Gudríd and many others that year from Iceland was a Dutchman named Jan Jantzen, alias Mourat Rais. Like the well-known Simon Danser, another renegade European called "Captain Devil," Jantzen captured ship passengers and kidnapped villagers, bringing them back to Algiers to be enslaved. Gudríd Símonardottír was one of them.

REYKJAVÍK WASN'T what I'd expected. Neighborly and hip, the center of the city was concentrated around a dozen charming streets, always crowded with well-dressed blond people on cell phones. There were music stores, hair salons, vegetarian restaurants, cafés, bookstores, galleries, and antique shops. Clad in corrugated metal and painted bright yellows, reds, and blues, the houses flowered with window boxes and pocket gardens and offered glimpses into tiny courtyards. But this miniature Copenhagen soon flowed out into broad highways, industrial parks, subdivisions, and apartment blocks, looking for all the world like any medium-sized city in North America, complete with SUVs parked in supermarket parking lots.

I'd been given the use of a spacious basement apartment in the house belonging to the Writers' Union of Iceland. The staff was on vacation and the offices upstairs were closed, so I had the complete run of the place. What a luxury to have a kitchen, washer and dryer, phone, fax, and computer. Fortunately the director was still available to put me in touch with people to help me with my research, and it was in this way I came to be invited for lunch at the house of Steinunn Jóhannesdóttir, an actress turned playwright, who was now researching and writing a historical novel about Gudríd Símonardottír, or Turkish Gudda, as she came to be called.

Steinunn had played the part of young Gudríd for the National Theater of Iceland years ago. A playbill showing Steinunn, ethereal and earnest, was framed on the wall of the living room. At fifty, Steinunn was still a bit ethereal, with shoulder-length brown hair, lightly freckled skin and the considered movements of someone trained for the stage. "The part of Gudríd had a big effect on me, but I didn't feel the play did justice to her. When I wrote my own play about her, *Gudríd's World*, I made Gudríd an old woman, looking back on her life." Since that play was produced, five years ago, Steinunn had delved deeper into the subject, traveling to North Africa, Paris, and Amsterdam, digging into archives, writing her back into history.

Outside the window, the afternoon sky was the opaque gray of a newly painted battleship, a typical Reykjavík summer's day. Rain occasionally spattered the glass ill-naturedly, as if trying to punish the potted geraniums inside for daring to be red. In front of us, on the dining room table, the lunch plates of cheese and sliced, dried mutton had been pushed away, and photo albums were open to scenes of minarets and courtyards, to yellow and cobalt-blue tiled interiors and to fountains splashing in the midst of jasmine-draped gardens. You could almost hear the fountains echoing the cry of the muezzin.

Gudríd spent nine years as a captive in Algiers, at a time when that city was at its peak as a Mediterranean power. Before the advent of the Ottoman Empire, Algiers was only a small town on the coast of North Africa. But under Turkish military rule, it had grown to a city of between 100,000 and 130,000 people, a polyglot community of Turks, Maghrib natives,

Christian slaves in Algiers

Moriscos (expelled Spanish Moors), Jews, renegade Christians, and captives from every corner of the world. Society was ruled strictly, from the top down, with a bureaucracy that encompassed every aspect of life. There were hundreds of titles, from "Sequestrator of unclaimed property and supervisor of cemeteries" (one job) to "collector of the tax on mulberries."

At the top of the heap was the Ottoman ruler called the *dey* or regent. According to Steinunn, Gudríd ended up in the *dey's* household. There she worked, without pay, of course, but still managing—perhaps with extra services—to accumulate, very slowly, money toward her release. For the Algerians had no objection to allowing their captives their freedom if they or someone else could pay for it. The slaves in Algiers made up from fifteen to twenty percent of the population. Between 1621 and 1627, there were twenty thousand Christian captives in the city.

A pastor from Heimaey had been released within the first year, in order to arrange with the Danish king for ransom money.

Gudríd, being related to clergymen in Iceland and one of the few Icelandic captives who could read and write, eventually managed to get one of her letters delivered back to Iceland. The story of a Christian woman trapped on the heathen Barbary Coast launched a belated effort at redemption from the Danish government. The Danes collected taxes from the Icelander's fish catch and farm assets; the king contributed money as well, and eventually several dozen of the Icelanders were ransomed and taken back to Copenhagen by ship. About half of that number, nineteen, eventually returned to Iceland. Gudríd handed over all the money she'd saved over nine years; it wasn't enough to free her son, however, and at the last minute she had to leave him behind when the ship sailed for Copenhagen in 1636.

Steinunn and her daughter cleared away the lunch plates, and Elin went off to meet friends while Steinunn and I looked through photo albums that charted the travels she'd undertaken in search of more information about Gudríd. Given that the Islamic Salvation Front and its terrorist splinter groups had begun targeting foreign tourists who visited Algeria in the nineties, Steinunn and her husband decided to travel to Algeria's neighbor Morocco to get a feel for the old North African cities. In Rabat they happened across an antiquarian bookshop with many arcane and beautiful books in French. In one volume, Steinunn found exactly the illustrations she was looking for of seventeenth-century Algiers.

From the sea, Algiers looked, as it was meant to, like an impregnable fortress, a tight geometry of white, able to withstand siege and shelling. But behind the harbor defenses and fortifications it was a place of fountains and baths, markets and bake houses, "very like an egg in its fullness of houses and people," as one observer wrote. The houses, washed thickly with lime, were built close upon each other, walls sloping inward as they rose from ground level, so the roofs were almost joined. The streets were narrow and sloped inward as well, toward a central drain; a man on horseback could barely get through most of the streets; it was difficult to walk two abreast. These streets had no names and no obvious directions; you'd need a good memory to find your way.

Women, of course, didn't move freely around the city. The institution of the harem had come from Turkey, where the Ottoman rulers kept thousands of women odalisques, their children, and servants sequestered in luxurious rooms with no exit to the outside city. Every other harem was modeled on the Grand Harem in Istanbul. The women had nowhere to go except from room to room or up and down stairs. Sometimes they climbed to the rooftop terraces for a view, and from there they could jump or climb ladders to neighboring households. The enforced confinement of these women has been glamorized in hundreds of British and French Orientalist paintings.

For art books, too, sprawled open on Steinunn's table; they showed lushly patterned paintings of women reclining, half-dressed in silk harem pants and embroidered vests, a cheroot or hookah in hand. Some of the paintings were of the baths, or hammams, where men and women could spend the day, separately, washing and steaming, being scrubbed and pummeled, oiled and perfumed. Scenes of voluptuous women half-veiled in water or steam, and lounging all over each other, while black servants scrub them or feed them sweetmeats, are staples of such painters as John Frederick Lewis and Jean-Léon Gérome.

We looked at the paintings with a mixture of fascination and revulsion, then turned back to the photo albums. Steinunn's photographs of Rabat and Tangiers began to merge with those of Paris, where she had lived for two months, spending every day at the museum at L'Institut du Monde Arabe. Steinunn's long fingers lingered over the photographs of Paris; she was clearly back in a warmer climate that smelled of oranges and coffee. Her last trip had been to Amsterdam, to look in the archives of the maritime museum there for evidence of the renegade Dutch captain, Jan Jantzen. When I asked her how soon she planned to finish her book, I had the sense that she was in no hurry to leave the magic places she was remembering and conjuring up in fiction. "Oh, it will take a long time," she said, with a writer's sigh, but she didn't seem unhappy about it. "I keep uncovering more of the story. I've found records of the amounts all the Icelanders paid in ransom; I've found material on Jantzen and his family life. I know I'm going to have to write another volume of my novel about what happened to Gudríd after she left Algiers."

The second half of Gudríd's life was as extraordinary as the first. At the age of thirty-nine she arrived in Copenhagen, there to be "reindoctrinated" as a Christian after her years with the infidels. A young Icelander, a ministerial student named Hallgrím Pétursson, was put in charge of the released captives. Within a short time he and Gudríd had formed a passionate relationship and she was pregnant. Since, as far as anyone knew, Gudríd still had a husband in the Westmann Islands, this was fornication, pure and simple. The two of them were packed off to Iceland under a cloud. They soon found out that Gudríd's husband had drowned some time ago, and they quickly married. Hallgrím began a career as a minister in a settlement to the north of Reykjavík, on the Hvalfjord.

There Hallgrím began to write religious poetry and songs. In years to come he would be revered as Iceland's greatest spiritual poet. Hallgrím Pétursson is the John Donne of Icelandic literature, the author of the great cycle *The Passion Psalms*, often put to music and sung in choirs all over the world. One of the psalms is sung at every Icelandic funeral.

"It's said, however," Steinunn told me, "that when he gave a sermon, Gudríd would go outside the church and sit looking at the fjord. They said she never really readjusted to life in Iceland after all those years in Algiers. Many people believed she must have converted to Islam and wasn't really a Christian. And then, of course, she had been a slave in the *dey's* house, and a slave, well . . ."

Our eyes went back to the art books, where in the heavily patterned rooms of red and dark blue, the white flesh of captive women shone like silk.

NOT FAR from Steinunn's flat is the cathedral named after Turkish Gudda's husband. Hallgrím's Church rises up from a square that, violently windswept as it was when I approached on a summer's day, must be a terrible challenge to cross on a dark, snowy winter morning. The steeple is a beacon; it stands over two hundred feet tall. Inside, the church holds twelve hundred people. It has an airy plainness of purpose, its whiteness unrelieved by iconic decoration. Nothing could be more different from the swirls and flourishes of Arab color and form I'd been looking at in Steinunn's photographs.

I sat in a hard pew, relieved to be out of the wind, and read the small pamphlet about the church. Without knowing the story of Turkish Gudda, I would have been more receptive to the description of Hallgrím: "He influenced the nation's spiritual development perhaps more than any other person." There was no mention of his early adulterous romance, or indeed of his wife at all. I couldn't help wondering whether Gudríd had found any happiness when she returned to the North. She must have wondered about her son: Was he still alive? Did he live as a slave or did he convert, as had so many of the Christians? Should she have stayed with him, after all?

Wouldn't she have longed for Mediterranean warmth and color? Iceland engages only one primary sense: sight. There are no smells of mint and saffron; you can't finger an aubergine or pomegranate, stroke silk or satin, trail your hand in scented water. The tang of highly spiced food is absent here. The lunch I'd just finished of cheese and dried mutton had filled my stomach but not my imagination. No wonder the Icelanders were suspicious of Turkish Gudda. She'd sampled delights that were unknown in Iceland, that encouraged lasciviousness and wantonness. Could she really be a Christian after having lived among the harem, worn layers of veils and perhaps been the plaything of some wealthy pasha?

A man becomes the closest thing to a Lutheran saint the Icelanders have; a woman is nicknamed Turkish Gudda and shunned. A man gets a cathedral; a woman gets a footnote in history.

Though if Steinunn had her way, perhaps that would change. I thought back to Steinunn turning the pages of the photo album on the table in front of us in slow, considered movements, as she told me stories about the twisting streets of Rabat's souks, rich in smells of mint and figs and ripe fruit. Far from accepting that it was a nightmare place to which Gudríd had been kidnapped, Steinunn saw the appeal of the orderly, enclosed world of the harem and the hammam, where fountains splashed and the muezzins called in the distance. Perhaps it

wasn't only a desire to unravel the mysteries of a strange fragment of Icelandic history that had led Steinunn to the tangled
cities in North Africa, and to museums in Paris and Amsterdam,
but a longing to be changed by what she felt and saw. To physically visit a place, to immerse oneself in a strange world, was
what I was doing myself. My memories of mountains and waves
and wind, the act of walking down a street in Stromness or
looking for Betty Mouat's house in Shetland had enriched every
dry fact, every statistic and anecdote.

Tomorrow I was flying to Heimaey myself. In months to
come, I would turn the pages of my own album for friends, just
as Steinunn had turned them for me, explaining dreamily, "Here
we are in the Westmann Islands, where Gudríd Símonardottír
was kidnapped by Algerian pirates."

At sea again, if only in a tour boat with fifty bird-watching
Spaniards, I gazed over the railing into the water as we rocked
our way into an island cave. The sun glanced off the cheese-
holed volcanic walls, lightened to amber by guano. Sunlight
seemed to enter the cave with us, its celestial gold becoming our
gold, nets of gold folded wave by wave in water so turquoise as
to seem deliciously swimmable. In the echo of the cave, a woman
suddenly began singing "Summertime," and "The leeving ees
eesy" came at us, improved in tone, from all directions.

This was the denouement of an exhilaratingly brisk cruise
around Heimaey and other smaller islands of the Westmann
chain off the south coast of Iceland. We'd motored close enough
to the lava cliffs to see that they were not as sheer as they
appeared, but wrinkled and pitted like pale brown cardboard. In
every pit and crevice, along every ledge, a bird was nesting.

Topmost were the gentle kittiwakes, who could nest on next to nothing. This was their own protection against marauders, who could not find a purchase on the finger-sized outcroppings that formed the nurseries of the kittiwakes. Lower down were razor-bills and Brünnich's guillemots. Both had black heads and wings and snowy breasts, but the razorbill, a small auk, had a thick, parrotlike beak. They were pelagic birds, spending winters at sea and breeding in the Far North in summer. They stood side by side on the cliff's ledges, at deck height, long lines of sports fans rooting for the other team, jeering and heckling as we sailed slowly by. Closest to the surf breaking at the feet of the cliffs were eider ducks, while, high up, on the green pate that crowned the islands, were the tunnels and burrows of the puffins, thousands upon thousands of these sociable little birds, who like to stand around gabbing like old people reminiscing, but whose tiny-winged, heavy-bodied flights over the ocean's surface always seem to bear the hallmarks of anxiety.

Surrounded by parka-headed Spaniards with serious zoom lenses, digital cameras, and camcorders, I was out of my league with a small pair of binoculars and my Collins' *Birds of Britain and Europe*, which I couldn't even open properly because of the wind. No matter, I was happy. I'd only been in Iceland a week, but my Faroese funk had been dispelled by the free spirits I found here. When I asked an Icelander if I could do something, he or she almost invariably thought a moment, and said, "Yes!"

Our tour boat had bounced from island to island in search of more nesting birds and had finally come to rest here, in the echoing aquamarine chamber of the moberg cliffs, where an icy breeze blew off the water, where the loops and coils of the sub-merged golden net at the opening to the cave entranced and warned. The half-visible webbing made me think of Ran, the

Norse goddess of the sea, who lived in a great golden hall under the ocean with her husband, Ægir, and their nine daughters. It's said that Ran steered a ship with one hand, while with the other she swept her net through the waves. With this net, this golden net, she snared sailors and carried them to her underwater palace, and there they lived as if they were on earth. To die by drowning was "faring to Ran" or "falling into Ran's hands." Many sailors, knowing her love for gold, carried coins in their pockets to allow them to enter Ran's domain, her bed. *Ran-bedr*, the ocean floor was called.

The Westmann Islands, off Iceland's forbidding south coast, are above the Mid-Atlantic rift, where the continental plates are pulling apart, and where the earth's liquid-hot center escapes through the break in the plates to surge upward, sometimes in spectacular ways. Beginning in 1963, the island of Surtsey was created from the waves over a period of four years of eruptions. Ten years later, on Heimaey, a volcano blasted forth, very near the homes of a number of unlucky Icelandic fishing families. That cone is Eldfell, "fire mountain"; it increased the island's size by fifteen percent. Burnt orange and black in color, the volcano's cone still smolders in places thirty years later. This morning I'd flown from Reykjavík to Heimaey, a journey of about twenty minutes. Our twelve-person plane could only come in at an angle between two mountains, and the wind was not cooperating. With nothing between these islands and Antarctica to the far south, the Westmanns are one of the windiest places in Iceland; gales have been clocked at 120 knots. The plane turned on its side, easily, as a Frisbee lurching in the breeze, and gave us a close view of red-ochre mountains frosted with lime green, a bright blue sky in the wrong place—down—but still very beautiful.

Myth places Ran's golden palace near the island of Hlesey, which could perhaps have been the island of Hellisey in the Westmann chain. Hellisey is home to a great many gannets, but no one else. From the air it has the shape of a half-submerged horseshoe, clearly the visible C of a volcanic cone, with one side eroded and open to the sea. I found it interesting that, unlike the Celtic storm and sea goddesses, Ran had a home. In fact she was, like few Norse mythological figures, in a stable relationship with many progeny, everyone in the household working together. Ægir kicked up the storms at sea, Ran cruised underneath gathering drowned souls, and their nine daughters helped out however they could. The nine daughters, the waves, had these names: Cold One, White One, Grasper, Howler, Heaven-Bright, Billow, Comber, Dip, and Bloody-Haired. Medieval Icelandic poets called them "the claws of Ran" and described a time "when hard gusts from white mountain-range teased apart and wove together the storm-happy daughters of Ægir, bred on frost."

Who were these nine daughters or ocean giantesses? Saxo Grammaticus wrote in his *History of the Danes* of "the Nine Maidens of the Island-Mill, who far out beyond the skirts of earth, set the ocean moving as if a quern were being turned." There are also Celtic links. Hilda Davidson, in *Gods and Myths of the Viking Age*, points to a Celtic story about nine giant maidens of the sea who mothered a boy among them:

> In the tale of Ruad, son of Rigdonn, Ruad was crossing the
> sea to Norway with three ships, when the vessels ceased to
> move. He dived down to find out the reason, and discovered
> nine giant women, three hanging on to each ship. They
> seized him, and carried him down into the sea. There he
> spent a night with each in turn, and then was allowed to

continue his journey. They told him that one of them would
bear him a child, and he promised to come back to them
after he left Norway. But after a stay of seven years he
broke his promise, and went straight back to Ireland. The
nine women discovered this, took the child 'that had been
born among them,' and set off in pursuit, and when they
could not overtake Ruad they cut off the child's head and
flung it after his father.

The maidens turning quernstones are sisters of Finnie and
Minnie, the giant bondswomen whose revolt off the coast of
northern Scotland caused the sea to turn to salt. Whirlpools
are created in cauldrons, like those of the Cailleach, who turned
her laundry bright with foam. Celtic mythology makes frequent
reference to cauldrons of regeneration and cauldrons of plenty,
and these cauldrons are usually said to come from the Land-
Beneath-the-Waves. In the Norse tale "The Lay of Hymir" the
story is told of a visit by Thor to the golden hall of Ægir and
Ran. "Brew some ale for the gods," Thor demands. Ægir,
angered at the peremptory tone, says coolly, "I've no cauldron
that would hold enough. Bring me a cauldron, Thor, and I'll
brew ale for all the gods." None of the gods know where to get
such a cauldron, until one-handed Tyr volunteers the information that his father, the giant Hymir, has a huge cauldron five
miles deep, a "water-whirler." Tyr and Thor eventually manage
to reach Hymir's hall, where they find not one, but nine cauldrons. Hymir smashes eight of them, but Thor and Tyr manage
to steal the ninth for Ægir, who then becomes "the ale-brewer."
The sea could be Ran's Road, a highway of death, but it could
also be a golden palace, a storehouse of plenty, with a cauldron
that never stops brewing, a cauldron of regeneration. It is of

course of interest that Hlesey or Hellisey is shaped like a cauldron, is in fact, a volcanic caldera.

The Cailleach was a storm goddess who lived close to shore and used the rocks and currents to stir up whirlpools. Ran ranged freely through the northern seas, whisking up storms with her daughters and husband and then lying in wait, like a giant spider at the bottom of a web of waves for sailors to fall into her embrace. The famous poem by Egil Skallagrímsson about his drowned son has these lines:

> The sea-goddess
> Has ruffled me
> Stripped me bare
> Of my loved ones
> The ocean severed
> my family's bonds
> The tight knot
> That ties me down.

Although she was called the wife of the sea god and queen of the drowned, Ran had perhaps once been the great goddess of the sea, with Ægir (more a giant or personification of the sea than a god) a later addition. Ran's nine daughters, says one mythology dictionary, indicate the presence of a college of priestesses. Some sources speak of the girls as mermaids not waves, but I like their Eddic names—Howler and Grasper—"storm-happy daughters." Could any phrase give a better sense of being at one with the elements?

◎   ◎   ◎

I WENT to the town's library to ask about Ran and her possible home in the Westmann Islands, and was directed upstairs to the museum. The guide was a wild-eyed man of seventy-five who lunged at me with a terrifying handshake and shouted, "Hello, hello, hello! Sign the guest book, sign the guest book. Seattle, Washington. SEE-attle. Come with me. Now this model shows what everything was like before the eruption. You see, SEE-attle? Nice and quiet. Then—*boom*! You've heard of the eruption? You know the eruption? Everyone around the world knows the eruption. I didn't leave the island, I saw it all. One of the few, one of the few."

When I tried to interrupt with a question about Ran and her undersea palace—"Was it the island of Hellisey?"—he dismissed me. "Ran. Ran, you say, Ran? Maybe. Maybe not. Come with me. Look at these photographs of burning houses. Lava bombs. Flying ash and cinders. Gas. Look at the gas masks in these cases. Five thousand people lived here. They all left that night. I didn't go. I lived on a hill outside of town. I saw it all."

The photographs were shocking. Half the town was buried under ash and many other homes were on fire. It looked as if the new volcano would close the harbor, too, with a steady gush of lava moving oceanward. The fishing community, the richest in Iceland, could not bear to see this happen. An Icelandic scientist suggested a radical solution: pumping water in great volume from the sea and directing its stream at the lava in order to deflect its course. The harbor was saved and, in fact, improved.

"Well, that's how it was. That's how it was."

He was bouncing up and down next to me, making a dash for a display case, rushing back and taking my arm to make me follow after. There was no way to look at anything in the rooms without him telling me what to think about it. When another pair of tourists entered and the guide seized on them ("Welcome, welcome. *Benvenuto! Italianos? Sí, sí, sí.* Roma, Roma, Roma. *Venga!*"), I escaped. Even going down the stairs I could hear him assuring them, "I was there. *Io. Io.* I was there."

It was the time of year when the sun stays up long past her bedtime. Even after every shop—there weren't terribly many— had closed on Heimaey, the light blazed coldly on, scouring the empty streets like a gold-bristled broom. I had dinner and took a walk. The worst-hit neighborhoods of Heimaey were still under tons of lava and ash, but other sections had been bull- dozed and built up again, this time with modern, split-level ram- blers that wouldn't have looked out of place in Florida or California. The homes often had large picture windows, draped in gauzy curtains, with small Greek or African statues visible on the sills. Surrounded by green lawns, bordered with low shrub- bery, the only thing "Icelandic" about these houses were the chunks of dark-gray basalt, often oddly shaped, that decorated many of the front lawns. Some were at least four feet tall; many had purple-hearted pansies planted around their bases.

I circled back to Heimaey's harbor with its view of the bright green hills and moberg bird cliffs. I leaned against a bollard and looked into the water, where there were still faint strands of gold reflected from the sun. Ran's net? Or something woven by the Norns, those three figures of fate? No one knows just where the word *Norn* comes from, but one etymology ties it to the Indo- European root *ner,* which means "twist" or "twine." The Norns were those who worked with the threads of destiny; they twisted and twined them to form a life, and at some point, Third or Skuld, the goddess in her destroyer aspect, cut the thread. In eighth-cen- tury Ireland an abbot wrote, "I invoke the seven Daughters of the Sea who fashion the threads of the sons of long life."

Other myths said it was a serpent, not Ran's family, who stirred up trouble at sea. In 1957, Roger Corman, king of the B flick, directed a movie that even for him was extraordinarily silly. *The Saga of the Viking Women and Their Voyage to the Waters of the Great Sea Serpent* was shot over a period of ten days along a California beach and in Monument Valley. Half the women wear flaxen Brunnhilda wigs, and all are statuesque in short, belted tunics. When the story begins the women are worried about what has become of their men, who set off some weeks ago in a ship and haven't been seen since. Should the Viking women stay and wait or should they go in search of the men? There's conflict between an evil, dark-haired girl and a blond heroine, but in the end the women pull a longship down to the shore and get in. Not long after, what looks like a storm comes up, but it's not a storm; it's a whirlpool, caused by a giant sea serpent.

Once Christianity was established in the North, there were other explanations for whirlpools, or "ocean whirls," than the sea serpent or Ran and Ægir. The *King's Mirror*, a late-medieval Norse text, describes such a phenomenon:

> It is called hafgerdingar [ocean-whirl] and it has the appearance as if all the waves and storms of the ocean had been collected into three heaps out of which three great waves form. These so surround the entire sea that no openings can be seen anywhere; they are higher than lofty mountains and resemble steep overhanging cliffs. In only a few cases have men been known to escape who were upon the sea when such a thing occurred.

Far off the coast of Iceland, where I would not venture on

this trip, midway between Snæfellsnes and Cape Farewell on Greenland, was such an ocean whirl. Sailing directions from the nineteenth century mention that the sea broke strongly in that area and the cause was believed to be volcanic. When Eirík the Red and his followers sailed to Greenland in the first colonizing effort, only fourteen of the twenty-five ships made it. The rest were lost at sea, perhaps caught up in the ocean whirl and destroyed.

I preferred thinking of a whirlpool as the *umbilicus maris,* "the navel of the sea." Even though the vortex led downward, perhaps to the hollow center of the earth, perhaps to Ran's realm, it was the spiral shape the stirred waters made that intrigued me. So often when I imagined the shape of a whirlpool, I seemed to see it from above, its coils resembling a labyrinth, a circular path leading to a center. It was that inevitable center that fascinated me. In a labyrinth you picked your way closer to the heart of things, via paths that often dead-ended. In a whirlpool you were funneled along with the flotsam and jetsam of your life into the core depths. Either way, you came to the center, or as close as you were able.

Did I believe in destiny? I thought back to my arrival on the west coast of Ireland over two months before, to my first glimpse of Clew Bay and my sense that, beginning with Grace O'Malley, I had so many lost and forgotten stories to discover along these northern coasts. I thought back even further, to a day by the tide pools of Cape Cornwall, when I lay on the warm rocks in the September sun and read a book about women pirates. Where are the stories of women and the sea? I want to know them, I'd decided.

Had fate spoken to me then? Had the Norns made me take my journey around the North Atlantic? Had they brought me all the way to Iceland to show me something important? The Norns were said to be present at birth. They were the name givers; they decided what would happen to you. My practical, prosaic side reminded me that it was a film option on one of my books that had given me the resources to make this trip. I believed in daydreams, I believed in risk taking; I didn't really believe in destiny. It was easier to believe that I'd been handed a ball of thread, a clew, and that my work was to follow it and see where it led. If I looked hard, I could just see the faintest thread of gold down in the darkening waters of Heimaey's harbor. Was I making my fate or was my fate making me? Or was I perhaps weaving a net myself, a net of clews? I listened for the unexpected voice inside that had told me so recently to change my name. But for now it was silent.

CHAPTER XIII

ICEBERG TRAVEL

Snæfellsnes Peninsula, Iceland

THERE WERE once two sets of cousins. Helga and her sisters were the daughters of Bard. Red-cloak and his brother were Thorkel's sons. The cousins grew up together on the lava-licked edge of the Snæfellsnes Peninsula in the far west of Iceland. There was rivalry between them. "The sons of Thorkel wanted to rule the roost because they were stronger, but the daughters of Bard would not allow themselves to be subdued any more than they were able," *Bard's Saga* tells us.

One winter's day, the cousins were playing down on the beach, and the playing was fierce as always, especially between Red-cloak and Helga. An ice field was just offshore and a floe had broken away and drifted very near land. Helga and Red-cloak pushed each other back and forth until he shoved her onto the floe. There was a thick fog that day and a strong wind. Just as Red-cloak pushed Helga onto the chunk of ice, a gust caught the floe and she was carried out to the ice field. That night the entire ice field moved away from the coast and out to sea. Helga had no choice but to cling to the ice as it drifted. But, as the saga tells us calmly, with no hint of the miraculous, the ice field drifted so quickly that within a week Helga arrived in Greenland, where she was rescued by Eirík the Red. The historical Eirík, the father of Leif Eiríksson, had led the colonization of Greenland in 985, which would put Helga's purported voyage about a thousand years ago. You could argue that Helga was the first woman to make a solo crossing of the North Atlantic, however accidental the journey and unorthodox the vessel.

"And this," said Gulli Bergmann dramatically, "is Deep Lagoon, the very beach where Helga was pushed onto the iceberg!" Black pebbles like a million hard droplets from the dark center of the earth covered the half-circle of the bay. Behind us was an alien forest of grotesque and gorgeous lava formations through which Gulli had just led me and a German couple and their teenage son. At our feet were crusty orange tangles of seaweed that glowed vividly against the black pebbles when wet. The air was so clear, so bright that I lost depth perception, couldn't judge whether anything was distant or close.

"Amazing," I said. "Wow." I frequently said these paltry words in Iceland, though today I'd stopped gasping, "Wonderful," since that always caused Gulli to burst into song: "It's wonderful, it's marvelous. . . ." He was a great fan of Frank Sinatra and other crooners as well as of Broadway musicals.

We stood back from the waves as they crashed and pulled at our feet. The ocean was rough here, and vast, and Greenland was far away. Although I'd come to the Snæfellsnes Peninsula in great part because of this strange saga episode, now that I was here, I could still scarcely picture it. The story began in the same sort of gender rivalry I remembered from my own childhood, when I tussled with Johnnie next door over which of our imaginary racecars was fastest; yet Helga's tale quickly veered into the fantastic.

"Is there any basis in history for Helga's voyage to Greenland?" I asked Gulli.

"No," he said, amending, "Well, who knows? The whole of *Bard's Saga* is a mix of the supernatural and the ordinary. Bard was the son of a troll mother and of Dumbur, a giant king from

up in northern Norway around the Barents Sea. He grew up
living in caves in the Norwegian mountains. He lived in a cave
when he first came to Snæfellsnes. *Bard's Saga* explains why
Iceland has the energy it has, the mysticism. It wasn't just
Norwegians who came here. It was Sami, the Laplanders, from
the far north of Norway. Anytime you read about a troll, for
instance Bard's mother, you know it's a Sami person. And then
there were the Celts; you know Celts don't just mean the Irish.
The Celts go back to Babylon, when Nebuchadnezzar threw the
tribes out of Babylon and one of the tribes got lost. Somehow
these people, Celtic-Jewish people, ended up—after some centuries in Russia—in Iceland, as slaves brought from Ireland.
What do you think of that?"

"Wow."

Gulli was in his late fifties, a big-hearted, irascible, red-faced
bear of a man who had once had a successful clothing business in
Reykjavík and now, with his wife Gudrún, ran a small New Age
resort at Hellnar on the Snæfellsnes Peninsula. Last night, just
having arrived, I'd been seated next to Gulli at the long dinner
table, and after an hour, I'd been worried how our excursion
today would go. He'd begun with Schumacher's *Small Is Beautiful*
and had ended up ranting about the intractable nature of human
greed. "What we have to deal with constantly is the beast in
man," he said several times. "I tell you, the beast in man is our
worst problem. Not pollution, not AIDS, not murder and rape.
These are all results of the beast. The beast is what we must recognize." His face turned a violent tomato and his blue eyes
flashed. The Germans, a photographer and his wife and son,
looked as taken aback as I felt. Gulli's views were certainly not
the droopy, feel-good type of New Age wisdom. He was a
Communist for one thing, and a passionate environmentalist.

Gudrún had smiled reassuringly at me last night, and had rolled her eyes slightly when Gulli got to the part about the beast in all of us. She was a classic beauty—a softer, more tranquil Vanessa Redgrave—with a long braid of silvered blond hair. She believed that the ancient conical volcano covered by a glacier that loomed above their community was a power plug and a potential source of the spiritual awakening of humanity. She'd written a small book about this mountain, full of references to Egyptian pyramids, ley-lines, and psychic research. In spite of this, she was a practical sort. At this moment she was back at the resort, wearing her bright blue overalls and wielding an electric saw. She was building another new cabin for visitors, while Gulli took me and the Germans out for the day to places of interest nearby.

"After Helga was pushed onto the ice floe, her sisters went home to Bard," said Gulli, rattling black stones in his meaty palm. "Bard went looking for his nephews. They were only eleven and twelve, but he showed them no mercy. He threw one of them into a ravine and the other off a cliff. Then he got into a big fight with his brother Thorkel, and Bard broke Thorkel's leg. At the end of his life, Bard disappeared into the Snæfellsnes glacier. He's still in there, people believe. He's the guardian of the mountain, of the glacier, a nature spirit."

"Do *you* believe he's still in there?"

"Of course."

Neither Gulli nor Gudrún were unusual in Iceland in their supernatural beliefs, though they were probably among the few to attempt to run a New Age resort. The Icelanders are a worldly and sophisticated population; people travel abroad regularly, and almost everyone is linked to the Internet and plugged into a cell phone. Literacy is universal and the per capita consumption of books is the highest in the world. Yet there is a persistent belief in nature spirits—elves, fairies, gnomes, and other hidden people—who inhabit the landscape, particularly lava beds and formations. In a town not far from Reykjavík, Hafnarfjördur, where I'd recently visited the maritime museum, the tourist bureau was selling a colorful hand-drawn map of the town's environs, with all the places where the hidden people live. Most remarkable, perhaps, was that the map included a message from the mayor, which blithely stated,

In Hafnarfjördur, we have known for a long time of another society coexistent with our human one, a community concealed from most people with its dwellings in many parts of the town and the lava and cliffs that surround it. We are convinced that the elves, hidden people and other beings living there are favourably disposed towards us and as fond of our town as we are.

I'd seen lava in Hafnarfjördur, but it was very wet the day I ventured there, and the hidden people must have been inside, reading a nice book (or did they now have elfin computers to send and receive email?). Here in Snæfellsnes, in the thin bright air, the lava was shockingly vibrant and alive. There was so *much* lava, too. Some of it, the agglomerations above the Deep Lagoon, looked like flames of frozen rock. The cliffs at the edge of the land were basalt, the hardest lava, Gulli told us; it came from the center of the crater. A more crumbled lava made up the fields below the huge mountain; it had spewed from the volcano or been crushed by the advancing and retreating glaciers and spread across the plain. Imagine churned-up, jackhammered asphalt stretching as far as the eye could see. Lurid with yellow-green lichen, the land pulsed like a painting under black light. The shore was lava, too, but eroded into a slope of smooth ball bearings. The surf rolled in, white over black pebbles, and when it rolled out, all the pebbles, every single one, moved and knocked together.

The German family with us picked their diligent way along the crunchy black beach—the father taking photographs, the boy climbing lava aggregate, the mother looking slightly worried— while Gulli stared at them pensively. Earlier this morning he'd made an anti-German joke, then asked if they were offended.

"To be honest," the mild-mannered German photographer had said, "yes."

"Things never went too well for Helga, starting from being pushed onto the ice," said Gulli to me now. "In Greenland she fell under the protection of Skeggi, one of Eirík the Red's men. She lived with him there and helped him fight off a troll attack; later she traveled with him to Norway. But when they returned to Iceland, Skeggi went back to his farm and got married to someone else. Helga was heartbroken and never recovered. Her father came and got her, but she couldn't stand the sight of him. She was a poet. She said this verse:

Soon will I seek to leave.
My sorrow does not fade
for the waster of wealth.
I must wither away
for with passion hot and heavy
I loved the heaper of riches.
So my sorrow I cannot hide.
I sit alone, I tell my tragedy.

We walked back and forth on the beach, as Gulli attempted to get the attention of the Germans by pointing at his watch. "Helga never liked men afterward. She spent one winter in someone's house, often playing her harp because she couldn't sleep. A Norwegian came to her at night. They struggled and when they parted, his right arm and his left leg were broken."

"It's one of the strange things about the sagas," I said, "that they're always so specific. His *right* arm and his *left* leg."

"Many people thought she was a troll. But she was a nature spirit, too. She couldn't live in houses for the most part. She was usually in small caves. There are many caves named after Helga in Iceland."

He continued, pulling me down to the water. "This is what you need to know about Iceland! We believe in the divine in nature and that is the Celtic heritage. And now they want us to celebrate a thousand years of Christianity this year, and the government is spending millions on it. What a waste of money. That is not the Icelandic religion, not really."

Gesturing at the big green waves, Gulli said to me, "It's important to work with the energy of nature. When you stand in front of the wind, shout 'Kari, kari, kari.' When you stand in front of the ocean, shout 'Ægir, ægir, ægir.'" We stood and shouted for a while until the Germans came back. Doubtless they thought we were calling them.

THE SNÆFELLSNES Peninsula is riddled with craters, some of them lined with moss, like green nests, and with caves. Not far from Hellnar is the so-called Singing Cave, where Bard is rumored to have spent his first winter in Iceland. At the end of the afternoon, after many hours of driving around the

peninsula, our two cars charged up the steep one-way road
that led to the Singing Cave and gave us a grand, stomach-
twisting view of the lava fields and sea below. It wasn't only
Gulli's enthusiasm that made me think this one of the most
extraordinary landscapes I'd ever seen. The hardened lava
flow covering the plain below us, right down to the sea cliffs,
was blackened as if the last eruption had been recent, not centuries ago. Waterfalls spurted out of the hills and at almost
every turn we saw some aspect of the glacier, and some new
coloration that ranged from shadow blue to lemon ice.

The Germans, I noticed, had gotten quieter and seemed
exhausted. Perhaps this accounted for the fact that when Gulli
had squeezed us into the tiny cave and demanded that we sing
something, they balked completely. "We don't know any songs,"
said the photographer.

"Don't be ridiculous. You have folk songs, you have your
national anthem. What is your national anthem?"

"We don't sing our national anthem," said the woman, as
stubborn as her husband.

"Barbara, you sing!"

I obliged with "Michael, Row the Boat Ashore." It sounded
extremely good in the acoustical cave.

Then Gulli gave us a rendition of Iceland's national song,
and it made him proud and a little teary. The Germans looked
sad. The melancholy fact is that Germans are not allowed to be
patriotic the way Icelanders, for instance, can be. I thought their
son could probably have given us a good rendition of any song by
U2, but he wasn't asked. Instead, Gulli broke into "Oklahoma,"
and I joined him.

Back at my little pine-paneled cabin in Hellnar, I wrote up my
notes before dinner. I scribbled down everything I remembered

Gulli saying, even the confusing bits (Pope is keeping Icelandic sagas in basement of Vatican?? What *about* Nebuchadnezzar and the Celtic-Jewish people?). Then I rested, thinking of Helga. Much as I was entranced by the story of Helga's iceberg journey to Greenland, I couldn't imagine it as very likely. Yet even as saga or myth, it's one of the few tales I'd come across on my travels of a woman making a voyage alone. Not until the mid-twentieth century would women cross oceans again in solitude. We know, of course, that all the women who colonized Iceland arrived by boat, and that some of them journeyed farther, to Greenland or back to Norway or to Ireland or the Hebrides. Here and there in the Icelandic histories and sagas are a few tantalizing lines about women voyagers. In *Celtic Women* Peter Ellis mentions several Irish women who bore the name Muirenn (Sea-fair), "one of whom is said to have led a band of Irish travellers to Iceland and is mentioned in the Icelandic *Landnámabok [Book of Settlements]* in the form of 'Myrun.'" Aud the Deep-Minded's ninth-century journey from Scotland to Orkney, the Faroes, and Iceland is well documented. It was not far from here that she first put in after crossing the Atlantic. Another saga makes mention of a widow, Thorunn, who commandeered a boat to return to Norway after her husband died in Iceland. There was also a woman called Thorgunna. She appears in *The Saga of Eirík the Red* as the Hebridean lover of Leif Eiríksson, who had been blown off course on a voyage between Greenland and Norway. When he was ready to leave those Scottish Isles, she asked to go with him, but he demurred because she was nobly born and it would have been seen as abduction. She told him she was with child and would send her son to him and would herself come to Greenland in the end.

The Icelandic sagas, most of them written at least two hundred years after the events they describe, are a tantalizing brew of biography and history, sometimes quite realistic and specific and sometimes mixed with bits of skaldic verse from earlier times and with ghost tales, all of it completely readable and not quite reliable as history. In the sagas the supernatural and violent are anchored by the minutiae of verisimilitude. Hauntings and dreams are bracketed by meals; acts of vengeance take place while people are tending the sheep. Often, after peculiar and tragic events, characters just return home to a spouse who asks, "So where have you been?" Helga had zoomed off on an iceberg, yes, but afterward she fell in love with a man in Greenland, went to Norway, then returned to Iceland, where she lost him to another woman. She was heartbroken, and that sounds like the story of a real woman.

The sagas had given me some of the oldest and most interesting stories of women at sea; yet what stories might there have been, what stories might have been lost or deliberately forgotten or unrecorded? What was the origin of the story about Helga on the iceberg? Had there ever been a woman who voyaged across the oceans alone? Had women ever traveled together by ship without men?

That night after dinner I decided to walk to Arnarstapi, about four kilometers distant, by way of a coastal path that led through lava fields and overlooked a coast of blowholes, arches, and bird cliffs. With the crash of surf and the screech of birds, it was not a still evening, but there was quiet underneath. How strange the situation of sea birds: so free in the spaciousness of the air, but as crammed together as tenement dwellers when it came time to nest. When I first set off on my walk, there were patches of green here and there, with ragged and alarmed black sheep precipitously chewing, but after a while there was only lava.

All day I'd looked at lava, crumbled, exploded, cracked. No longer as raw as when it was first spewed forth, now much of it was covered with moss, pale yellow with a gray or green tinge. All day similes had gone through my mind, and oddly, many of them made me hungry. The lava fields looked like vanilla cake batter poured over a thick jumble of dates, walnuts, and chocolate chips. In the sun the moss could also look like lemon yogurt spooned generously over granola.

This evening, with a fish and potato dinner inside me, and with the shadows falling over the path, I could more easily picture the beautiful, heartbroken Helga frying up a plucked puffin in a cave, or one of the hidden people playing a game of checkers in a lava community center: gnomes, probably. Gnomes were very tiny, only about twelve centimeters tall, while lovelings were slender, the size of ten-year-old children. Light-fairies resembled lovelings, angels, and flower-fairies, and were mainly to be observed in nature, especially near lakes. Dwarfs, on the other hand, were the size of three- to five-year-olds, and they were not as nice as some of the others; they could be temperamental or unfriendly. Angels, of course, were radiant and good, and so were mountain spirits, who could be immensely tall, and who beamed out life force. It wasn't really so difficult to see the lava formations as resembling small houses and apartments.

I was someone skeptical of the supernatural, or so I said. My Christian Science upbringing had made me steer clear of the psychic world. Table rappings, ghosts, spirits, and fortune-telling were all anathema to Mary Baker Eddy and her followers. The truth of the universe was sunny and perfect; perhaps there was another altogether murkier substrata to life, but all we had to do was turn away resolutely and it would disappear. Ley-lines and pyramids and clairvoyant visions about Mount Snæfellsnes were not a language I could speak; in fact, I was inclined to mock them. Yet, it was also true that all the fairy tales and myths I'd read as a child had left their mark on my imagination. I could believe in magic—of a certain kind. Abstractions never spoke to me, but the poetic always did. I couldn't feel myself traversing a ley-line deep below the lava shore, but yes, if I looked closely, I could imagine Helga in a cave or a dwarf peering out of an indentation in the volcanic rock. Some say the early Icelanders peopled the empty land they found with gnomes and spirits to make it less lonely. Others say that the hidden people were really the first inhabitants, whom the Vikings pursued and wiped out. (This may be a reference to Irish monks, who may have been here in small numbers when the colonizers first arrived.) The Irish, of course, had tales of leprechauns and fairies, the little people who still play a role in the Irish imagination.

At Arnarstapi I had a cup of tea in the café and wandered around the tiny fishing village, where a towering statue of Bard had been constructed many feet high near the edge of a cliff. He seemed to have been built from stone Legos, so rectangular was he, with a massive head and legs you could walk between. On the way back to Hellnar I was torn between a grand sense of freedom at being out so late at night in such a mysterious and unfamiliar landscape and a shrinking unease. The blackened lava piles through which the path wound along the coast, the eerie long single notes of the gulls, the chill wind, and the still-light evening all conspired to raise goose bumps. It didn't make me feel any more grounded to know I was on my way to ask advice about the inner voice that had directed me to change my name. At ten-thirty Gudrún was going to read my Viking cards at her kitchen table.

◎   ◎   ◎

AFTER THE reading I went down to the sea again. I felt curiously awake, though it was almost midnight. Behind me, the
glacier of Snæfellsnes was faintly rosy with something between
a sunset and a sunrise reflecting off its icy surface, a pink-
lemonade snow cone. A rowboat knocked against a short concrete jetty. It was a measure of how accustomed I'd become to
the constant harsh cries of the gulls and other sea birds that I
thought of the evening as quiet, and a measure of how accustomed I'd become to the northern summer that I thought of
midnight as evening.

A slight mist rose off the surface of the water, a crocheted
white spread over a dark-blue comforter. Mist and steam had
come up twice in my Viking cards, in the form of the Sweat
Lodge card. I was unclear about my name change, unclear how
to explain it to myself or to others, the imaginary chorus with
unsmiling faces that would sing the slow baritone question:
Whaddya mean / Change your name? Not only did I have the
miasma of the Sweat Lodge in my cards, but I was a Libra to
boot. "That's the Libra tendency," Gudrún sighed (she was one
herself). "Always this need to ask the opinion of others, to consider their reactions, to please them."

"But I'm so stubborn," I'd protested. "I've always gone my
own way."

"That doesn't mean you don't care about what people think
of you."

We'd been sitting at her kitchen table, a plain wooden one,
with the cards between us. Gulli had been reluctant to leave us;
he'd wanted to talk about the film *Erin Brockovich.* Eventually he
appeared, wrapped in a large bath towel, on his way to the

sauna. There were no candles, no mystic music. The house was wood-paneled and pleasant, filled with family photographs. Gudrún wore a blue work shirt and jeans; her voice was light and firm, not spooky. She gave me a glass of water, and set a tape recorder going, in case I didn't remember afterward what we said.

She had me shuffle and cut the cards. "No one shuffles cards like an American," she'd laughed. "It's like you're playing poker on a riverboat."

The Viking cards had brightly colored drawings, a northern tarot of Thor and Odin, ravens and dragons and Norns. I'd said I had only one question to ask the cards—not should I change my name, for I knew I had to, but what did it mean to do so? Soon I was talking about my father, the orphan, and how Wilson had been his name for us, for the three of us who had survived my mother's death.

A bowl had turned up in my reading; it signified abundance and my difficulty accepting it, and then the Sweat Lodge, swirling with mist and steam. "All you need to do is to open the door and clear your head," Gudrún had said, smiling. "Easier said than done, yes? But that's how you get out of the mist." She'd watched me turn over another card, this one the Shield. "That's good. A shield is something you can hold in front of you. It will protect you when people ask you why you're changing your name."

"You have your shield, and here, yes! When you come out of the sweat lodge, the ship will be waiting for you," she'd said as I'd turned over the card with a Viking ship on it. "The Ship card indicates the exploration of new worlds. A new name might be just what you need to make the journey."

"They say that when we reach seven times seven years

we're ready for our life's purpose," Gudrún had added as she'd collected and stacked the cards after the reading. Gulli had come tiptoeing noisily back from the sauna, sweating, red and merry, but at a look from Gudrún, he'd vanished into their bedroom. "You're forty-nine. You can have a new name. You don't have to ask permission. But you have to be willing to get onboard. When the Vikings went out in their ships, they had no idea what was ahead of them. You have to be willing to leave the harbor. Like the women you're writing about."

Now, down by the water, I considered the rowboat thumping gently against the pier. If it had been a kayak, perhaps I would have been tempted. Helga hadn't even used a ship; she'd gone by iceberg, by chance of course; yet all the same, she'd arrived.

"Ocean, ocean, ocean," I said, and then louder—much louder: "Wind, wind, wind."

CHAPTER XIV

LEIF'S UNLUCKY SISTER

Reykjavík and Glaumbær, Iceland

JULY 17, 1006: *A tall woman, red-haired, stands at the bow of her ship, looking back at the vivid green banks on either side of Eiríksfjord. The barren gray mountains of Greenland seem so close in the bright summer air; the icebergs, in fantastic shapes and sizes, sail serenely in the turquoise water. The ship is jammed with livestock and everything they'll need to sustain themselves for the journey and to re-create their lives on the other side of the ice-strewn deep waters, far south of here. Vínland, her brother Leif has called it. Axes and stone lamps, wooden barrels of dried mutton and porridge oats, casks of water, even a loom—all make it hard to move around the ship. The woman wears a long woolen shift, with an apron front and back, attached by shoulder straps with oval brooches high on her chest. From a chain strung between the brooches hang scissors, knife, needle case, and keys. The farms she has known since childhood are receding in the distance; the icebergs grow larger, the wind stronger. The sail fills. They are away.*

A THOUSAND years ago Freydís Eiríksdóttir set off from Greenland on a summer's day, with her husband Thorvard and crew, in a wooden clinker-built ship with a single square woolen sail she'd most likely helped to weave. Following the route Leif Eiríksson had pioneered, they sailed north from their home in

Eiríksfjord, in the southerly Eastern Settlement, up the coast of Greenland, and crossed over to Baffin Island, where the Davis Strait was narrowest. Keeping land in sight, they worked their way down the coast of Labrador to the northern tip of Newfoundland. There, at the site the sagas call Straumfjord, now known as L'Anse aux Meadows, Freydís, Thorvard, and the others moved into the turf houses that Leif had constructed and left for members of his family and other Norse settlers to use as they further explored the region he called Vínland.

Freydís Eiríksdóttir was an adventurer at sea and a leader on land. Like Grace O'Malley, she came from a clan of skilled and courageous seafarers who ranged across the northern seas. Her father, Eirík the Red, had colonized Greenland with his followers; her three brothers explored the coasts of Greenland and Atlantic Canada. One of them, Leif Eiríksson, is the first known European to have landed on the North American continent; he predated Columbus by five centuries. Freydís is one of the most vigorous women in the Icelandic sagas, but her name isn't always mentioned in connection with the famous Vínland voyages described in *The Saga of Eirík the Red* and *The Greenlanders' Saga*. When her name does come up, it's often with a nervous laugh or a shudder. For if history is written by the victors, it's also written by those who can write. By the time the tales of the Norse, who made those perilous voyages across Davis Strait, were carefully inscribed on vellum in the thirteenth century by Christian scholars in Iceland, Freydís Eiríksdóttir's accomplishments were ignored in favor of the terrible deed she'd allegedly instigated while in Vínland.

Unfortunately, all we know about Freydís comes from these two sagas. In *The Saga of Eirík the Red*, she's described, depending on the translation, as "arrogant," or "very haughty," "a virago," "overbearing," or "man-like," with a husband who is "rather feeble," "not a very imposing person," or "nobody." We are told that she "had been married off to him mainly for his money," and also that she was pagan, like all Greenlanders of this era. Although her brother Leif was celebrated for having converted Greenland to Christianity around the year 1000 A.D., it's likely his reasons were more political than religious; the Greenlanders continued their allegiance to the old Norse gods for some time.

If Freydís was haughty, that pridefulness would doubtless have come from being one of Eirík the Red's children. A hot-tempered Norwegian who'd been banished for murder, Eirík fled to Iceland, where he was soon causing trouble as well. After several murders he was banned by the Icelandic parliament, the Althing. He made an exploratory trip to Greenland, and returned to convince others to return with him to a country of lush virgin meadows, and fewer testy relatives demanding revenge. In Greenland Eirík was at the top of the heap, and so were his sons. Things were a little different for Freydís, a girl born out of wedlock. Haughty she may have been, but probably also resentful.

Freydís, like her brothers, no doubt sought to better her social and financial standing in the community. It wasn't easy to become rich—or even comfortable—in Greenland. Unlike the rest of the Norse, who traded and farmed from the Baltic to Normandy and Ireland, the Greenlanders had little arable land (though, in fact, they had more arable land per capita than the Icelanders). The lush virgin meadows were only a narrow strip along the southern coast of Greenland, and would soon be grazed over; there was no timber for ships, and no nearby trading partners. When Bjarni Herjolfsson was blown off

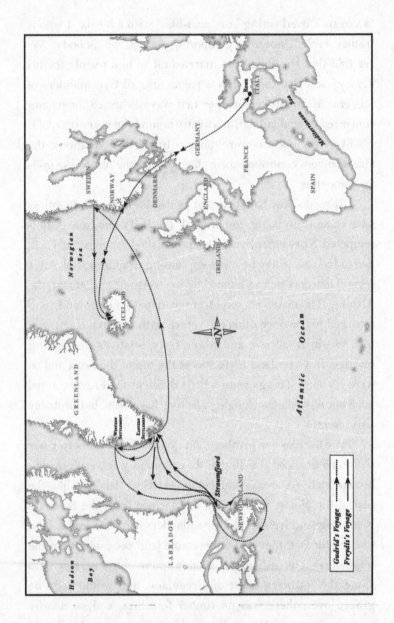

The voyages of Freydís and Gudríd

course on his way to Greenland from Iceland, he ended up farther west and south, in sight of an unknown shore. Bjarni sailed
north until he reached the latitude of Greenland, then east. It
was Leif Eiríksson who, fifteen years later, set off to explore
what Bjarni had only glimpsed: a land of forests, a sea of abundance.

The forests of Canada, with rich pastures, rivers, and bays
teeming with fish, seals, and whales, must have seemed a magnificent opportunity for Leif and those who came after him.
They may originally have thought of colonizing, but unlike
many of the places where the Norse had staked a claim—the
Faroes, Iceland and southern Greenland—the new country was
inhabited. The Norse most likely used their base at Straumfjord
in northern Newfoundland as a gateway to further explorations
down the coast to Nova Scotia and New England or inland to
New Brunswick (all of which have been proposed as possible
sites for Vínland).

Freydís's expedition was only one of several to Vínland, and
possibly one of the last, though we can't count on the authors of
the sagas for strict chronology. According to *The Greenlanders'
Saga*, she undertook this journey in conjunction with two
brothers from Iceland, Helgi and Finnbogi, who'd arrived in
Greenland by ship. Freydís visited them over the winter and
asked "if they would join her with their ship on an expedition to
Vínland, sharing equally with her all the profits that might be
made from it. They agreed to this."

Freydís and Thorvard had their own vessel and crew, and
together the two ships departed. Already Freydís is depicted in
the saga as underhanded, taking thirty-five able men, when the
agreement had been for each ship to take thirty. Women, who
may have been servants, slaves, or concubines (or perhaps all

three), were presumably not part of this equation. The Icelandic brothers made land at Straumfjord first and moved into the houses Leif had left. Upon her arrival Freydís protested this arrangement, arguing that Leif had lent them to her, not the brothers. Haughtiness perhaps, but also a sense of her family's social standing and its bonds.

When Freydís told them to leave, Helgi responded, "We brothers could never be a match for you in wickedness." In a huff, they abandoned Leif's buildings and constructed new houses farther away. The summer and fall were spent in felling timber, fishing, hunting, and exploring the new land. What the sagas don't tell us about daily life, archaeology can. The original site at L'Anse aux Meadows was discovered in the 1960s by Helge Ingstad, a Norwegian writer, and excavated under the direction of his wife, the archaeologist Anne Stine Ingstad. They found remains of three turf longhouses, and a few objects, among them a needle and a spindle whorl. There was work for the Norse to do, but not as much as in the warmer months, and a winter could be long, especially if there was bad blood.

> When winter set in, the brothers suggested that they
> should start holding games and other entertainments. This
> was done for a while until trouble broke out and ill-feeling
> arose between the two parties. The games were abandoned
> and all visiting between the houses ceased; and this state of
> affairs continued for most of the winter.

Eventually, as *The Greenlanders' Saga* tells it, Freydís set up a situation in which she was the innocent victim of the two brothers. She went to Finnbogi early one morning and asked if the Icelanders would exchange ships with her, as theirs was larger and she was eager to go away. "I shall agree to that," Finnbogi said, "if that will make you happy."

Rather inexplicably, seeing that Finnbogi had agreed to her demand, Freydís returned home, woke her husband and said that the brothers knocked her around when she offered to buy their ship. She goaded her husband to avenge her honor, threatening to divorce him if he refused. He and the other men then marched over to the Icelanders' camp, broke in, tied the men up, and dragged them out of their turf house. The saga continues:

> Freydis had each of them put to death as soon as he came out.
> All the men were killed in this way, and soon only the women were left; but no one was willing to kill them.
> Freydis said, "Give me an axe."
> This was done, and she herself killed the women, all five of them.
> After this monstrous deed they went back to their house, and it was obvious that Freydis thought she had been very clever about it. She said to her companions, "If we ever manage to get back to Greenland I shall have anyone killed who breathes a word about what has just happened. Our story will be that these people stayed on here when we left."

They returned to Greenland in the summer, following the opposite route up Labrador to Baffin Island, across the Davis Strait and south. They were wealthy now, loaded with timber and furs, and at first, perhaps, everyone expected the Icelandic brothers to follow, equally loaded down with goods. Eventually the story of the massacre leaked out and Leif discovered what Freydís had done. "I do not have the heart," said Leif when he heard the news, "to punish my sister Freydís as she deserves.

But I prophesy that her descendants will never prosper."

"And after that no one thought anything but ill of her and her family," the writer of *The Greenlanders' Saga* concludes.

This story has, for a long time, intrigued and baffled me. Why would one of the leaders want half the expedition crew killed? Was it possible that a woman, even a bad-tempered Viking, would take an axe to five women she'd worked alongside for months? Even if they were slaves? How had this blood-thirsty tale made it into the Icelandic sagas, and did it have a purpose beyond its purported truth?

Although Freydís wasn't Icelandic herself, she was probably born here, and I hoped in Iceland, home of the sagas, to find some answers to my questions about this notorious woman. I most wanted to know why, given how far she ranged, she wasn't seen for the seafaring explorer she was. Although I could understand the financial reasons for her trip, I thought she must have had other reasons—wanderlust, curiosity and a strong desire to prove herself fearless—to impel her from the safety of home out into the almost unknown ocean.

In the harbor of Reykjavík, on a glass-bright summer morning with the icy whip of the Arctic in the north wind, a Viking ship prepared to set off for a voyage to the New World. Clinker-built from pine and oak, the *Islendingur*'s prow swept high up off the water, more like a sculpture than a boat. That sweeping prow and broad beam would keep it from foundering in the rough seas between here and Vínland. The shallow draught would help it ride out gales as well as glide on and off shore. A single tall mast was placed amidships; from there the heavy square sail could be hoisted from the yard.

"Come onboard," said Ellen Ingvadóttir, and I hopped over the side.

The *Islendingur* had a deck, unlike ships from the past, where the cargo had been stowed in the hull and covered with ox hides, and livestock jostled for room with three or four dozen people. On this upcoming voyage from Iceland across the North Atlantic to the New World there would be only nine people, all of whom would sleep in bunks. It wasn't luxurious, but compared to conditions in the Viking Age, it was extravagantly comfortable. Ellen showed me a small galley and a toilet secreted away. "I don't usually show people the toilet," she said. "Most of the media have an unhealthy obsession with our elimination arrangements, especially mine." She was to be the only woman on a crew captained by Gunnar Eggertsson, who'd built this ship himself about four years ago. It was a faithful replica of the Gokstad ship dated 900 A.D., excavated in Norway, in 1880 and now displayed in an Oslo museum. They'd be setting off in about a week for Greenland and from there to Canada and down the eastern seaboard to Manhattan.

Six feet tall, large-boned, with a mature woman's figure, Ellen was bigger than a couple of the men on the ship, but still not quite someone you'd expect to find getting ready to cross the North Atlantic in a seventy-five-foot wooden sailing vessel. When I'd met her at her office, she'd looked every inch the successful woman professional: blond hair pulled back in a black bow from a strong, attractive face, big clip-on earrings, a flowing suit, and low heels. A certified court interpreter and translator, Ellen ran a translation bureau with a staff of eight. She was also head of Iceland's National Organization of Conservative Women (since one of their goals was to increase the number of women active in politics via participation in the

The *Islendingur*

Gender Equality Council, I could only surmise that an Icelandic conservative was different from one in, say, South Carolina). But in her youth Ellen had participated in the 1968 Mexico City Olympics, on the Icelandic swim team, and like most Icelanders, she was resilient and versatile. "In such a small country," one Icelander had told me, "we don't have enough people to go around. So all of us have to wear many hats." One of Ellen's hats included participating in this millennial voyage in honor of Leif Eiríksson's discovery of Vínland in the year 1000.

"We'll be retracing the route of the Greenland and Vínland

expeditions, stopping at something like twenty-four ports. There's a lot of PR involved, setting up contacts, translating, talking to the media; I'll be keeping the ship's log, too, in English, on our website. Naturally I'll be doing my share of the ship's tasks," she said, glancing at the three men who had jumped off the *Islendingur* to have a smoke on the dock. "I'm really tired of being asked by people how it's going to be living with eight men in such close quarters for several months. We'll be busy. There will be a lot of work to do and no time to worry about appearances. Of course," she added wryly, "somehow or other I'll have to pull myself together for the television cameras in port. I'm a little worried about the hair washing."

I could sympathize. On this chill windy morning, I'd clamped the knit watch cap I'd bought in Orkney over my disheveled hair and wrapped my neck in a scratchy woolen scarf. I was wearing long underwear and a bulky Icelandic sweater under my green rain slicker. I'd felt like a large androgynous gnome making my way to Ellen's office. It was hard to be both elegant and warm on this trip. I could hardly imagine battling waves and storms only to come into foreign ports under camera surveillance.

The *Islendingur* smelled clean, of tar and wood oil and sawdust. Because of the wind, the ship was in motion even tied to the dock. I tried to imagine myself among forty to fifty people shoulder to shoulder on this rocking vessel, all our worldly goods piled around us: knives and scythes, barrels of water, sacks of feed and seeds, dried fish, whey; precious woven wool for sails and clothes, spindles and needles. I tried to imagine other ships around us, loading up as well with families hopeful and afraid. In the summer of the year 985, twenty-five ocean-going *knarrs* departed Iceland to help Eirík the Red colonize

Greenland. Only fourteen of the vessels arrived in Greenland, the rest driven back or sunk by heavy seas.

Later colonists also suffered from foul weather: A girl called Gudríd Thorbjarnardóttir set off from under the shadow of Snæfellsnes Mountain with her family in the spring of 997; they didn't reach Greenland until the end of October. Apparently Gudríd didn't harbor terrible memories of the ocean journey; within a few years she was voyaging farther north up the coast of Greenland, to the Western Settlement, with her husband, Thorstein, Eirík the Red's son. After his death she married the Icelandic trader Thorfinn Karlsefni and they decided to try their luck in Vínland. That expedition probably lasted several years; with them came as many as a hundred Greenlanders and their slaves, in search of the rich resources Leif had described.

Gudríd's sea journeys are told in *The Vínland Sagas*. She and her husband Karlsefni spent two or three years in the New World, and Gudríd gave birth to a son, Snorri. After clashing repeatedly with the natives, the colony sailed en masse back to Greenland; the following year Gudríd and Karlsefni went on to Norway to sell their rich harvest of timber and furs. Already wealthy, Karlsefni was now even better off. He and Gudríd returned to a farm in the north of Iceland. But Gudríd's travels weren't over. After the death of her husband—and no longer young—she set off on a pilgrimage to Rome, crossing first to Denmark, and then going overland from there. Other Icelandic women made the same voyage, it appears. In a register of medieval pilgrims at the Swiss monastery of Reichenau, a page devoted to Icelanders lists four women's names from the eleventh century, most likely highborn women who would have had companions and servants.

After centuries in which the most common image of a

Viking was a wild-eyed warrior with hairy legs, who wore a
bronze helmet and wielded an axe, centuries in which the very
word *Viking* meant "man" and the voyages to Greenland and the
New World were perceived as male enterprises with Leif "the
Lucky" Eiríksson as the single hero, quite recently a new
figure—female—has entered the picture to become part of the
myth of the Vikings' westward expansion. Even before arriving
in Iceland, I'd come across Gudríd's name in a brochure for a
new translation of the complete Icelandic sagas.

In Reykjavík, I found that Gudríd's star was definitely on
the rise. A local playwright and director, Brynja Benediktsdóttir, had written a play about her life, and Jónas Kristjánsson,
saga scholar, had recently published a novel. Gulli and Gudrún
Bergmann, back on the Snæfellsnes Peninsula, had been
working to have a statue of Gudríd erected there, near her
birthplace, and up in the north, in Glaumbær, where Gudríd was
said to have spent the remaining years of her life as an anchoress
after returning from Rome, there was a monument. Even Ellen
and crew had gotten on the bandwagon; they mentioned Gudríd
in their promotional material and Ellen planned to take the
opportunity as the *Islendingur* came into port to talk up this seafaring woman to a public ignorant of Viking heroines.

But of Freydís Eiríksdóttir there was, oddly, not a word.

"IT'S TIME that Gudríd was acknowledged," said Jónas
Kristjánsson to me a few hours later as we sat in a café in central
Reykjavík. I was feeling a bit the worse for wear. After leaving
Ellen, I'd ventured into a hair salon, removed my tight watch
cap and asked for help. I didn't want to meet a manuscript spe-
cialist, professor emeritus, and novelist looking like a gnome.

The stylist had recommended something called Hár Hónnun (Hair Honey), which quivered in its plastic jar like a musical instrument from another planet. I thought it was a gel, but it was more like glue; my hair was now plastered down like sticky chunks of wood.

But Jónas treated me very courteously; I could see he was having trouble with his sparse hair today as well because of the furious cold wind. He combed it down carefully before ordering coffee for us, and bringing out a copy of a novel he'd written about Gudríd Thorbjarnardóttir, *The Wide World*. Now retired from his long-held position as director of the Árni Magnússon Institute, which was built especially to house the old vellum books from Iceland's past, he was turning his energy to fiction.

Eventually I brought up the subject of Freydís Eiríksdóttir. Why didn't she get more recognition as a pioneering seafarer?

"Ah, Freydís Eiríksdóttir . . ." Jónas looked away.

It was a common reaction: an embarrassed laugh, a rolling of the eyes, a sigh. Earlier today Ellen Ingvadóttir had groaned when I mentioned Freydís, as I might if someone wanted to enthuse about what a strong role model for women Margaret Thatcher had been. The kindest description of Freydís I'd come across was "hot-headed." Other sources were far more pejorative. "Arrogant" and "greedy" were two of the lesser epithets; "bloody" and "murderous" two of the worst.

"Who knows exactly what the truth is?" Jónas said when I pressed him about whether he believed that Freydís was really so evil. "The fact is we have only the sagas to go on and they were written between two and three centuries after the events. Perhaps Freydís had some reason to do what she did. Perhaps someone didn't like her."

Perhaps it was a question of blame. After Jónas had

departed, I sat for a while longer in the café, reluctant to face the freezing wind. I took out my copy of *Women in the Viking Age* by Judith Jesch. Jesch is part of a new generation of Scandinavian scholars who have applied feminist theory to accepted history. She takes a cool view of the oft-made claim that women in the sagas were strong heroines: "Because the women of the sagas of Iceland are *not* portrayed primarily as objects of desire, many critics have been fooled into overlooking the stereotypic ways in which they are portrayed."

In a section called "Iceland's Vengeful Housewives" Jesch dissects the image of the female inciter who appears in so many of the great family sagas. Unlike their mythic predecessors, the Valkyries, these literary women almost never employ violence themselves, either with fists or weapons. Instead, they use cruel jibes and threats to create situations in which their men, unable to stand being taunted any longer, break down and murder someone.

Iceland in the thirteenth century, when the sagas were written down, was a country riven by blood feuds, the Sicily of the North. The democratic institution of the parliament with its lawgivers had almost collapsed. By 1235 civil war had broken out, and in 1262 the Icelanders submitted to the Norwegian crown. The lack of centralized authority had, while creating a more classless society, also resulted in family-enforced punishments and increasing civil disorder. In looking for someone to blame for the disintegration of their society into warring factions, the saga writers lit upon the not completely novel idea of pointing the finger at women. Freydís fits right into this scenario of women who whet, except that, not content merely to goad, she takes the axe into her own hands at the end to become a mass murderer.

◉ ◉ ◉

Playwright and director Brynja Benediktsdóttir was one of the only Icelanders I met willing to entertain a different view of Freydís. A few days after my coffee with Jónas, I walked over to Brynja's house for lunch. The rooms were dark mustard with wide-planked wooden floors; a lace-curtained window offered a view of the Tjörn, the small lake near the city's center. There was a shiny black grand piano, an antique four-poster bed in a corner, and a very random collection of chairs.

"My play, *The Saga of Gudríd*, is based on both sagas, particularly *The Saga of Eirík the Red*. That's the one with the most information about Gudríd and her husband Karlsefni. One of the things I was most interested in writing about was the interaction between the colonists and the native population. You know, the reason that the Vínland settlement failed was not lack of resources. The world climate was warmer then; there was plenty of everything, timber, game, fish, fruit, and they were in addition very resourceful people. But they had no concept of how to deal with a native population, the people they called *skrælings*. There had been no significant native population in either Iceland or Greenland when these countries were settled, so the encounters with the inhabitants [perhaps ancestors of the Mi'kmaq or the Innu] which had begun with some friendliness, quickly deteriorated into suspicion, attacks, and counterattacks. That's really the story of *The Vínland Sagas*, the attempts and ultimate failure of the white settlers to understand and acknowledge the people already living there. It foretells the failure of the Europeans five hundred years later!"

At sixty, Brynja had been in theater most of her life. Her blond hair was short; her face composed and open. She had the contented, busy air of a successful impresario. She showed me clippings from newspapers in Sweden and Ireland, where her play had been performed. Her favorite performances had been in Greenland. She patted an unusual necklace of carved bone on her chest, which had been given to her by Greenlanders.

Brynja saw Gudríd and Freydís as mirror images. The purpose of putting Freydís beyond the pale was to raise Gudríd's status. It was all about religion, about deconstructing Iceland's pagan past and assigning blame. "The descendants of Gudríd were bishops, a long line of them. One of them was trying to put together a good Christian lineage to impress the Vatican. When the story of Gudríd was written down, Gudríd was elevated as Christian and quite devout. After she and Karlsefni returned to Iceland he died, and then she went off by herself on a pilgrimage by ship and foot to Rome. When she returned, she became a nun and an anchoress. Freydís, on the other hand, was a bastard and a pagan, and comparing the two women made Gudríd look wonderful. Some scholars now think that part of the purpose of *The Saga of Eirík the Red* was to elevate the courage and goodness of Gudríd and Karlsefni so that her descendants might be canonized."

I knew too little about the intricate belief systems of the pagan Norse to even guess what sort of heathen Freydís might have been. Would she have sacrificed animals at the shrine of Odin, or perhaps to Freya, the Norse goddess of fertility? Freya introduced divination to mortals, and her cult of followers, many of them women, included seers and foretellers. Freya was also known for bringing discord among the gods. But before Freya joined the complicated pantheon of Norse gods, and was relegated to a lesser position as female troublemaker, she'd been the Great Goddess herself. Freya. Freydís. Was this the reason the churchmen who wrote down the sagas had it in for her?

Leaving Brynja's, I walked over to Hallgrím's Church, where a statue of Leif Eiríksson towers over the square. Although it was presented to the city by a group of Americans in 1930, it embodies the centuries-long pride the Icelanders have taken in this native son (though he actually lived in Greenland most of his life). One of the reasons that Leif was called "the Lucky" was that he seems to have led a charmed life, and that's emphasized in the sagas. As charismatic as his father, Leif comes down to us a born leader. The stories of him reminded me a little of those told about Grace O'Malley. They had a certain prideful pleasure. Here was someone well respected, well remembered, and well loved, who reflected only good upon the race.

Freydís was no Grace O'Malley, but was she really Lizzie Borden? In *The Saga of Eirík the Red*, the one Brynja had used as the basis for her play, there's no mention of Freydís as a psychopathic killer of her own sex. In that saga, Freydís barely appears, and seems to be on the same expedition to Vínland as Gudríd and Karlsefni. But her brief appearance is, in fact, heroic. When the Norse were attacked by the Indians, the male settlers ran off, but Freydís, heavily pregnant, stood her ground, calling to them, "Why do you flee from such pitiful wretches, brave men like you? You should be able to slaughter them like cattle. If I had weapons, I am sure I could fight better than any of you." She snatched up a sword from a slain man and faced the *skrælings*. Pulling down her shift to show one of her breasts (possibly to indicate she was a woman), she slapped at it with the flat part of the sword and frightened the natives off.

What was the truth of the events so long ago in Greenland and Vínland? Was Freydís a heroine or a murderer? What happened to Finnbogi and Helgi and their followers? Perhaps one of the ships was no longer seaworthy enough for the return home, and the Greenlanders, under the direction of Freydís, did take the remaining ship and sail off, leaving the Icelanders behind. Perhaps when the two ships set a return course for Greenland after their stay in Straumfjord, the Icelanders didn't get back safely. Their absence gave rise to rumors; the rumors were pinned on Freydís. The Norse were a violent people; we can only speculate about events so long ago. The important thing *is* to speculate, to keep the possibilities open.

What continues to strike me about the legend of Freydís is what a closed book it is to many scholars and researchers, and how easily it's assumed she turned murderer. In fact, there's no other example in saga literature, replete as it is with women's jealousy, hatred, and goading, of a woman who kills in such an outright fashion. Whatever her accomplishments, however great her courage at masterminding an expedition to a distant shore and organizing life under difficult circumstances, it doesn't seem that Freydís could get her companions to like her, much less love her as they did Leif. I didn't find it easy to believe that Freydís had ordered all the Icelanders to be killed, much less that she'd hacked the Icelandic women to death with an axe, but I didn't have a problem believing she lacked an outgoing, lively personality that made men want to follow her anywhere.

Grace O'Malley, like Leif Eiríksson, had an innate gift of leadership, a trustworthiness and verve, a charm and power that made her sailors and warriors overlook and even celebrate her gender. Freydís was tough, but that toughness inspired hatred, not admiration, at least in the medieval churchmen who transcribed and reinterpreted Iceland's oral tradition. Many scholars now consider the sagas more fiction than truth, just as much for what they say about medieval Christian belief as what they say about their pagan Viking forebears. But if the sagas are fiction, then why don't more scholars question the intent of the stories about Freydís?

I looked up at the statue of Leif's massive legs and barrel chest, the cloak swirling down his back, the helmeted head arrogantly tilted back, the gaze calm and lordly. He held the traditional double-headed, long-handled axe of the Vikings. In his hands it was a symbol, so expected as to seem unremarkable, of domination and confidence. It hardly even looked like a weapon meant to kill people, just an extension of his powerful body.

THE SILVER river cut a swath through green meadows where horses grazed by the hundreds. North was open ocean, the Greenland Sea; yet the day had a fluted balminess. I was in the delta valley of Skagafjord, in the north of Iceland, a part of the country generally warmer in summer than Reykjavík. Not that it was tropical; it was more like Wyoming or Montana, an impression reinforced by the proliferation of Jeeps and trucks on the roads, and the lack of inhabitants. There were few villages in rural Iceland, and the convenience store attached to a gas station was the social hub. Most of the interior was lava or gravel desert, or glacier or mountain; the sparse pastures and farmlands clustered around the edges of the country, especially around large bays or deep fjords like this one. The farming population, though once much larger, had never been large enough or wealthy enough to create many towns with schools, churches, banks, and offices. Yet some of the farms had been social clusters in themselves, supporting and sheltering several dozen people.

Today I was visiting Glaumbær, an old farm now turned

into a museum. I didn't know which was more remarkable, being inside the warren of dark, dirt-floored rooms that seemed to be dug out of earth, the home of Mr. and Mrs. Badger and their children, or standing outside and watching how the grass rippled over the roof and the low sod walls, some set with glass windows. These turf farmhouses were built up from loaves of sod in horizontal rows, the sod placed on the diagonal in a herringbone pattern. Over the years the sod had hardened and the colors had softened. They were a ravishing marble of rose, burnt sienna, and yellow ochre. From a short distance, the rounded outside walls looked as if they'd been quarried in Italy.

One of the reasons the buildings at Glaumbær had remained intact was that, although they were only one or two centuries old, they were built on land that was said to have been farmed by Thorfinn Karlsefni and Gudríd Thorbjarnardóttir, and their son, Snorri. Not far from the farmhouse was a verdigris-weathered bronze statue, about two feet tall, on a rock. A woman stood on a ship, one hand on the upward-sweeping prow. With the other arm she hoisted a baby on her shoulder. He had the fully formed, small adult limbs of a medieval baby Jesus; uncradled and alert, he stood on his mother as if her shoulder were a crossbar on a mast.

I was glad to see Gudríd honored, but what a curious, feminine memorial it was, small and maternal, so unlike the enormous statue of Leif in Reykjavík. Gudríd's iconography was Madonna-like. Her potency was in having given birth to Snorri and a line of bishops, her rediscovered importance to Icelandic history seemed to lie in modesty, faith, and willingness to follow where her father and husbands led; though perhaps, on her own at the end, traveling to Rome, she'd finally known independence.

I sat down on the grass and began to sketch the small statue

**Gudríd Thorbjarnardóttir
with her son Snorri**

of Gudríd. I remembered how two months ago, in Ireland, I'd
tried to imagine my travels as *an thuras,* a counterclockwise
journey around relics and sacred sites, with a ritual performed
at each one. Over the weeks, I'd found a few historical traces of
women's lives in the buildings where they'd lived. There were
the dormitories of the herring lassies, the big houses built by
Christian Robertson in Stromness, the dismantled croft house of
Betty Mouat, the castles of Grace O'Malley. They were not
exactly monuments or sacred sites, and I'd performed no rituals
other than to take photographs. This statue of Gudríd on a ship
was the first marker I'd found specifically placed to recognize a
woman's achievement as an explorer and seafarer. I used to

think of statues as part of the vague background of city life, busts of forgotten city fathers and obscure poets hidden in park foliage, or bronze horses rearing up in traffic circles. But journeying with a historical purpose had made me look at how figures from the past, especially women, were remembered and how their memory was enshrined. Most women, even the greatest, had no memorials at all—Freydís Eiríksdóttir, for one, whose bad name had lasted a full thousand years.

"And after that no one thought anything but ill of her and her family," *The Greenlanders' Saga* concluded Freydís's story. All the bravery and endurance that shine through the account in both sagas about her expedition are dismissed. She was arrogant, greedy, and a murderer, and that's all one needs to hear to judge her. The legend of Freydís as killer completely usurps the story of Freydís as adventurer. Yet I found myself wanting to know all kinds of details about the powerful, pagan, and possibly vengeful Freydís Eiríksdóttir, not so much whether she killed anyone, but what it was like to sail through Arctic waters in a wooden ship. What it was like to see icebergs and whales, to steer by the light of the stars, to only guess at what you'd find on land, or whether you would find land at all.

So often the sea has marked the boundary of women's geography. Beyond the shore we could not go—or so we learned. If the ocean is a place of imagination, women were not encouraged to dream of it; we were forbidden to imagine ourselves at sea, much less to dream of discovering new lands. It was Freydís's imagination I was most interested in; I knew she had one.

I stretched out on my back on the grass and looked up at the big, fast-moving, lush blue sky of northern Iceland, thinking about Ellen Ingvadóttir's upcoming voyage on the *Islendingur*. This time a woman was keeping the ship's diary, a woman was logging on to the Internet to tell the story of reaching Vínland. If only Freydís had been able to write down her adventures, if only Freydís had had a little laptop to tell her tale. Would she have written, *August 15: Killed five women with an axe today, good riddance*, or would she have written something completely different?

Saw the coast of a new country today. It is wooded and fertile. I look forward to exploring this vast new continent. The possibilities for me here seem endless.

CHAPTER XV

A WOMAN WITHOUT A BOAT IS A PRISONER

Tálknafjördur, Iceland

"You must take abyss lessons," proclaimed Professor Lidenbrock to his nephew Axel in *Journey to the Centre of the Earth*. Jules Verne was describing their ascent up a church steeple to prepare for the exploration of the Snæfellsnes volcano, but he could just as well have been talking about driving a small rental car along the switchbacking mountain roads on the way to Iceland's Westfjords. Unpaved, with no dividing line and often only a single lane, without guardrails of any sort, the road wound up and down and around the deep inlets on the northern side of the Breidafjord.

"What a view! You don't know what you're missing," said my friend Tess. She'd arrived from Seattle a few days ago, bringing news of home but, unaccountably, not a single sweater. Her confident ebullience on the road both cheered and petrified me. I didn't want abyss lessons. I was grateful that she was at the wheel, but my terror at plunging over the side to a sheer fall into the water below was compounded by the sight of her driving with one hand, snacking on Fritos and Icelandic licorice with the other, while gazing out in rapture over the high volcanic plateaus. I'd tried closing my eyes at the worst parts, but the worst parts all began to merge together, and finally I had to make her stop the car so I could lie down in the back seat with a jacket over my head. The only thing that made me feel better

251

was recalling that Ellen Ingvadóttir, the woman about to cross the wild northern seas in a replica Viking boat, had told me she'd been deathly afraid when her husband drove them around the Westfjords.

Tess and I were on our way to visit an eighty-year-old historian, Thórunn Magnúsdóttir, in the remote fishing village of Tálknafjördur. Ever since I'd arrived in Iceland, several weeks before, her name had come up. "*She's* the one you should talk to if you're interested in women and the sea," people said. "She knows about Skipper Thurídur, our great fishing foremother; she knows all kinds of things about Icelandic fisherwomen. She's written a book about them."

If Iceland is shaped like a baseball mitt, then the huge peninsula called the Westfjords is the thumb poking up north by west into the sea, albeit a thumb with hundreds of indentations. In a country of heart-stopping scenery, the rocky bays, white sand beaches and dark, anvil-shaped mountains of the Westfjords arguably provide the most spectacular views. Although the Westfjords peninsula makes up only one-tenth of Iceland's land mass, it has more than half of the country's total shoreline. On a bright day in summer, especially if one is in a car and protected from the biting wind, the landscape can seem oddly reminiscent of the American Southwest: how New Mexico might look if the states west of it broke off and left the mesas at the edge of the sea. The reason so many of Iceland's mountains have that uniform height and bread-loaf appearance is that the volcanic eruptions occurred under a thick mantle of ice during one of the glacial periods. Instead of forming high peaks, the mountains flattened under the pressure of the ice even as they rose.

We'd chosen to drive around the vast Breidafjord rather

than cross it by car ferry (we'd do that on the return). The only other way to get to the Westfjords was by plane from Reykjavík and then bus. But I'd wanted to get a sense of the Breidafjord. Not only had some of the earliest settlers, like Aud the Deep-Minded and Eirík the Red, lived on or near its shores, but this huge bay, shaped like the mouth of a whale gobbling minnows (twenty-seven hundred islands have been counted), was known as the food larder of Iceland. At difficult times in the country's history, when much of Iceland was starving, the Breidafjord provided fish, shellfish, seaweed, and seal meat. Few of the small islands had farms. The inhabitants lived on sea-bird eggs and fished all year. It had one of the strongest fishing cultures in Iceland, and historical sources suggest that in the eighteenth and nineteenth centuries women fished in this bay in almost equal numbers to men.

Head hidden under my jacket, I thought about Halldóra Ólafsdóttir, who lived on an island in the Breidafjord in the eighteenth century, during some of Iceland's worst times, when the volcanoes spewed poisonous ash and the northern coastline froze much of the year. Halldóra had a twin brother, whose boat she skippered. Nicknamed Clubfoot, she was a forceful helmswoman who competed hard against her brothers and, it's said, would only have a female crew. When famine drove settlers from the north of Iceland down to the Breidafjord, she and her twin brother took them in. They ferried the refugees from the shore to the islands, and made sure they didn't eat too much, too quickly, for starving people often died when they were given food.

At the University of Reykjavík, the librarian of the women's collection, Erla Hulda Halldorsdóttir, had shown me a book on women's work in Iceland, which included information on women fishers and shellfish collectors. "A woman without a boat is a prisoner," the chapter on women in the Breidafjord was called, a twist on the Faroese saying, *Bundin er batlos man*, "Bound is a boatless man." The symbol of the Women's Association of the Breidafjord was a single woman in a small boat with its sail up. The material included oral histories with women who'd been born in the nineteenth century. Gudný Hagalín, for instance, learned to steer a boat and scull when she was twelve.

> She wanted to go to sea and did so often with her father as well as accompany him on foxhunts. She was a little proud of accompanying her father on such trips while her brothers sat at home. Her father wanted to teach her to carry a gun, but her aunt forbade it, saying that he was raising Gudný as if she were a man, not a woman, and that the girl was learning no women's work.

Another woman, Rósamunda Sigmundsdóttir, also grew up on boats.

> Rósa was not big, but well-formed and amazingly strong. One of her most prominent features was that she always got enough to eat. She could keep up with any average man rowing . . . She knew very well how to trim sails. After the gaff sail came to the islands, and sheets had to be loose when tacking, no one held on to the jib better than she did. . . . She liked sailing . . . And she could really haul in the catch.

Then there was Gudrún Jónsdóttir, who was "a great, heroic

fisher, not less than Skipper Thurídur . . . she was an outstanding helmsman." She used to go out fishing with her sons, even when the weather was bad and even when she got old. She thrived on rough seas and used to say, "I'll take the rudder, boys."

The car had braked on a slight incline. The crunching of Fritos stopped.

"What's happened?" I asked, blind, muffled, fearing the worst.

"We're up on top of the world, in the middle of absolute nowhere. And there's this *huge* statue by the side of the road. I have to take a photograph."

I crept out and, true enough, there was a statue of a giant man, constructed from massive stones, by the side of the road. It's said that the highway crew who put these mountain roads in had built it and had given the giant the face of their boss. I stood outside briefly. Around us were flattened mountains, and in the distance snow-covered peaks. Below us, fallen boulders and gravel washes led the way back to the Breidafjord, austerely beautiful, like a lake in a desert. It looked, as many landscapes in Iceland did, just formed, prehistoric, as if human settlement were yet to come.

"It's not so bad right here," said Tess. "We're going down. You could come back up here if you want. Of course, according to the map, we still have five fjords to drive around and a lot more of these mountain roads."

ASIDE FROM these high gravel roads without guardrails, I'd liked Iceland ever since I arrived from the foggy Faroes. One of the things that most impressed me was a seemingly collective attitude toward remembrance. This was a country dedicated to history and to family, which to them were often the same. In spite of rushing headlong into the twenty-first century, they retained old habits, still speaking the same form of Old Norse that had long vanished from most other parts of Scandinavia, still recalling and celebrating the deeds of ancestors as far back as the early settlement of Iceland in the ninth century. Iceland had begun as a pioneer culture, where everyone's help was needed to survive, and continued as a vassal state of Denmark, ground down by poverty and disease, by trade restrictions and taxes. In this country, everyone who could work had to. Through it all, through centuries of smallpox and leprosy and volcanic eruptions and poor crops and brutal laws, the Icelanders had held on to their heritage, especially to the literature of settlement and saga, and to the memory of heroic ancestors.

Like most male-oriented societies, Iceland's official histories tended to downplay the achievements of women. But at the same time, because Icelanders had saved so much of the past and because they loved genealogy, they had records of many women who'd been fishers and boat builders. These women weren't strangers, but often relatives. And they knew their relatives. So, in contrast to the sometimes blank looks I'd gotten elsewhere in the North Atlantic, here in Iceland people wanted to tell me stories of seafaring women.

Brynja Benediktsdóttir, the playwright who'd tackled the story of Gudríd and Freydís, had also written a play about a skipper called Salome from up here in the Westfjords who rowed with other women. Her husband divorced her because he said she acted like a man. Brynja also told me about Gunna the Footless, who started out as a fisher, but after suffering frostbite and the loss of her foot, turned to building boats and became well known for it. And everybody had told me about Thurídur Formadur, or Skipper Thurídur, the greatest fisherwoman of them all, whose story I was soon to learn from the woman who knew most about her.

"Eat, eat," urged Thórunn Magnúsdóttir. "Do you like it?"

"It's an interesting breakfast," Tess said, looking at the paper-thin gray flatbread, the tough curls of dried cod and the wet scoop of what seemed to be chocolate pudding on her plate.

"This is very typically Icelandic," said Thórunn. "*Skyr* is thick cultured milk, full of health. I have been eating *skyr* all my life for breakfast. Of course," she added, "it should not be chocolate *skyr*. I made a mistake with the label at the grocery store."

We'd arrived in Tálknafjördur yesterday afternoon and were staying with Thórunn in her sunny flat on a hillside overlooking the small harbor. It was more like a college student's apartment than an old lady's: bright prints on the walls, lots of books. There was something of the student still in Thórunn, too, a guileless enthusiasm. Like a British schoolgirl, she wore a white shirt buttoned up to the neck and a plain wool skirt with white socks and black shoes with straps. Her dark hair was short, straight, and parted on the side. Her glasses were bottle-thick, and she moved slowly and methodically, but in general she looked far younger than eighty. She'd been born in 1920 in the Westmann Islands and had had two husbands, one of whom had fought in the Spanish Civil War, and five children. Like her parents, Thórunn had been active in the trade union movement and in later years became an ardent feminist. She'd gone to the university in the sixties and again in the eighties, when she'd earned a masters in history based on her research on women fishers in the southeast of Iceland from 1697 to 1980. Growing up in a fishing community, she'd heard many stories about women who fished; one of her female ancestors had crewed with the famous Skipper Thurídur.

The remarkable history of Skipper Thurídur was part of Thórunn's dissertation, but there were other stories and accounts of women fishers from much earlier in Iceland's history. The only trouble was keeping Thórunn on track. Last evening she'd spent an hour telling me her adventures in China during the 1995 International Women's Conference in Beijing, and this morning she'd shown me a book she'd written on Romania, as well as her collection of Bulgarian art books—all before I'd had my first cup of coffee.

I nibbled at my flatbread and opened my notebook. I'd read a précis in Danish of Thórunn's dissertation on Icelandic women fishers, but was eager for the details. "Last night," I began, "you said you'd used parish registers, court cases, tax records, the census in Iceland, local history, family genealogies, and oral sources."

"Don't forget the Annals of the Bishops," she said. "That is how I found some of the earliest material. The bishops of Iceland had to keep records, you see, and for instance, in 1554 one of them writes about a fishing boat capsizing. Nine men and three women drowned. In 1640 there is a note in the annals about another boat sinking with eleven men. The owner of the boat is listed as 'Katrina.'

"And of course one of the early fishers from the north was Björg Einarsdóttir, born in 1716. She was the daughter of a priest, but the times were very difficult. In that century the weather was often cold and wet so the crops failed, and then there were eruptions and earthquakes. Her parents sent her to a farm in Eyjafjördur and she ended up living there most of her life. She had a boat. She was a poet. She had a foreign lover, a man left onshore by a ship from another country. She wrote him a poem about his poor rowing:

> You have to row better, my dear.
> You shouldn't fear slamming
> Your oars against the sea
> Tomorrow it will recover.

"When she was old, she was reduced to begging. She rowed her lover out to another foreign ship and sent him on his way. Those were very terrible times," Thórunn said pensively. "Do you know Iceland's history? Do you know about the famine years? What about the government?"

"Of course I'm curious about everything to do with Iceland," I said a little nervously. "But what I'd really love is to hear about the women. I'd love to hear about Skipper Thurídur."

Thórunn fetched a book that seemed to be a full-length biography of Skipper Thurídur. "It's all here."

"Yes, but in Icelandic."

"Such a pity. You speak Norwegian. A year or two of study and you'd be able to read Icelandic. Then you could read our sagas, the history. You really should know more of our history." She waggled a finger and smiled. "But in the meantime, I'll tell you the story of Thurídur Formadur . . ."

THURÍDUR EINARSDÓTTIR was born in 1777 on the south coast, near Stokkseyri, the daughter of a skipper and farmer at Stéttir Farm. Her brother Bjarni started fishing and Thurídur begged to go as well. In those days women in Stokkseyri often rowed out with men, but it was less common for girls. One day when she was eleven, her brother was ill, so her father took her out instead.

As the biography tells it:

As soon as her tackle hit bottom, a fish took the hook; it was haddock. Thurídur began to pull it in and did not lack courage, but things would not go smoothly. She was inexperienced, had little stamina, and her sea mitts were an obstacle. For a while, either Thurídur hauled in the line, or the haddock pulled it out through her hands. Then one of her mitts fell off; she seemed to get a better grip then and threw off the other mitt as well without letting go of the line. The haddock began to tire, and Thurídur finally got it. She immediately paid the line out again, and another haddock took the hook. It went the same way with this one as the first. So it went time after time. As soon as Thurídur's line reached bottom, another fish was on the hook. Actually, she hardly had the strength for haddock then, but she quickly learned a technique for hauling in that kept her from tiring without giving the fish enough line to get loose, and she always got it in the end. Her father saw that allowing her to fish was worthwhile, as she caught more than most others. He therefore had leather clothing as well as sea mitts made that fit her, and he allowed her to keep half of what she caught that spring and the next two springs after that.

This was the beginning of Thurídur's fifty-year career as a fisher and skipper. It was also the beginning of her reputation for luck, as well as for wearing men's clothing. After her father died when she was fourteen, she began to row for her brother, who had inherited the family's boat and farm.

> This was regarded as a novelty, that a girl under twenty would be treated the same as full-grown men when the catch was divided. However, the deckhands thought this was fine because Thurídur both caught more fish than anyone else and was quickest and most energetic at every-thing, and then she was especially confident and clever at finding solutions, deliberative and clear-headed, so that people on the ship often referred matters to her if a lot rode on the outcome, and she was deemed to find quick and good solutions.

Her prowess as a rower was no mean feat off the south coast of Iceland. Although the fishing was rich because of a shelf extending offshore, there were no harbors. That partic-ular coastline was dangerously jagged with volcanic reefs, sharp as black scalpels. The fishing was usually done in the winter and spring, before the planting on the farms began, and a storm, especially a snow or ice storm, could descend at any time. Nothing could be seen, hands turned to ice at the oars, and the reefs were invisible until they sliced the hull. No one could stay out in such weather; worse yet was the return to land. The boats were heavy with fish, and the waves crashing into shore made it difficult to maneuver the closer to land they came. Many skippers tried to stay out fishing as long as the weather held, but that meant they often didn't get back in time. So often the boats overturned close to shore, in full view of those who stood there ready to help unload the catch.

This is what happened eventually to Thurídur's brother, Bjarni. When his boat capsized offshore, he thrust his axe head into the bottom of the boat and managed to hold on as he shouted for help. But the seas were too rough and the wind too strong. Like so many others, he drowned as those who stood on shore watched helplessly. Thurídur's "luck" had much to do with caution. After rowing for her brother for some years, she went to work for a skipper called Jón Thórdarson, known for his large catches and his bravado at tempting fate.

> Jón was known to stay rather a long time at sea and be daring in how much he loaded his ship; but Thurídur was cautious in this as in other matters and had the integrity to tell him what she thought. But he was always amenable to reason, and he usually followed her suggestions. He noticed that Thurídur always urged a timely return to shore, and that later was not better. It also happened that Jón reproached deckhands for something, but not with the tact or reasonableness that seemed appropriate. Thurídur then always answered on their behalf and smoothed everything over. From this, they got used to letting Thurídur answer for them whenever necessary. Thurídur was also fun to be around, talkative and uplifting at sea or ashore. Word got around that Thurídur would be a good skipper.

And this is what happened. She was given a boat in 1816, when she was thirty-nine, and was its skipper for fourteen years; in 1830 the fish off Stokkseyri were scarce, and she moved, as did others, to Thorlákshöfn, where she skippered another boat for ten years. She retired from fishing in 1840, at sixty-three, but continued farming and lived to the great age of eighty-six.

Like most women who fished, Thurídur wore pants and a shirt under traditional outerwear made of water-repellent seal-skin. At that time in Iceland it was illegal for a woman to wear men's clothing on land, so she always switched to a dress when she was in public. On one occasion, however, after a robbery had taken place in the district, Thurídur was called in front of the local magistrate to testify. Not that she was a witness, but the judge thought she might know something about the perpetra-tors. She'd been tarring her boat, and hadn't had time to change from her male attire. She apologized to the judge, and he told her, "I have already heard that you go about in men's clothes every day. However, to do so, you must apply for a permit, and I shall obtain this permit for you if you give me a clue about who the robbers were at Kambur."

Although Thurídur feared for her safety if she testified, she was able to identify the stitching on a pair of shoes left behind at the robbery, which led to the capture and imprisonment of the thieves. From then on she wore men's clothing in public, though one source says that three times she was maligned for doing so. Each time she sued the men for slander, and each time she won.

Thórunn's grandfather, Jón Jónsson, had been one of her first sources for family stories about Skipper Thurídur, for his mother and grandmother had both worked for Thurídur. His grandmother Ingibjörg had been a deckhand on Thurídur's boat for sixteen seasons. "My grandfather was a good historian," Thórunn told me. "He always got the names of people. Women were never just wives or mothers to him. He wrote down their names and what they did. Ingibjörg and Thurídur were very close, and Ingibjörg lived with Thurídur before she married. My grandfather told stories of storms at sea. There was a ter-rible storm once and two boats were out; the boat with all the women rowing got back into shore while the other boat went under and everyone drowned. Many stories were told about this and other storms and perils. My grandfather said he believed the women's accounts more than the men's. Why? Men are so often drunk when they tell about their sea voyages." What was true, what everybody says, is that Skipper Thurídur was counted a very lucky captain and many people wanted to crew with her.

Skipper Thurídur was an unusual woman, but apparently very attractive to men. She had many offers of marriage, and probably several lovers, one of whom gave her a child. Sadly, the little girl died at age three. Thurídur married once, when she was in her early forties. According to Thórunn, the young man, only twenty-three, crewed on her boat and said he'd leave if she didn't marry him. "So she did, because she needed him on the boat, but it didn't work out and they divorced. All of them wanted to take away her independence, but she ended all the relationships without any rancor.

"To appreciate living with a woman of so many talents, men have to be great themselves," Thórunn, herself divorced, added tartly.

A FEW hours later Tess, who had gone out for a walk as I took notes, returned and we set off for the sports center that every Icelandic town has. Here in Tálknafjördur a windscreen protected the outdoor pool and gave an illusory sense of heat. As we settled into the embrace of the pool, cerulean-tinted, slightly sulfuric, with the dry brown mesas looming around us, and a bright azure sky above, I felt I'd been transported to a Palm Springs resort. Floating on my back, in spa comfort, I couldn't help thinking of the desperately hard lives most Icelanders had lived up until only a few decades ago. I told Tess what I'd learned about Thurídur, and how I was trying to understand the large number of women who'd gone fishing in Iceland for almost three hundred years. There had been women fishing—women in their eighties!—in the Breidafjord until the last twenty years or so. So many names, and so many stories of luck, skill, and courage. Tess listened as I enumerated them, and laughed at one point.

Skipper Thurídur

"You said there was a woman called *Salome*? That's a change. I thought half the women in Iceland were called Gudrun and the other half were called Gudrid. I keep wondering, how do they keep everybody straight?"

I'd been muddled, too, though now I was getting more used to it. Still, when Thórunn had brought out her family's genealogy book, full of variations and repetitions of the same names, I'd found myself asking, "If no one has the same last name as her grandfather or father, much less relatives who went further back, how do Icelanders know who their relatives are?"

Thórunn had looked at me strangely. "We *know* who we are," she said. "We're a family of fishers, historians, and musicians."

I'd told Tess soon after she arrived in Iceland that I'd felt the call to change my name. Now I brought it up again, not sure whether to be firm in my decision or to ask advice.

"Well," she said diplomatically. "It's your choice. A big choice, though."

"Wilson's not right now," I said. "I don't feel connected with it anymore."

"But what about publishing? Isn't it too late to change your name? What will happen to your books? Won't it be confusing? What is this new name anyway?"

"I'll find it," I said confidently, then paused. "Actually, I have no idea how."

"Maybe it will find you . . ." She still seemed uncertain. "I've always known you as Wilson. I *liked* Wilson."

But I noticed she was already using the past tense.

WHEN WE returned to Thórunn's apartment, we found that she had organized a small gathering for us. She'd asked three teenage girls who fished with their fathers to join us for soft drinks, cake, and cookies. Two were sisters, Gudrún and Erla Thorsdóttir, and the third their friend Birna Tryggvad. Erla, sixteen, had broad shoulders, fluffy-fine light hair and a very freckled face. She wore an Adidas sport shirt and had several studs in her upper earlobe. Her elder sister Gudrún was also tall, with a serious round face and blond hair pulled back in a ponytail. She spoke American English well and idiomatically though she'd never been out of Tálknafjördur. She planned to go to university the following year and eventually to study law. Birna, in a black ski cap pulled down over her ears and platform shoes the size of astronauts' moon boots, seemed less mature and prone to snorts of laughter.

All three girls fished during the summers with their fathers, mostly for cod, off the coastline of the Westfjords. "We go out early in the morning, set the lines and then come back and winch the fish up and cut their throats," said Gudrún matter-of-factly. "It's a summer job for us, we've done it most of our lives. We only fish because our father has a boat. Girls who don't come from fishing families don't go out fishing. So I guess we're lucky; we're able to help our families and save money for ourselves. We have more money than the girls whose families don't have boats. But we wouldn't go on our own; we would never ask a man if we could go out on his boat."

"You wouldn't want a boat yourselves?" I asked. "You wouldn't think of becoming a fisher yourself?"

Gudrún and Birna looked decisive. "No. Our brothers will take over from our fathers. We'll do other things."

Erla, making her way through a large slice of cake, seemed slightly more wistful. "We're not strong enough to fish," she said, and her elder sister confirmed it: "Men have more strength, and strength is needed for fishing."

Tess and I couldn't help glancing at Erla and back at each other. Erla had told us she played basketball and soccer; she was about five foot eight and had shoulders like a linebacker.

Thórunn poured everyone more Fanta Orange and urged more cake on us. "But your aunt—your father's sister," she said to Erla and Gudrún, "she fishes for a living."

Erla perked up. "Yes, she's strong."

Gudrún shook her blond head. "Our aunt wouldn't fish if she wasn't part of the family business," she explained to us. "Our grandfather had eight children and all of them had four to six children, so we're a big part of the population of the village. His company has eight boats. But our aunt usually goes out fishing with her boyfriend," she added. "Some women might fish *before* they get married, but hardly any afterward, when they have children."

Tess coughed slightly. "You know, strength isn't the only thing. When I first started as a carpenter's apprentice, when I was twenty-two, I was surrounded by young men twice as strong as me, who could pick up heavy objects without blinking an eye. Because I was physically smaller and weaker, I had to learn other ways of lifting and carrying. I had to use my head. As the years went on, I saw these guys' backs go out. By the time we were all forty, many of them were on painkillers just to get through the day. Now they were interested in learning ways to lift and carry that didn't put such a strain on their bodies. I found I was no longer physically weaker than most of them."

The girls looked at her solemnly, but perhaps with some skepticism. At sixteen, at eighteen, it's almost impossible to imagine being forty. Besides, fishing wasn't how they imagined spending their adult lives.

When we'd finished with the cake and Fanta Orange, all of us gathered at the apartment's big picture window that looked down over the village and the harbor. The girls lovingly pointed out the different boats pulled up at the wharf; of course they recognized each one.

"That's a good boat. That's *our* boat," said Erla.

It was a mild, sunny day in Stokkseyri, a village of perhaps a couple hundred souls. Tess and I had made our way safely back over the high mountains and across the Breidafjord, a ferry journey of four hours. We'd then driven south, circling around Reykjavík down to Iceland's south coast. The tide was out and jagged volcanic rock stretched far offshore. A reek of sea wrack and bird guano pulsed in the morning sun. A sea wall had been built along the shore and behind it sheltered houses, some covered with stucco and some with rusty galvanized cladding. There was a processing plant that looked permanently closed, and a feeling that the little settlement had seen better days. I asked at the gas station for the house of Thurídur Formadur, and at first the attendant looked quite surprised. He led me outside and pointed down the road.

Although I'd been hearing about Skipper Thurídur ever since I arrived in Iceland, I didn't expect much in the way of a memorial. In fact, I was prepared for a few stones to mark the foundation of her fishing shack. Instead, along the road that ran through the village, we found a tiny, well-tended house that one of Beatrix Potter's characters could have inhabited, constructed of dry-wall volcanic rock with a steeply angled turf roof that fit snugly over the walls. There was a small window set into the wall, and a black-painted door with a high sill. Above the door was a wooden sign with the words carved into it by hand: "Thurídur's Cabin." The door was only about four and a half feet tall; you had to duck to enter. Inside were three beds, one after the next, on each side, with a little ventilating hole in the center of the roof. In olden times, I knew from having visited Gudríd's farm at Glaumbær, Icelanders didn't have tables or chairs, because of the lack of wood. They sat, slept, and even ate meals in their beds. Very frequently two people shared a mattress.

Around the back of the little house was a sod wall, and to the side was a stone bench near a weather-proof plaque with a drawing of Thurídur, wearing a jacket and top hat, carrying a riding whip and looking like a young George Sand. Under the drawing was what seemed to be a short biography and a history

Thurídur's cabin

of fishing off the south coast. My grasp of written Icelandic was improving slightly; I could make out the fact that in 1890 there were forty-six cabins like this in Stokkseyri. This was the only one remaining; it had been refurbished and maintained as both an example of how fisher folk lived in the old days, but also as a monument to Skipper Thurídur.

Sitting outside on the bench, I began to draw a picture of the little house. Out at sea the waves whipped up a froth. You'd have to be a good sailor, not just lucky, to navigate these shores and bring a boat in through these black, knife-sharp reefs. You'd have to have been a good sailor, too, to fish in the Breidafjord, which was no protected narrow inlet, but a great, rough sound.

Could a woman be recognized as a good sailor? "Devillish" is what the Orcadians called Janet Forsyth, while Annie Norn was bewitched. Some of the Irish—not her victims—may have praised Grace O'Malley; the English were more ambivalent: She was called "a woman that hath impudently passed the part of womanhood," but also "a most famous femynyne sea capten." Icelanders seemed far more accepting of their seafaring women.

Of Gunna the Footless who became a boat builder, of Halldóra Ólafsdóttir, who competed against her brothers and would only have women on her crew, of Rósamunda Sigmundsdóttir, well-formed and amazingly strong, who could really haul in the catch, of Gudrún Jónsdóttir, who thrived on rough seas and used to say, "I'll take the rudder, boys," and of Skipper Thurídur, the greatest of them all—of all these women they said, "They're Icelanders, they're ancestors; they are my family."

CHAPTER XVI

SEAWIM

Tjøme, Norway

The romance of the sea, that's what you're suffering from.
You'll have to stop reading all those adventure stories about
the exploits of seawim and stick to books for boys instead.
Then your dreams will be more realistic. No real menwim
want to go to sea.

—Gerd Brantenberg, *Egalia's Daughters*

In 1864 Sven Foyn invented the automatic harpoon gun. He
was a Tønsberg boy, and so it wasn't surprising that much of the
basement floor of the Tønsberg Museum was devoted to the full
arsenal of lethal weapons used to slaughter and process whales.
From primitive spears to stationary harpoon guns with a powerful charge, from flensing knives to old pots used for boiling
the blubber, everything was here except the whale.

I was visiting the museum with Gerd Brantenberg, a
Norwegian writer and old friend, who had a house nearby, on the
island of Tjøme in the Oslofjord. I'd flown to Oslo from Reykjavík,
and had taken the train to Tønsberg, looking forward to some
days of rest at Gerd's house, where I could swim and sail, before
heading up the northern coast on the steamer for my final voyage.

Tønsberg is one of Norway's oldest towns; the famous Oseberg ship, from approximately 820 A.D., was excavated from a Viking burial mound nearby. For over a hundred years Tønsberg was a whaling port as well. In addition to the whaling exhibits (large and lovingly maintained, in contrast to the exhibit at the maritime museum in Oslo, which was modest and discreetly captioned only in Norwegian, in deference to the sensibilities of international visitors), the Tønsberg Museum had a floor called "The Seaman's Life" full of colorful objects collected from the seven seas: carved curios of wood from the Far East, jade from China, ivory from Africa; conches; stuffed parrots, models of Chinese junks; Japanese dolls in kimonos, Kente cloth, balsawood rafts. Even through the glass of the display cases there was a faint tang of market haggle on the timbered wharves of exotic ports.

Gerd's father, a doctor, had shipped out on a whaling expedition to the southern ocean for a season in 1946. The war and the German occupation of Norway had just ended; he left behind a wife and two little girls. The doctor worked on the big ship, "the Cooker." The smaller boats did the hunting and harpooning, and then would bring the whale back to the large ship to be boiled down. "When he came home," Gerd said, "he had a suitcase full of presents. There was flowered cloth from Cape Town, I remember. My mother made the bolt into dresses and we always called them the African dresses." The little girls could hardly believe what he told them about New York. "The lights were on there twenty-four hours. In the middle of the night it was as bright as day."

Gerd's father had a friend who was a radio operator on a tanker. When the girls were growing up, he used to bring them presents from all over the globe. He was her father's age, but he fell in love with Gerd. When she was twenty, he suggested that she go with him on his ship, a Swedish tanker, and help him with his work and see the world. Gerd's father was incensed. "He said, 'The only women who go to sea are whores,'" Gerd told me, leaning against a display of sextants and compasses. "That was enough for me. I slammed the door when I left."

Gerd was onboard for ten days. "There was nothing between us, though he would have liked to have married me. He was a gentleman. We were supposed to go to Venezuela, but at the last minute the orders were countermanded. We did get to Stockholm."

Gerd thought of going to school for a year to become a radio operator, one of the only things that women could do on a ship in the early sixties, but instead she went on to the University of Oslo to study English literature. She was an early and fiery spokeswoman in Scandinavia for women's and gay liberation and published several amusingly didactic books before turning to serious fiction with a series of funny and wrenching semiautobiographical coming-of-age novels. In Norway she's much admired for this trilogy, while elsewhere she's mainly known for her razor-sharp satire of gender roles, *Egalia's Daughters*.

I'd first heard Gerd read from that book at the International Feminist Book Fair in London in 1984. *Egalia's Daughters* is one of those rare feminist titles that hasn't dated, perhaps because its subject is the justification of power, a theme that is always with us. It's set in a mythical land called Egalia, where the wim have all the power and the menwim have very little. The only future that Petronius, the son of the director, Bram, sees before him is curling his beard, wearing a peho (the equivalent of a bra) and finding a wom who will provide for him and bear the children he will raise. There is a breathtaking brazenness to the manner in which the wim explain why they have always had freedom and money and the primary role in society. Their arguments are familiar. Men have used them the world over to justify their oppressive power over women. Reversed, the explanation for why wim are best suited to run the world makes hardly any more sense, but is just as convincing to those who spout it. Within pages we're rooting for Petronius and his young menwim friends to overthrow the strictures that crush their dreams.

I'd reread *Egalia's Daughters* before beginning my journey and was struck, as I hadn't been before, by all the seafaring references. Egalia is an island nation and all the wim go to sea as sailors or fishers. They laugh at the soft young menwim who dream of glory as spearfishers, and when Petronius is reluctantly taken aboard a fishing expedition, the captain, Liz Bareskerry, lectures him, "But you must understand, Petronius, that for a wom, the adventure is a reality. . . . Menwim always think that what wim do is full of sheroism and splendour." The fishing trip ends badly, with the wim getting drunk and fighting over young Petronius, and declaring once they get back on land, "Menwim at sea are nothing but trouble."

"Where did you get the idea for the setting of Egalia?" I asked Gerd, on the drive back to Tjøme from Tønsberg. "Was it the islands and skerries around here?"

"I was probably imagining Copenhagen. I was a teacher in Denmark during the early days of the women's liberation movement there, when I was thinking about all the ideas that eventually went into my book. Copenhagen, Queen of the Sea—you know that song from the film *Hans Christian Andersen* with Danny Kaye? No?" She began to sing it for me:

Wonderful wonderful COP-enhagen
Salty old queen of the sea

A more perfect summer afternoon there could hardly have
been, and few places on earth can be as enchanting as the
southern Norwegian coast in the summer. Construction has
been restrained; the white wooden houses, each with their red,
blue, and white Norwegian flag, cluster above coves of
smoothly sloping granite. The air is crisp and clean, the ever-
greens dark and fragrant. Soaring over the span that connects
Tjøme to the mainland, with a regatta of white sails crossing
the channel below us, with Gerd singing ebulliently, "Salty old
queen of the sea," I should have been very happy. In fact, I was
burdened with the realization that the sore throat I'd woken
with this morning had not gone away, but was an indicator of
something worse to come.

One of Gerd's neighbors recommended a tablet called *Vekk i
Morgen*, "Gone Tomorrow," which supposedly contained raw
milk antibodies from cows nursing their young, but it hadn't
done the trick. As the day went by in Tønsberg I felt increasingly ill. My head was enlarging and my nose swelling and dripping. From time to time I gave a suspicious sneeze. After
months of perfect health I suddenly had a head cold. I could
hardly believe it. Gerd and I had big plans for the next four days.
We were going to swim and take out the rowboat through the
skerries and at some point her old friend Tove would show up in
her yacht and take us out on a sail around the Oslofjord.

I went to bed early, hoping to shake it, but awoke the next
morning feeling as if aliens had pumped my head up to three
times its size as an experiment. Fever made my skin tingle. I
could hardly swallow.

"You don't want to go swimming?" demanded Gerd, whose maternal instinct was faint. "But this is perfect weather. You won't find warmer water than now. And the rowboat—surely you can go out in the rowboat?"

For a person who, as far as I could tell, lived on crispbread, cheese, Marlboros, tea, and beer, Gerd had a remarkable physical robustness. Almost sixty, she was nut-brown with hardly a gray hair, and scrambled over the rocks like a kid. I dragged myself after her to her family's bathing place on some smooth granite boulders above the sea, but there I balked. I spread out my towel and looked at my anemically colored limbs. It had started raining in Seattle the previous November and had poured until the day I left home in May. Whereupon it had been rainy, foggy, windy, and cold two and a half out of every three days all summer. I had an excuse to be pale, but along with my cold, it made me feel subhuman and certainly not briskly, athletically Norwegian.

Eventually Gerd gave up trying to coax me in for a dip. She stripped off her suit and plunged off the rock, swimming vigorously back and forth and shouting out, "You don't know what you're missing!"

Tjøme is the Martha's Vineyard of Norway. It's been a summer residence for the bourgeoisie for several generations and more recently has become the home of choice for the Norwegian superrich. "He's a shipping magnate. He's a millionaire," Gerd would point out tan, round-bellied men in bikini swimwear, negotiating their yachts through the channels off our bathing rock.

Gerd was no millionaire, of course. Her grandfather had made money during prohibition as a pharmacist who had distilled spirits to spare for the thirsty. He had unaccountably bought up a farm and a great deal of property on Tjøme back when it was less known and much cheaper. Sales of this increasingly desirable real estate had kept Gerd and her younger sister in funds for years, which was good, since even a best-selling author in Norway can't quite manage on royalties. Once Gerd just kept the large old farmhouse on Tjøme for summer holidays, but in recent years she'd decided to rent out her flat in Oslo and live full time on Tjøme. She clearly loved the place and relished her family's standing as real estate moguls among the millionaires. Recently she and two other writers had been interviewing people on Tjøme for a collection of oral histories. Gerd had spoken with the queen of Norway, Sonja, who, like Gerd, had grown up spending holidays on the island and who now maintained a summer residence with the king not far from where we were.

As the day ended, all I was hoping was that I could pull myself together sufficiently for the sail around the Oslofjord. When exactly was Tove arriving, anyway?

"With sailing people, you never really know," said Gerd. "The wind and so on. And then, well, Tove has always been very unreliable."

She showed me a photograph of her friend, black-haired and bronzed, with a bright white grin. "She looks like a gypsy, but she grew up very rich, very spoiled. She's been sailing all her life; she's always owned her own boats. She's never married, though she's had a hundred lovers. She's sailed all around the Mediterranean, in Australia. She's crewed in several transatlantic races. The men—the male sailors—are horrible, she says. She has to pick one and stick with him the whole voyage. Otherwise, it's hell."

I was wild to meet Tove. I was set, to the point of childish

eagerness, on the hope of going out into the fjord on a big sail-
boat with an experienced yachtswoman. I wanted to take a close
look at a woman who had sailed across the Atlantic. I yearned to
hoist sail with her in the Oslofjord. In my fevered state I was
sure that my journey in search of seafaring women would be a
complete failure if this did not happen.

"We'll see," said Gerd.

TWO DAYS passed. I could feel the cold gradually migrating
out of my head and into my chest. I carried big wads of toilet
paper from the outhouse, paper that took on a greenish tinge.
Gerd tried to be sympathetic, but I was convinced she thought I
was the dullest guest she'd ever tried to entertain. I sat around
coughing up phlegm and went to bed at nine o'clock in broad
daylight. She did not cook herself or ever eat anything that
resembled a fruit or a vegetable (though she did swill down two
tablespoons of cod liver oil every morning and had her whole
life, which perhaps accounted for her sturdiness), but she took
me shopping for orange juice and soup mix and carrots.

She was eager to show me her island and took me on long
walks where I gradually fell behind. I was weak and feverish,
though I recognized I was in a kind of paradise. The skerries offshore were formed of granite, as was the larger island of Tjøme
itself, but where enough soil had built up in Tjøme's interior to
make meadows and farms possible, the skerries had the arid look
of partly submerged desert isles. All of them had lichen, orange
and blood red, with seaweed at the waterline, but only a few had
scrub oak or a tough, juniper-like thicket growing in their
crevices. Most were bare: pale cool gray in the morning,
becoming golden in late afternoon. The granite outcroppings

on Tjøme were the same bare stone, not quite smooth, more like
nubbled silk; you could clamber and slide over their slippery
salt-and-pepper hides all along the outer shores of the island.
Inland there were corridors of beech and birch, with stream-
trickled meadows opening among the piles of boulders and outcroppings. Wild raspberries grew by the side of the paths, and
finches and nuthatches rustled in the hazels.

"Before the main road came to Tjøme, this is the way the cars
would come," said Gerd, showing me an overgrown lane with a
natural pavement of granite. "When we came up the hill, my
sister and I had to get out so the car would be lighter, and so we
could open the cow gates for my father." The interior of the island
was full of such secret byways and magic groves. It had the old-
fashioned Scandinavian summer magic of a Bergman film, like
Wild Strawberries, a different feel from the beach huts and speed-
boats and huge yachts only a few hundred yards away. "When I
interviewed Queen Sonja, she remembered all these places, too—
the barn where we used to jump down from the hayloft, a swing
that was set among the trees." Perhaps because Gerd had so
recently talked with Sonja, the queen came frequently into conversation. Had socialist Gerd become a monarchist? But then,
most Norwegians *are* ardent monarchists, in their egalitarian way.

All this talk of the queen set me thinking about the two
women whose remains had been found not far from here, at
Oseberg, in a ship grave from the Viking age. One woman was
older and one much younger; no one knows for sure which one
was the queen and which her servant. That at least one of them
was a woman of great importance there is little doubt, for only
the elite of Viking society were buried in ships of such splendor.
Many scholars believe she was Queen Åsa, the grandmother of
Harald Fine-Hair and probably a powerful woman in her own

right, though nothing is now recalled of her life and deeds.

The discovery of the Oseberg ship marked the richest Viking burial mound ever found. With its refined lines and exquisitely carved dragon prow, the ship was preserved for approximately eleven hundred years in a bed of blue clay. Archaeologists were able to rebuild it using ninety percent of the original wood, and it now stands in a specially built museum in Oslo, along with a wealth of intricately carved objects also discovered in the mound—a large bed, an oak chest, a cart with wooden wheels—as well as pots, dishes, and textiles. I had seen the ship in Oslo and an unguarded replica of it outside the Tønsberg Museum.

Ships have long had connotations of death and rebirth in many cultures. The word *ship*, or *skip* in Norwegian, comes from the Old Norse word *skop*, meaning fate. The ship was a symbol of the goddess Frigga; she was connected to the ship-shaped graves of the Norse. The English word *frigate* probably comes from Frigga. Some scholars trace the shape of Norman churches to the Viking burial mounds, which were laid out in the form of a ship. Churches always have a nave, from the Latin *navis*, or "ship," also the origin of the word *naval*. It's curious that our umbilical cords are tied off in a word that conjures the sea.

The ancient Welsh sent their dead back to the waters, and sang dirges known as "Giving-back-to-the-sea Mother." A Norse expression for death was "to return to the mother's womb." There are other etymological associations with the special vessel used for Viking funerals. It was called *ludr*, which meant boat, coffin, and cradle (probably coincidentally, *ludder* in contemporary Norwegian now refers to a whore). This vessel of death and rebirth was a feminine noun, a teasing reminder, perhaps, of why, when so many gendered nouns have gone by the board, sailors cling to calling a ship a *she*. Perhaps it's a crucial recognition that ships are the daughters of the mother, the sea.

GERD AND I reclined on towels most afternoons on the smooth granite outcroppings above the water, which bloomed with pink and violet jellyfish, and periodically Gerd jumped in naked and came out much refreshed and ready for a Marlboro. She rowed off by herself and returned. She told me more stories of her life, and also bits of natural history. She had come to know all the birds coming through the islands, and what the plants were called. The hundreds of islands, holms, and hummocks of the Oslofjord were called a *skjærgård*, or "garden of skerries." Together we waited for Tove, and Gerd pointed out the million-aires. "It's their favorite thing, to cruise around all summer with the wife and kids and visit different islands on the Oslofjord. I've heard the wives don't like it much. They never get to do any-thing, never get to steer, only get to cook and wash up. Some holiday, huh?"

Other than the rowboat and a leaking kayak, Gerd didn't have a ship. She said she'd once wanted very much to learn to sail.

"I was eighteen, living at home in Fredrikstad. A friend and I saw a very inspiring film called *Windjammer*, about a sailing school in Oslo. My friend and I hitchhiked to Oslo to see if we could get on the *Christian Radich*, which was the name of the clipper ship where they taught sailing. We stood on the dock and called up, 'Halloo,' to the bridge. Finally the first mate came to the bridge's little porthole. 'I'm sorry,' he said, 'the school isn't for girls. We can't have girls onboard.'

"'Why not?' we called back up. It was 1959. We stood on the dock, strong, young, and eager.

"There was a silence and then he said, slowly, 'You see, we sleep in *hammocks*.'"

Of such rejections are satiric novels born. But *Egalia's Daughters* is far more than a revenge fantasy, though there is an aspect of "Now see how it feels!" to it. The blustery control of the wim is delicious fun at first (When Bram gives birth, she does it in the birth palace with a full musical chorus urging her on), but becomes oppressive. Why can't the menwim go to sea? Why can't they dream and realize their dreams? There's nothing physical to hold them back, only family expectations and social punishment. When the menwim begin to ask questions, to step out of line and to organize, we cheer them on.

MY LAST afternoon in Tjøme Gerd had to drive to Tønsberg to get her computer fixed, and I elected not to go but to sit on the rocks with a book. I went down to the little beach where the sand was chunky with half-digested rocks and the rubble of shells. The ebb tide had exposed the rounded shapes of boulders in the cove. Those farther out wore rockweed like shiny brown toupees; the tide had turned and was beginning to cover them again. I lay on my stomach on a smoothly polished warm stone close to the shore. In high tide it was submerged, but now the green water only lapped at my toes. I turned my head to the Oslofjord, eye-level with the water. I was still looking for Tove, that salty old queen of the sea, even though Gerd thought it was increasingly unlikely she would arrive before I left for my voyage north.

The smell of salt and sea wrack was strong in the sun. I trailed my hand in the water, which was coming closer, and touched something pleasingly slippery, a length of kelp with air sacs. Some bladderwracks are called sea bottle or sea whistle. This length was like a brown rope with hard bubbles. I explored it with my fingers, trying to squeeze the bubbles to make them pop as I did so often as a child on the sands of the Pacific, but these sacs had thicker walls. How did the air get in them anyway? I tugged at the rope, but it must have been long and attached somewhere I couldn't see. I still had the fuzzyheaded-ness of illness, but the worst of it had subsided as long as I didn't strain myself and start coughing. My nose was stuffed up, but I could smell the sea, and other senses seemed enhanced. The water shimmered and shapes formed on the horizon. Somewhere in the Oslofjord a woman with streaming black hair and bronze skin was standing at the helm of her ship. She could have been Grace O'Malley heading for Clew Bay, a rambling garden of skerries, holms, and hummocks much like this. She could have been Queen Åsa, taking a cruise in the dragon ship that would become her coffin.

I was lying on the rock with my head turned toward the water. The granite was warm beneath me, like the smooth back of a seal, or a stone hill. Gradually I felt lifted, upward. The tide was coming in. I could just stay here, a limpet on the rock, and be washed over, an island that emerged and disappeared with the tides. Or I could float and move with the current. I could drift or paddle right out to sea. The other day Gerd had told me the poetic Norwegian expression for drowning: *Han ble med sjøen*, or simply *Han ble*. "He stayed with the sea. He stayed." I had no intention of drowning, but I liked the idea of being one with salt water, of staying with the sea. The word *sjø*, or "sea," with its soft "sh" beginning, its open vowel, as in *beurre* or *bleu*, was a long drawn-out three letters. It sounded like the tide coming in, going out, the inhalation and exhalation of the vast deep ocean.

CHAPTER XVII

TROUSER-BERET

Drag, Norway

THE DRAG Guesthouse did not look promising. For one thing, it was closed. And for another, it had a sign on the door announcing that a band called Absolut Vodka would be performing tonight, and that they were "guaranteed to play 60% of the evening." I could see through the windows that my prospective room was down a very short corridor off the bar.

I'd traveled up to this hamlet, on one of the octopus-armed fjords of a very convoluted coastline above the Arctic Circle, on perhaps the most quixotic search of my entire four-month journey. I was looking for stories, for any traces at all, of a Sami woman nicknamed Buks-Beret, or Trouser-Beret, who had been the renowned skipper of a fishing boat in the first half of the nineteenth century. If I could find anything out about her, it would be in Drag, or around the Tysfjord, where a sizeable Sami population still lived, and where the Árran Center, a Sami museum and cultural gathering place had recently been erected. Once called Lapps or Laplanders, the Sami had begun to reclaim their language, history and culture in the last thirty years, if not their ancestral land.

Back in Seattle, it had amused me to tell friends I'd be looking for Beret "in Drag," for Beret had received her nickname, of course, for her habit of wearing men's clothing when she went out fishing. Now, as I stood in front of the guesthouse,

marooned so unpicturesquely at the edge of an asphalt parking
lot leading to the small ferry dock, I thought of another, more
unfortunate meaning for *drag*.

To get here, I'd traveled this morning by bus across the
island of Hamarøy, called in tourist literature "Hamsun's
Kingdom." For it was here that an uneducated adolescent Knut
Pedersen began his lengthy transformation from farm boy into
modernist European writer. He took the name Hamsund from
the farm where he worked, and later dropped the *d* to create his
new name. This taking of a farm or place name was common in
a country that abounded in Jon Jonsens and Jens Jenssens. In
Iceland the patronymic system had remained fresh with each
generation, while in Norway it had stultified, so that sometime
in the late 1880s, people began using hereditary names and
women began taking their husband's name. A 1923 law required
everyone in a family to have just one last name, and for that to
be a hereditary name, the father's. The result was an even
greater abundance of Hansens, Olsens, and Nilsens.

But there was an earlier naming pattern that intrigued me,
and this was the custom of adding the farm "address" to the
patronymic, so that a woman who lived on a farm called Vik
might be called Ellen Andersdatter Vik. If she moved to another
farm or place called Holm, she'd be called Ellen Andersdatter
Holm. In this system, as in Iceland, the first name was primary;
the second name gave your ancestry and the last name placed
you.

It might be nice, I'd thought, leaning against the bus
window, taking in a landscape of marsh and stunted white birch,
shallow bays dotted with shore birds, to take the name of a place
as *my* name. Should I call myself Greenwood, after the neighborhood in Seattle where I lived? Barbara Wilson Greenwood?

Did the place you came from have to be a real place, or could it
be imaginary? What about taking a name that was from a language not your own? I'd read about Chinese students in
English-language classes adopting all manner of fanciful
English names, from Magic Johnson to Medusa to Satan.
"Satan" was adopted by a Ms. Zhou, who said she liked the name
for both its sound and its supernatural connotations.

I was Irish, but I was also Swedish. My father's grandparents had left Stockholm with their two young daughters in the
first years of the twentieth century and had ended up on a farm
in Illinois. I never knew my grandmother Gladys, nor did my
father; she died when he was only two. But because I looked so
much like her, I always had a feeling of closeness to her. Why
not take a Scandinavian name? I could call myself something to
do with the sea: *sjö* in Swedish, *sjø* in Norwegian. *Sjo, sheu, shoe,* I
tried out quietly, practicing English pronunciations. It had a
nice sound, but an unfinished one.

I LEFT my backpack leaning against the door of the guesthouse
and walked toward a large wooden tent-shaped building on a
hillside above the ferry parking lot. To my great relief Lars
Børge Myklevoll, the director of the Árran Center, had heard of
my interest in Trouser-Beret and was expecting me. I followed
him downstairs through the museum to his office with more
gratitude than he could probably realize. Although I'd gotten
used to a fair share of blank stares and disavowals of any knowledge on the subject of women and the sea all through my
journey, it had been in Norway and with Norwegians that I'd
felt most snubbed. The curator of the Nordland Museum in
Bodø had said firmly, "A man would rather take a twelve-year-

old boy fishing than a woman. There were no women fishers in
northern Norway. The taboo was too strong against them." I'd
also had email brushoffs from several prominent academics in
Tromsø, one of whom was a specialist in Sami studies. "Of
course I know the story about Buks-Beret," he responded
crisply when I wrote asking for information. "But my impression is that the sea and its activities were man's domain."

A friend in Tromsø had put me on to Buks-Beret in the first
place by sending me an article from the 1970s that mentioned
her briefly in the context of gender-role patterns in northern
Norway. What had intrigued me about the article was its contention that in Sami communities, unlike in rural Norwegian
fishing and farming society, men's and women's roles had been
more egalitarian. Men did the cooking so that the women could
weave, and women often participated in hunting and fishing. It
wasn't usual for a woman to captain a Lofoten fishing boat, but
it was something that *could* happen in the *sjøsame* culture. The
sjøsamer were the Sea Sami, or Sea-Finns as the Norwegians
called them. They were, unlike the Sami who still owned reindeer in the far northern interior of the Scandinavian countries,
mostly assimilated by now.

Lars, whose grandfather was Sami, had trained as an
archaeologist, but he clearly had gotten some exposure to feminist and progressive social anthropology. To my surprise and
delight, he soon began to talk about the taboos and prestige surrounding fishing in the North. "Myths have a function whether
people are aware of it or not. Myths strengthen the roles
between the sexes, and emphasize what is prestigious and what
is not. Taboos keep women in their place. Taboos also disguise
reality. There were men who did not have sons, who took their
daughters fishing. The taboo made it seem as if that was not

Women carrying fish from boats, northern Norway, late 1800s

happening." As for Trouser-Beret, he knew little about her, but was fascinated. "The Native Americans have a tradition of cross-dressing," he said cheerfully. "Berdache acknowledges that not everyone can be confined to gender roles, and that there is a place for a third sex."

Male transgressions against gender roles, Lars reminded me, were actually punished more heavily than female boundary blurring. Men whose wives were ill or dead were permitted to do housekeeping, childcare, and other women's work. But if a man stayed unmarried or chose farm work over the sea, he became a laughingstock, was called an old maid, a weakling, a good-for-nothing who should wear a skirt. Women were less punished by social sanctions and verbal scorn, which only underlines the fact that labor traditionally associated with men has much more prestige, no matter who does it.

Lars and I compared notes on Beret. At the University of

Bergen library I'd tracked down an oversize travel book with engravings of dramatic cliffs and fjords published in 1882, at a time when Norway was drawing tourists the way Alaska does now. The author, traveling by ship up north, mentions the Lapp community of Tysfjord, and a remarkable woman who belonged to that group, twenty or thirty years prior. The author writes that he heard she was the skipper of her own boat, with her husband as first mate, and that she was accustomed to wear men's clothing, hence her name, Buks-Beret, or Trouser-Beret. A later reference in a Norwegian encyclopedia of the 1920s refers to Buks-Beret as "the pride of the Lapps."

I'd also discovered that in the early part of this century a young woman named Inga Bjørnson, the niece of one of Norway's most famous authors, Bjørnstjerne Bjørnson, used to come and stay with her mother's sister and her pastor husband at the parish Evenes, one or two fjords from Drag. Inga, an adventurous girl, became interested in collecting stories about the local Sami people and in 1916 published a small book called *Dundor-Heikka*, or *Tales of the Lapps in Their Own Words*. It was mostly written in dialect and I found it difficult to wade through, but I did find two chapters about an expedition Inga Bjørnson took in search of the descendants of the famous Trouser-Beret. Inga had heard the tales about Beret; she knew she was a boat captain who rowed to the Lofoten fishing. "It wasn't difficult for Beret to find a crew to go with her," she wrote, "because she was so lucky with the sea. She could make the waves go quiet." After much searching, Inga tracked down the granddaughter of Beret, who told her many stories: how good-looking and strong Beret was, how she rode a white horse, how in addition to being a captain, she was also a peddler, a midwife, a butcher, and a shooter of bears. "She was better than a man," said Beret's granddaughter, adding that Beret lived in a loving relationship with her husband and six children.

"I have good news for you," said Lars, after we'd been talking hard for an hour or two. "I discovered that the great-great-grandniece of Beret lives just across the fjord, in Kjøpsvik. Her name is Hilgunn Pedersen and she's the town's local historian. I called her and told her about you, and she said that if you wanted to come over to Kjøpsvik, she'd tell you all she knows about Buks-Beret. And if you want, she'll take you to the place Beret lived."

I immediately agreed. Not only was I delighted by the chance to talk to a relative of Beret, but leaving Drag also meant I wouldn't have to listen to Absolut Vodka for sixty percent of the evening.

"WELL, THE first thing to understand is that Buks-Beret didn't live on the Tysfjord at all," said Hilgunn Pedersen. "She lived on the Efjord and that's where my father and his father were born, and I was born there, too." To many of us, one fjord above the Arctic Circle may be just like another, but to a historian with Hilgunn's love of facts, not to mention family pride, such a mistake was grave. That Trouser-Beret had been claimed by the Tysfjord Sami had opened the way for other serious errors about the legendary character to creep in, for instance, that Beret's husband went fishing with her, as her first mate.

"He never went to sea," said Hilgunn. "He was from inland Sweden, a carpenter who learned to be a boat builder. He wasn't used to the sea. Besides, he had to stay home and take care of the children while she was out fishing for months at a time."

We were sitting around a low table in Hilgunn's living

room, with a pot of coffee, papers, and books spread out before us. Sven, Hilgunn's housemate, eighty years old, leathery brown, and silent, sat watching TV in a recliner nearby. On the way from the ferry Hilgunn had managed to tell me some of their story. Sven and Hilgunn's late husband had worked together in the cement factory nearby. Sven had nursed his ailing wife for six years; after she'd died, he started to help Hilgunn nurse her bedridden husband, who was ill for eleven years. Now Hilgunn and Sven lived together, and were planning to move this fall to the Canary Islands.

Books on learning Spanish lay here and there around the room, and a computer sat in the midst of piles of genealogical records and papers. Hilgunn was in her sixties, blond and lively, with wide cheekbones and curious eyes. Hilgunn's grandfather was full Sami; she hadn't realized she had Sami blood until she eventually went to school. It wasn't, in the fifties in Norway, something of which to be particularly proud. Now Hilgunn is the unofficial local historian and genealogist, who knows an enormous amount about how the Sami lived and who was related to whom. Like Thorúnn Magnúsdóttir in Iceland, she based her research on old tax and property records, the bound volumes of marriages and christenings. She'd become a pro at reading wavery old script, which is how Lars Børge Myklevoll at the Árran Center had first come to know her.

"People just repeat the same old stories. If they bothered to look, they'd easily find out the truth. The records are there. People just don't want to do the research," she complained good-naturedly.

She spoke English very well, and I was glad, for the stream of history pouring out would have been a chore to get down fast enough while translating from Norwegian to my language.

Although I'd learned Norwegian in my twenties and could read it well, it always took some time to get up to speed when I visited the country.

According to Hilgunn, Trouser-Beret was born Beret Johanna Paulsdatter in 1794 in Kvæfjord, not far from Harstad. Her father was a nomad reindeer herder, who had followed the traditional yearly migration of the reindeer over the mountains from Sweden to the fjords and islands of Norway and back again. At some point, he decided to stay in Norway and raise his family there. Beret came to the Efjord with Peder Thomassen in 1824, and she died there in 1868. She had seven children (one died very young).

Every winter she went fishing with a Sami crew, and apparently everyone was eager to row with her, for it seemed she was able to quell the waves with a look. They said she was the most capable in the whole fjord and gave orders in a way that they all felt scared of her, with one hand on the tiller and the other on an oar, rowing backward. She wore a full suit of skins. When she traveled as a peddler, she wore Sami dress and mounted a white horse. She helped at many births, both animal and human. She owned a mill for grinding as well. "She was said to be clean and reliable, and to always keep her word. *What she said was akin to Amen,*" Hilgunn finished up.

"There were other women who fished around her, who supported themselves by fishing," Hilgunn added. "I've run across them in the records. There was another one they called a Buks-Beret around here. She was Birgit Pedersen, a widow with a daughter. It was a derogatory name of course; all around the north of Norway, if a girl got out of line, was too tomboyish, that's what they called her: Trouser-Beret. I was called that myself. But let's go out for a drive; we'll look at where Birgit Pedersen lived."

It was about eight at night, still full daylight, but with the look of light filtered through ice cubes. The granite mountains around us slipped iron toes into the blue-gray fjord waters, and everything shivered. The landscape was alive. Hilgunn knew the history, and the geology, and the culture of the Sami, how they spent the winters in the outer fjords and summers at the fjord bottoms. They didn't have a concept of owning land, and for a long time coexisted with the Norwegians without sharing their values. The Sami continued to dress as before, to speak Sami and to make by hand many of their possessions. Because of their nomadism, the Sami were often doubly taxed, by the Norwegians and the Swedish governments. The earliest written reference to the Sea Sami is from 1584. It's an account of driving off a Swedish tax collector. Their nomadic life didn't fit with the tightening of the borders and with the eventual divisions of the North into separate countries. The reasons for suppressing the language and culture of the Sami came to be ideological, but for centuries the two peoples, Scandinavians and Sami, had lived side by side.

Hilgunn had me in the front seat; she spoke nonstop. Sven sat in back, preoccupied with his own thoughts. He hadn't said a word since I'd met him more than three hours earlier. The landscape was pearl gray and pewter blue in the lingering twilight. The white of the stunted birches was unearthly. Without sunshine, the North is dreamy, refrigerated, ancient. We stopped at a small bay where Birgit Pedersen had lived and fished with her daughter Benedikte. "Of course there were women fishing all along the coast," said Hilgunn as we got out of the car and looked across to the house where the women had lived. "They're in the tax records. If you were a widow—and many women were—you had to live somehow. There were

other women who lived alone, or never married, or who fished
with their husbands."

We got back into the car, Sven still inscrutable. He had a
large, beautiful hooked nose that, with his very brown skin,
wrinkled yet also drawn tight over his face, made him look like
an American Indian. I said to Hilgunn, "You said you fished as a
girl. Who taught you?"

"Taught me?" she laughed. "I remember fishing at five
years old. It was one of my first memories, how I managed to
catch a fish, but it was too heavy for me to get in the boat; my
father had to help. I was going out in a boat by myself and with
my younger brother by the time I was ten. Sometimes we
would go long distances. My father went to the Lofoten fishing
in the winter. When I was fifteen my father asked me to go with
him to Lofoten. We went for two weeks, then came home, then
went out again. This was 1951. There were no other girls on
boats. In the evening men from other boats would come by to
look at the man who brought the girl fishing. I was a Buks-
Beret. My biggest problem aside from the hard work—we had
to haul the long lines of cod up by hand in those days—was
peeing. There was just a bucket. Usually I waited till night.
Luckily it got dark early. I envied Buks-Beret's *tissehornet*, her
peeing horn. I used to hear that it had stayed in the family, but I
don't know who has it."

For this is also part of the Trouser-Beret legend, that Beret
had a reindeer horn with a hole at one end attached to her belt,
and when she felt nature's call on the boat, she would use it.

Back in Kjøpsvik, Hilgunn prepared sandwiches and we
watched the news. There was a long story about an eighty-five-
year-old man in Oslo who'd fought off a burglar. They interviewed the fellow from his hospital bed. "I told the boy who

attacked me that only one of us was getting away alive. That scared him. He didn't think I had it in me."

Sven watched contentedly.

I spent the night in a pension a few blocks away from Hilgunn's house, and the next morning set out with Hilgunn and Sven to the Efjord, where Hilgunn had been born and where Beret had built a house.

Hilgunn turned out to be an amateur geologist as well, whose rock collection was now on display at the Kjøpsvik community center. The area around the Tysfjord is a kind of chalk, she told me, which means this region was once covered by a shallow sea. They're still finding fossils of fish and birds in the mountains. When we'd stop the car for a look and I'd pick up a piece of rock, Hilgunn would often say, this is malachite, or quartz, or there's copper in this, too. The mountains didn't look to me like chalk, but they were, ancient and full of caves. In some of the caves researchers had found strange undersea fish skeletons; in other caves archaeologists discovered rock drawings from thousands of years ago.

Since we'd begun our journey, Hilgunn had mentioned the dates when this tunnel was built, when that road was completed. Some were as recent as the last five or ten years. "Before the roads," she said, "we traveled by boat. That was in my lifetime. Just imagine how people lived until fifty years ago." Desolate as it looked, this landscape was deeply inhabited, though it took a guide to help me see it. Hilgunn was always pointing to a cleft in the rock and naming it, or telling me that here was the pass through which the Sami herded their reindeer. The landscape, too—bogs, rock with heather and moss, waterfalls, coastal pine (some of the trees were short but five hundred years old), birch forests—was mysterious, nonhuman, crystallized into quartz.

We passed through a long tunnel and came out on the other side to the Efjord. The mountains in the distance were black, jagged, forbidding. This mountain chain between Norway and Sweden is called "the Keel" for it resembles the keel of a ship. The Sami had been famous for their shipbuilding craft; some say it was the Sami who built the longships that took the Vikings all over the world. Throughout the Tysford region, the Sami lived by boatbuilding from the Middle Ages to the eighteenth century, says A.W. Brøgger in *Viking Ships*, and the origins of their skill with boats goes back even farther. Old illustrations showed the Sami sewing their boats together with sinew, not hammering nails into them. Rock carvings from the Bronze Age suggest that the ancestors of the Sami had a boat culture; the boats depicted had ribs of wood and were skin-covered, usually with sealskin.

These boats carved on rock looked very much like the Inuit *umiak*, or "the woman's boat." It was not a kayak, which is found mainly in the North American Arctic, but a large open boat. The Arctic explorer Fridtjof Nansen wrote, "By Europeans it was named the woman's boat because in contrast to the kayak, it was rowed almost exclusively by women." The *umiak* is found over the whole Arctic, from Siberia to Greenland. Most common in the north of Norway was the Nordland boat, Hilgunn told me, as we began driving along the Efjord. That would have been the sort of boat Peder Thomassen, Beret's husband, built. The Nordland boat, clinker-built and single-masted, has remained essentially unchanged in design since Viking days. It once came in eight different sizes to accommodate everything from inshore fishing to coastal trading voyages. Smallest was the *faering* or

At the Theater in Oxon 1674.

Sami sewing boat with sinew

kjeks, probably from the Sami word *kjaex*, meaning "woman"—
that is, a boat handled by a woman. Most traditional for Lofoten
fishing was the *åttring* or *fembøring*. Trouser-Beret had a *fembøring*. Because people often rented rather than owned land, the
boat was the main piece of property to be purchased and passed
down. Salten and Tysfjord supplied the whole of Lofoten with
boats. The Sami who lived by the fjords had to pay a tithe of a
boat to the sheriff every year.

"That's where she took her boat out," said Hilgunn,
pointing across the fjord. "There, do you see? By that waterfall.
She had her mill there. The house was farther in, much farther,
by a lake called Dypvann. After she got the boat out, she had to
walk at least five kilometers, perhaps more, to the house."

There's a story that in the winter of 1832 Beret decided to
leave Lofoten before the fishing was over. Her crew protested;
they were doing so well that year. The fish were plentiful, and
the prices were good. Their protest didn't matter a bit; as
skipper, Trouser-Beret made the decisions. They set sail for
home a full month before the fishing was over. Early the
morning of March 22, they arrived in full sail here in the Efjord,

and she steered the boat right over to the spot Hilgunn pointed out. The moment the boat touched shore, she hopped out and told the crew to deal with the boat and the gear. She was late for something, she said, and hurried up past the waterfall to her home.

Inside she lit a fire in the hearth, boiled herself up some coffee. She took out her pipe and tobacco. There was time for a well-deserved smoke. Afterward she went into the bedroom and gave birth to her fifth child.

In Lofoten, Beret and her crew, like the other Sami, wouldn't have been welcome in the fishermen's cabins, Hilgunn told me as we drove on, Sven still silent as a clam in the back. They would have lived in tents they erected themselves. But here on the Efjord, she and her husband had a boat shed, a mill, and a house inland. Beret earned the money for the lumber from her fishing and Peder built them. "Her house burned down," said Hilgunn. "She had to build another. Oh, it was a sad story. First a man came to their farm with a weapon. Her young son Paul took hold of it. He had never seen a gun before. He looked into the barrel and somehow hit the trigger. The shot went right through his head. There were long days afterward when Beret just stayed in bed. Then the house burned down. The family just stood there, robbed of everything. Then, too, Beret lay down for eight days and refused to get up. But she had the courage to start again. The winter after those misfortunes she went fishing again in Lofoten. She made good money and with it bought material for a new house, so she and her family could move in before the next winter set in. They built the mill then, too."

We passed by a waterfall roaring down toward the fjord. This landscape made me shiver; it was alive in the way that Iceland had been alive, filled with names and memories, and something older than that, the skeletons of the nomads, the skeletons of fish and reptiles from a time when all had been tropical and warm. Now we were climbing; surely it was more than five kilometers that Trouser-Beret had to walk from the fjord to her lakeside home. But then, of course, she'd had her white horse. I pictured her in her colorful blue Sami tunic, with wadmal or skin trousers.

The sun was coming out and the landscape was transformed from harsh to bright. The lake had no firm shore; it was marshy at the edges, tea-dark, almost black in the middle, with white birches all around. I put my hand in my pocket, felt the sharp mineral edges of the rocks I'd picked up.

There were no traces now of their house, rebuilt with such courage after the fire. Dypvann meant "deep water," and it had been called that in Beret's time as well. Hilgunn remarked conversationally as we drove past, "Her husband took that name after a while. He was Peder Thomassen Dypvann. They were all Dypvann."

"Beret was Dypvann, too?"

"Yes."

"So then she had three names. She was Beret Paulsdatter. And Buks-Beret. And Beret Dypvann. Dypvann," I mused. "What a beautiful name. That's a name I wouldn't mind having. Could I take it, do you think?"

Hilgunn glanced at me a little strangely and rebuked me, as the historian she was, "You can't take the name of a place you don't live."

We drove a little farther, slowly, peering through the trees. Hilgunn had a zest for life that I envied, and more than that, a vocabulary, a deep remembering. I would like to know the names of all the rocks, all the lakes, all the trees. I would like to be from a place as fully as she was. Southern California, where I'd grown up, was buried under a million tons of concrete and asphalt. Greenwood in Seattle referred to a thick dark forest that had been cut down a hundred years before I moved there. In America it was hard to be from a place that wasn't constantly changing. Then Hilgunn said, "But you know, Beret had a fourth name; it was her real name that no one knows. I mean, it was her Sami name. People weren't allowed to write down their Sami names on the church registers, so they've been forgotten."

I didn't say anything to this, but I took it in. The sun struck the black water and the white birches. It didn't matter where I was from; I was here now. I could name myself. I could choose whatever name I wanted, whatever address I needed to call home.

CHAPTER XVIII

STATUE OF A WOMAN
STARING OUT TO SEA

Norwegian Coastal Voyage

THEY CALL it the Lofoten Wall, this island chain that seems to
rise up sheer and black out of the Norwegian Sea, frosted with
white in winter, emerald green in summer, jagged-spined as a
prehistoric beast. Our ship, the coastal steamer *Lofoten*, had
made the crossing from Bodø, a town just above the Arctic
Circle on the Norwegian coast. We were now approaching the
town of Svolvær at about seven on a cloudy violet evening shot
with gold. At the end of a rocky causeway in the harbor, high on
a pillar, stood a bronze statue of a woman, waving. Her long
skirt blew in the sculptor's breeze; she had a kerchief on her
head and a shawl around her shoulders.

I'd seen other statues like this on my voyages north, sometimes at the site of a terrible fishing disaster, where many men
lost their lives. There's a mammoth granite figure of a woman
at Gloup on the island of Yell in Shetland, recalling a terrible
summer storm in 1881 that swept away six fishing boats with
fifty-eight men. In the Faroes, at Gjógv, where two boats capsized in the surf in 1870 and seventeen men were lost, a monument portrays a cluster of three, a mother with her two children
clinging to her skirts. In Ålesund, Norway, a woman shading
her eyes and staring seaward perches on the edge of the harbor,
while farther north, in Rørvik's town square, looms a bereaved-
looking woman with her arms crossed below her chest, and a

Alfhild the Viking princess

small boy beside her. Invariably, the statues were called "The Fisherman's Wife" or "Waiting."

"This is the Fisherman's Wife," said a new acquaintance, Maggie, who'd joined me on deck with her friend Helen. "I read about it in the guidebook. She's supposed to be waving to the husband who's gone off fishing and might not come back."

"Oh, that's sad then," said Helen. "I thought she was waving hello to us!"

Maggie grumbled, "As if a busy woman would have time to stand around waving to some guy in a boat. She was probably milking the cows at home. Where's the statue of the woman milking the cows?"

"Where's the statue of the Viking woman warrior ready to go off pirating and raiding?" I asked.

"I know there were Vikings up here," said Helen, looking puzzled. "But the women didn't go to sea, did they?"

❂   ❂   ❂

Twelve centuries ago, long before Grace O'Malley commanded a fleet of pirate galleys that struck fear into the hearts
of the Galway merchants and put the English to flight, another
woman raider and warrior roved the northern seas in search of
loot and a good fight. She was the Viking princess Alfhild, and
her deeds, true or not, come down to us through the work of the
medieval historian Saxo Grammaticus, whose early-thirteenth-
century *History of the Danes* mixes genealogy, saga, and myth.
Fascinated with the heroic pagan past, this Christian scholar
knew enough to disapprove of the women warriors whose stories he told—still, he told them with relish. Some three hundred
years later another chronicler, the exiled Swedish bishop Olaus
Magnus, was also to write about Alfhild (or Alvild, as he called
her) in a chapter entitled "On Piracy by Noble Maidens," in his
comprehensive work, *A Description of the Northern Peoples*, first
published in 1555.

According to Saxo, Alfhild wasn't the only woman, like the
Irish pirate queen, to have "impudently passed the part of womanhood and been a great spoiler and chief commander and
director of thieves and murderers at sea." In fact, he recounts:

> There were once women among the Danes who dressed
> themselves to look like men, and devoted almost every
> instant of their lives to the pursuit of war, that they might
> not suffer their valor to be unstrung or dulled by the infec-
> tion of luxury. For they abhorred all dainty living, and used
> to harden their minds and bodies with toil and endurance.
> They put away all the softness and lightmindedness of
> women, and inured their womanish spirit to masculine

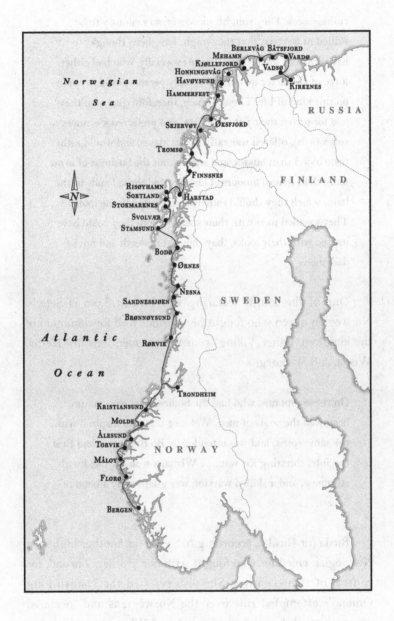

Steamer route up the Norwegian coast

ruthlessness. They sought, moreover, so zealously to be skilled in warfare, that they might have been thought to have unsexed themselves. Those especially, who had either force of character or tall and comely persons, used to enter on this kind of life. These women, therefore (just as if they had forgotten their natural estate, and preferred sternness to soft words), offered war rather than kisses, and would rather taste blood than busses, and went about the business of arms more than that of amours. They devoted those hands to the lance which they should rather have applied to the loom. They assailed men with their spears whom they could have melted with their looks, they thought of death and not of dalliance.

One of the tough seafaring warriors in Saxo is Sela, a Norwegian queen who fought her brother Koll for dominion of the kingdom. Other Viking women Saxo mentions are Hetha, Wisna, and Webiorg:

> On these captains, who had the bodies of women, nature bestowed the souls of men. Webiorg was also inspired with the same spirit, and was attended by Bo Bramason and Brat the Jute, thirsting for war. . . . Wisna, a woman, filled with sternness, and a skilled warrior, was guarded by a band of Sclavs. . . .

Rusla (or Rusila), according to Saxo, was another highborn Norwegian chieftain who fought with her brother, Thrond, for control of their country. She also resisted the Danish king Omund's attempted rule over the Norwegians and "declared war against all the subjects of the Dane." When Omund tried to suppress the rising, Rusla not only conquered them but also, "waxing haughty on her triumph," decided to tackle the sovereignty of Denmark. In this she failed, leaving the battlefield with "only" thirty of her ships. Obviously vexed, she met Thrond on her retreat and stripped him of his army. King Omund continued to pursue her, however, and eventually sent a great fleet to drive her from her kingdom in Norway.

> The king pursued her hotly, caught up with her fleet on the
> sea, and utterly destroyed it, the enemy suffered mightily,
> and he won a bloodless victory and splendid spoils. But
> Rusla escaped with a very few ships, and rowed ploughing
> the waves furiously; but, while she was avoiding the Danes,
> she met her brother and was killed.

The tale of Rusla and her many battles, as well as the even more compelling story of Alfhild was on my mind as I stood at the railing of the *Lofoten*, watching the turf-covered granite slopes behind Svolvær turn from dull olive to blazing emerald and back again, as the sun flashed in and out through clouds. For this was Viking country—*vik* means "bay" in Norwegian and is one of the possible origins of the name for the warriors who came out of the North to pillage, rape, and destroy, as well as to trade and colonize. Everyone knows that the Vikings terrorized the hapless Irish and Anglo-Saxons, but in fact there was also tremendous conflict among the different Nordic groups for dominance of the Baltic, North Sea, and Norwegian coastline. Most battles took place in the disputed passages of the Baltic and the fjords around southern Norway and Denmark, but there had been Vikings as far north as the Lofoten Islands. On the other side of Svolvær's peaks at Borg

was an archaeological site and reconstruction of a Viking chieftain's longhouse.

I tried to imagine a fleet of a hundred Viking longships with
dragon prows, massing for battle here in the Lofotens, with a
tall, keen-eyed woman in command. She would be wearing a
woven tunic, dyed blue, and a fur cloak around her shoulders.
Her hair would be pulled into a braid, her strong-jawed face
streaked with salt and sweat. Around her neck a torque of gold;
coiling up her muscular bare arms bronze bracelets in the shape
of snakes, and armbands wide as shackles. Nothing can give a
better sense of the robustness and splendor of Viking women
than to see (behind glass in museum cases) their heavy, barbaric
jewelry. Nothing, perhaps, except the size of their ships. For the
ships that Rusla and Sela and Alfhild would have commanded
were not the cargo-heavy *knarrs* that Aud the Deep-Minded or
Freydís Eiríksdóttir had sailed when they crossed the Atlantic
from the Faroes to Iceland or from Greenland to Vínland, but
sleek and deadly longships. These were to the *knarr* as the
Concorde is to the Conestoga wagon.

The longship was a flexible marvel of engineering, whose
axe-hewn, thin oaken planks overlapped clinker-fashion and
were riveted with iron. It could carry from sixty to as many as
one hundred oarsmen. With a stylized dragon or serpent
lunging high up the prow, round painted shields turned outward along the sides, and a massive square sail, often striped or
dyed bright colors, this was the fleet's war machine whose
dreadful shadow on the horizon caused Alcuin of York to write,
after the Vikings had attacked the holy island of Lindisfarne in
793, "Never before has such terror appeared in Britain as we
have now suffered from a pagan race, nor was it thought that
such an inroad from the sea could be made."

The struggles between Koll and Sela and between Thrond and Rusla were family affairs to begin with, and seem to show that women of that time felt they had as much right to power as their brothers. Then there were women like Alfhild, who took to pirating and war, not from a desire to claim or extend territory, but purely, it seems, for the adventure of it.

According to Saxo, Alfhild, the daughter of a lesser Danish king, Siward, was guarded jealously since birth in order that she could be awarded to a hero worthy of her—that is, someone who best suited a political alliance. In this case it was Alf, the son of Sigar, the ruler of most of mid-ninth-century Denmark. Alf stood up to the viper and snake that Alfhild's father had placed in his daughter's chambers to deter prospective suitors, but he was no match for Alfhild's indifference.

Instead of falling happily into the prince's arms, Alfhild showed a strange desire to dress as a male warrior and go off to enjoy for herself the pleasures and financial rewards of looting and battle. As Olaus Magnus writes: "Her determination to stay chaste was so steadfast that she began to reject all men and firmly resolved with herself never to have intercourse with any, but from then on to equal, or even to surpass, male courage in the practice of piracy." She must not have been the only maiden to have chafed at the restrictions of a woman's lot and to have "preferred a life of valour to one of ease," for she "enrolled in her fighting company many young women of the same inclination."

Both Saxo and Olaus Magnus give her a ship and a crew by accident. "She happened to arrive at a place where a band of sea-robbers were lamenting the death of their leader, who had been lost in war," writes Olaus Magnus. "Because of her beauty and spirit she was elected as pirate chief by these fellows and performed feats beyond a normal woman's courage."

What exactly these feats were, or whether she confined herself to plundering innocent trading vessels in the Baltic or, with her oarsmen and women, raided the monasteries and towns of England like other Danish Vikings, we'll never know. Alfhild seems to have kept the attention, however, of the Danish king and his son Alf, who "undertook many voyages in her pursuit." Like Lord Deputy Henry Sidney and Lord Justice Drury, whose dispatches from Ireland to Elizabeth's court plainly illustrate their mingled irritation with and admiration for Grace O'Malley, both Saxo and Olaus Magnus seem conflicted, praising the valor of Alfhild and her female crew as well as other pirate maidens, while retelling the stories in ways that emphasize their eventual defeat by death or subjugation.

Unlike Sela and Rusla, whose punishment was death, Alfhild had a different fate. She and her followers were pursued into a harbor, up the narrow fjord of Hangö in Finland, by the determined Alf. It's not clear whether either Alf or Alfhild knew their opponent's identity. Seeing unfamiliar vessels making for the harbor, however, Alfhild didn't wait to be attacked, but ordered her longships (for by now she had a fleet) out to meet the enemy head-on.

Olaus Magnus describes the battle thus:

> They began the sea-fight and sustained it on either side
> with high regard for their fame and courage. Then came
> the lucky moment the young man had been waiting for
> when he leapt onto Alvild's bows and, surrounded by sol-
> diers who were fresher and more numerous, forced his way
> right up to the stern, slaughtering all who withstood him.
> Borkar, his companion, struck off Alvild's helmet and, as
> soon as he saw the delicacy of her countenance, realized

Alfhild battles Prince Alf

that they should be going to work with kisses, not with weapons; they should lay aside their hard spears and handle their foe with more persuasive attentions. Alf was overjoyed when, beyond all hope, he had presented to him the girl he had sought indefatigably over land and sea despite so many perilous obstacles. He seized her passionately and straight away had her adorned with the most elegant and feminine clothing. Following the praiseworthy custom of his forbears, he married her and afterwards had by her a daughter, Gurith.

From Olaus Magnus's point of view, this is a very successful conclusion. For those of us thirsting for tales of women's valor on the water, for stories of sea fights sustained with "high regard for fame and courage," the ending is disappointing. What happened to Alfhild? What happened to Webiorg and her supporter, Brat the Jute? Were such women, who thought of "death instead of dalliance," so easily trounced?

◉   ◉   ◉

MAGGIE AND Helen and I were on day three of the
Norwegian coastal voyage, which travels up the Norwegian
coast from Bergen around the North Cape to the border with
Russia and then back again. They were doing the whole eleven-
day round trip. I was getting off in the Lofoten Islands, then
continuing on to Tromsø for a week, before beginning a series
of flights that would take me back to Seattle. It was late August
by now, and the shortening days made me think of home, even
as I longed to be at sea forever.

I'd met Maggie the morning of the first day out, when we
were sailing toward Ålesund. In her mid-fifties, plump and asth-
matic, wearing a large flowered blouse over several turtlenecks,
and a thickly crocheted blue cap on her head, she was a junior
high school teacher from a small town outside Sacramento.
Within twenty minutes I knew how much Maggie's house cost,
when she bought it, what it sold for last year, what her two
children did, and what they earned. This was her fifth trip on
the coastal steamer. She'd first traveled up to the North Cape
the summer of 1973; she'd even been on the *Kong Olav*.

"I was on the *Kong Olav* then, too!" I said. "I was a dishwasher."

It turned out Maggie had taken her trip in May, before I'd
started my job, but even if we'd been on the ship at the same
time, we probably wouldn't have met. "Just think, you could
have washed my dishes," she said, punching my arm in a friendly
way.

In the years since Maggie and I had made that first trip, the
ships of the line—*Hurtigruten* it's called in Norwegian—have
gotten larger. The *Kong Olav* was retired some years ago and
sold to Thailand; its sister ships, the *Lofoten* and the *Harald Jarl*,
were destined for a similar fate soon. These older ships were

being replaced by vessels with dance floors and panorama lounges, vessels that could compete with the massive cruise ships that plied Norway's scenic fjords.

No doubt about it, the *Lofoten*, especially after traveling on big car ferries like the *St. Sunniva* and the *Norröna*, seemed tiny and cramped, low in the water, an Alice in Wonderland change of scale. The doors opened heavily; the stairs were narrow, the corridors crowded. No lightweight materials here, but cast iron, many times painted, so that there was a thick skin of white, green, and black over every part of the ship. The wooden railings had been much lacquered; they had a skin of shellac, worn thin in places.

Still, like many passengers, I was attached to the old ships for their ambiance, and I especially loved the *Lofoten* for the memories it brought of my summer working on the *Kong Olav*, an experience that, like many during a hand-to-mouth, unstable period of wanderlust in my early twenties, seemed now both remarkably interesting and even amusing. Then, I'd been bitter about my low standing onboard, and wracked with anxiety about what to do at the end of the summer. I had been lonely at times and bone-tired from the long hours. But on this voyage, as a passenger, I'd found myself haunting the areas where the crew draped themselves over the railings to enjoy a smoke. I peeped into the kitchen, caught a glimpse of the cooks' and dishwashers' mess. The same jar of pickled beets seemed to be still sitting on the table amid overflowing ashtrays.

No cruise ship could ever replicate the feel of one of the coastal steamers, for the line had a long history in Norway. Inaugurated in 1893, at a time when the country didn't have railways or highways in the north, the coastal steamer connected towns and villages from Bergen to Kirkenes, bringing news, cargo, and passengers. News came no longer, but the daily ships, one steaming north and the other south, were still an event in some places, where small children might still wave as we came into or out of port. I found I was still fascinated, as I had been on the *Kong Olav* and during my childhood visiting the Port of Long Beach, to see the cargo being loaded and unloaded. Frozen fish came onboard; boxes of grapefruit and bananas and car parts were taken off. Occasionally a car swung on or off the top deck of the ship. The *Lofoten*, like the *Kong Olav*, could only fit four cars aboard at a time.

In Maggie, for all the ways we were different, I'd found a similar appreciation of the *Hurtigruten*. "There's nothing I'd rather do on vacation," she said, "than be on one of these ships and at sea. A cruise ship, no thank you. On a ship like this, it doesn't matter who you are, if you're alone, whether you're young and fit. The coastal steamer has a purpose—and you're part of it."

She and Helen had joined forces early on. A teacher from New Zealand, Helen was in her late twenties, attractive but shy, with beseeching blue eyes. Her mouth wore a practiced and brave don't-worry-about-me expression, but even her shoulders looked rejected. I'd seen her wandering around the ship the first evening, and she'd looked melancholy among the younger couples and out of place among the retirees. Maggie told me later that Helen's fiancé had dumped her in London, where they'd been staying with his brother. "And so she just decided, on the spur of the moment, to go to the North Cape by sea. I told her, 'To hell with him! This is the trip of a lifetime!'" Maggie chuckled, wheezing, "Does this mean I've had five lifetimes?"

The sun broke through, decisively, and cast a radiant gleam over the bronze "Fisherman's Wife" as we slipped past. She continued waving, not to us, but to the imaginary man fading out of sight. The verse of the skaldic poets in old Norway and Iceland often assumes a woman standing on shore, admiring the man setting off to sea. The skalds were employed, often by the courts of the kings and nobles of the Norse realm, to celebrate the battle victories of the ruler on land and at sea. One of them wrote:

> The prince's band can pull
> their oars straight out of the sea.
> The widow looks and admires
> the wondrous flight of the oars.
> Madam, there'll be much rowing
> till the tarred sea-tools fall apart.

Some Viking scholars, such as Judith Jesch, dismiss the story of Alfhild and other women warriors as male fictions based on stories of Amazons that date back to the ancient Greeks. Jesch suggests that these warriors (sometimes called Valkyries after the Norse god Odin's handmaidens who conducted slain heroes to Valhalla) were setups; after all, in the tales of Saxo and Olaus Magnus they invariably lose the battle and the kingdom in the end. Other historians are more sanguine. If the names of male nobles in Saxo correspond to other historical genealogies, why shouldn't Alfhild, Rusla, and Sela have existed?

Folklore that can't be proved or disproved presents a conundrum. I want to believe that parts of Alfhild's story might be true, that she turned pirate and performed "feats beyond a normal woman's courage." But I'm skeptical that she embraced Alf as robustly as he apparently embraced her. Her reaction to him isn't noted, and if the word "passionately" is removed from the sentence, "He seized her passionately and straight away had her adorned with the most elegant and feminine clothing," it might well sound more coercive than romantic.

In a corner of the Viking Ship Museum in Roskilde, Denmark, a former Norse stronghold and trading town near Copenhagen, are a mirror, some photographs and a row of pegs on which hang Viking clothing, men's and women's, in three sizes. For the girls and women there are a long white under-dress with full sleeves, a blue overdress, an apron gathered up at the shoulders and pinned with bronze oval brooches, and a long, fur-trimmed mustard-colored cloak. For the boys and men there are tunics and leggings and a short cloak edged with fur, secured at the shoulder with a stickpin. Just in case you should get any wrong ideas about which costume is appropriate for your gender, there are three pairs of photographs—boy and girl children, teens, and adults—to guide you.

But wearing male attire at sea, as Grace O'Malley, Trouser-Beret, and Skipper Thurídur could have explained, was more a matter of practicality than defiance. When Alfhild's warrior tunic and leggings, cloak, and helmet were stripped from her and she was once again "adorned" in dress and apron, it wasn't just a matter of gender being restored so marriage and mother-hood could begin. It was a signal that Alfhild's days at sea were definitively over.

I SAID goodbye to Maggie and Helen and spent several days in the Lofoten Islands before traveling onward on a different ship. This was the *Richard With*, one of the newer-generation coastal steamers built to resemble a cruise ship. On the *Richard With*, you could move about freely without bumping into anyone.

There was a cocktail bar, a library, and all manner of soft swivel chairs in front of floor-to-ceiling glass windows with spectacular views of narrow blue fjords and sharp granite mountains, of red fishermen's shacks and wharves, once the site of intensive winter fishing (this is where Trouser-Beret captained her boat), and now impossibly picturesque. Yet the *Richard With* was a more insulated world, whose very comfort made it seem sometimes as though we were passing through a travel video about the breathtaking Land of the Midnight Sun. To sit in a panorama lounge with a view of mountains and sea, with a novel on one's lap, was not the same as leaning over the railing and taking in great gulps of marine spray: salt water, fish, diesel, and a hint of frost from distant glaciers.

Still, it was the coastal steamer, and I loved the coastal steamer's route. Back in 1973 I'd joined the crew of the *Kong Olav* on a whim, after seeing an ad in a Trondheim newspaper during my second summer working in Norway. *Skipspike*, "Ship's Girl," sounded a lot better than stock clerk, the job I held at the time, and I was disappointed to find out that in this case it meant dishwasher. All that summer I slaved long hours and couldn't get the smell of fish and potatoes out of my hair. But I never tired of going out on deck and watching the coastline; I never tired of coming into port and leaving port. I could have done that the rest of my life.

The journey to Tromsø was short in coastal-steamer terms, just one night, just one last night sleeping in a cabin to the sound of the engines, just one more morning eating breakfast by a porthole, just one more port for a final disembarkation. I was sorry to have gotten off the *Lofoten* and often found myself wishing that I'd gone all the way up to the North Cape. I missed Maggie and Helen a little, the odd trio we'd formed by the end, shipboard friends with little in common except the voyage, three Norns at sea.

Yet in Tromsø, even with the weather getting colder and the days growing shorter, the time passed quickly. I had research to do and café lattes to catch up on. I went to museums and the university library, and even to the College of Fishery Science, a marvelous building in the general outline of a ship, with many festive decorative touches like portholes and fish-print drapes. The assistant director gave me a tour, loaded me with brochures and promotional material, and put me in contact with a few women who could tell me about women fishers. Another day I persuaded my friend Ragnhild to go with me to Polaria, a high-concept museum with little of interest except a model of how whirlpools are created. I'm afraid I taxed her patience by pushing the button again and again so I could see how the funnel swirled up from the bottom of the tall glass tank, faster and faster, until it became a tornado of white water with a wide opening on the surface. If ever there were a symbol for the once revered and now lost power of the feminine to create and destroy life, this was it. Call me the Cailleach, creator of sea cauldrons, the storm goddess now living in a glass box.

One afternoon I sat in the market square with my notebook, and sketched the statue before me: a large bold fisherman in a small boat, tilted at a vertical angle over two abstract curls of either wave or whale. His harpoon raised to strike, he was the epitome of action. All around the granite pedestal were bas-reliefs made of forged metal. One of them was a small tableau of two women and a small boy staring out at a ship. One woman had her hand on the other's shoulder; the boy wore a sou' wester and pulled impatiently away from his mother.

I'd just come from a meeting with Marit Husmo, who'd

done a lot of interesting statistical research on women in the fishing industry, and now I sat in the square, across from a man hawking fresh shrimp and a Russian woman selling lacquered boxes and dolls, reading through my notes. At the end of our talk I'd asked Marit about the custom of erecting statues of women staring out to sea, and she sighed. "Most women still work in factories, on the fish processing assembly line. That's the reality. There's no statue to *them*. There's nothing that reflects what women actually do."

It hadn't been until my last day in the Lofoten Islands that I'd tried to find out something about the Fisherman's Wife statue there, and about some of the other statues now being erected along these maritime coasts. Although most of these statues show women in old-fashioned dress—long skirts (the better to blow in the sculptor's breeze), kerchiefs and shawls— almost all have appeared in the last decade or so. When I finally asked, "Who's putting these statues up and why now?" the answers surprised me. Although the figures clearly drew on an iconography of mourning as old as Homer, most people didn't mention loss, but told me, "It's to acknowledge women's contribution to Norway's fishing culture. The men went out fishing and whaling, but the women did everything else. So this is a tribute to these women."

It seemed odd that the statues seemed to be appearing at a time when the old way of life was almost gone, when fishing was still tough but safer and less heroic, when women were encroaching on male territory in every way. The majority of coastal fisherwomen fished together with their male partners, I'd read; hundreds worked on factory ships, and thousands more in the industry as a whole. Even in earlier times, women had rarely stood around on shore waving and waiting. Their tasks,

Fisherman's wife

from milking to milling, from weaving to seaweed gathering and line baiting, from midwifery to childcare, were what kept the maritime communities alive; they had no leisure for sad farewells. To give tribute to women's endless labor ashore by showing them sadly waving or staring out to sea seemed entirely suspect. It didn't take into account Norway's own Trouser-Beret and her sisters, or Skipper Thurídur in Iceland, or the herring lassies of Scotland, all of whom had been hard-working women who supported themselves and their families from fishing.

Not to mention Grace O'Malley and Alfhild, and explorers and captains and sailors, who stayed at sea for months at a time, and whose wanderlust and expertise equaled that of men. It was, after all, pirates and seafarers, not herring lassies, whose boldness and transgressions captured the imagination. Women in the fishing industry—I looked at the pamphlets in my lap and my notes from Marit—were just as much a part of the wide lore of sea, but they weren't, you had to admit, heroines to live by, though they certainly deserved a statue or two.

If I'd discovered anything on my voyages, it was that women's maritime heritage was diverse: fishing *and* piracy, seaweed gathering *and* swashbuckling. Women's connection with the sea was about business *and* adventure, work *and* pleasure. About dressing as a man sometimes, about earning the respect of a crew, about making a living as a widow, about throwing off expectations. About taking passage on a boat to new shores, whether it was Elizabeth Taylor traveling to the Faroes, or Freydís Eiríksdóttir sailing to Vínland. About fighting with valor and keeping one's head when attacked. About standing on shore, and about sailing away.

The sailing away was the best part though.

At the beginning of my notebook was a sketch I'd done, months ago now, in Louisburgh, Ireland, at the Granuaile Heritage Centre. Tentative then, hardly knowing what I was recording, I'd copied the mannequin of Grace, in doublet and hose, with a sword at her belt, and one hand raised awkwardly to her forehead. It was the same pose, I realized, that the Fisherman's Wives were forced to take, but the meaning was entirely different. Grace O'Malley was looking out to sea for ships to plunder. She wasn't waiting for anybody.

WHEN I'D arrived in Tromsø, I'd found myself reluctant to disembark, for this was the farthest north I'd go on this trip, and yet I yearned to go much farther: up to Hammerfest and the North Cape, around the top of Norway to the Russian border. I wanted to book a small berth on the *Harald Jarl*, a ship even more like the *Kong Olav* than the *Lofoten* was, a ship that wouldn't sail again after this year. I often found myself walking by the docks at six in the evening, just when the coastal steamer pulled up its ramp, blasted its horn, and slowly moved away from land and out to sea again.

It was this rhythm of arrival and departure that I loved and had always loved most during my summer working on the coastal steamer. I loved the grinding of the engine as the pro-pellers churned counterclockwise to halt the ship, the *thunk* of the rope cables hitting the dock, the lowering of the metal gangway, the sudden silence as the engines stopped. I loved even more to hear the engines start up again, to look over the side and see the gangway disappearing back into the ship. A man on the dock would loose the ropes that were all that held the ship to the side, and they'd be winched up again into a coil. The space between the ship and the dock widened; for a second, no more, you could still have jumped the distance, then it was too late. You were separated from land. The ship hooted when we arrived and when we left, and in those blasts from the horn was everything I understood about departures and arrivals, about beginnings and farewells.

I stood on the Tromsø wharf many evenings watching the ships let go of land: the *Narvik*, the *Vesterålen*, the *Nordnorge*, all white and gleaming, all with their captain at the bridge and their crew at the ready, all steaming north. I stood watching their departures, and sometimes I waved to the passengers on deck, and envied them—but only a little.

I would take other voyages, I was sure of it.

Once, as a child, I'd stood with my mother on the pier in Los Angeles, waving goodbye to her friend, a woman sailing off for adventure in foreign ports.

Now I had become that woman.

"Goodbye, goodbye," I remember calling to my mother.

"Goodbye, goodbye," my mother had called to me. "Don't forget to write."

EPILOGUE

RETURN TO CLEW BAY

IT HAD been a few years since I'd first come to Clew Bay. Once again I'd traveled by the train from Dublin. Once again it was spring, the first day of June and a bank holiday. Once again sun sparkled green on the pastures and hills of Ireland, the holy mountain of Croagh Patrick a perfect cone in the distance as the train chugged into Westport Station.

I'd long wanted to meet Anne Chambers, the biographer of Grace O'Malley and the woman who'd done the most to put the pirate queen on the map. Although Anne lives in Dublin, she was here in Westport to help supervise the setting up of a statue of Grace on the grounds of Westport House, which belongs to Jeremy Browne, Lord Altamont, the eleventh Marquess of Sligo and thirteenth great grandson of Grace O'Malley.

Nearing the end of writing this book, I'd conceived a great longing to return to Clew Bay, the seascape of my pirate queen. In the mysterious way of things, no sooner had I decided on a short trip to the west of Ireland than I heard from Anne Chambers: The week I planned to come was the very week the Grace O'Malley statue was being installed.

We met in the lounge of the Olde Railway Hotel, a parlor so stuffed with horsehair sofas and wing chairs, birdcages, fern stands, occasional tables, pianos, and footstools that it seems hardly changed from Thackeray's time, when he visited Westport and pronounced the hotel "one of the Prettiest, Comfortablist Inns in Ireland." Tall and auburn-haired, Anne had an angular, animated face, generous and no-nonsense. Rangy in her jeans and jean jacket, she looked almost Western, as if she roped cattle in Wyoming.

I'd been living with the stories of Grace O'Malley for a long time now, but Anne had lived with them since childhood. She grew up in nearby Castlebar and spent her summers on the shores of Clew Bay. "I knew that some of the ruins and the castles had belonged to a woman they called the pirate queen, Grace O'Malley, but I never really knew if she was a real person, or if the stories were true. We didn't study her in history class; she wasn't even in the history books. I wondered if she was legendary, like Queen Maeve of Connaught."

Anne moved to Dublin; she worked at a bank and went to discos at night, like any person in her twenties. But she was still thinking about Grace. She started going over to the National Library during her lunch hours and after work, trying to satisfy her curiosity. "I knew nothing at all about how to do historical research," she told me. "I remember those state papers, learning how to decipher the faded handwriting, and my excitement when I found the letter from Grace to Queen Elizabeth."

The first edition of Anne's biography, *Granuaile*, came out in 1978, and since then it has always been in print, with a couple of revised editions as new material became available. For Anne, Grace has never lost her fascination and, in fact, grows more relevant as the years pass. "There's something modern about Grace. She was a career woman who had to balance business— i.e., piracy, seafaring, and warring—with a personal life of children, household responsibilities, and personal relationships. She wasn't patriotic; she was practical and pragmatic. She essentially got a 'prenup' agreement with her second husband. And she proved that she could do all this, be as tough as a man, without losing her femininity."

Granuaile was the beginning of Anne's writing career and her continuing interest in the tumultuous world of sixteenth-century Ireland, but in spite of her other projects, she'd never lost interest in Grace. She had a screenplay in the works, and a TV documentary. She was the energy and vision behind the Granuaile Heritage Centre in Louisburgh. She'd written count-less articles and been interviewed many times. She'd seen an orchestral piece, *The Granuaile Suite,* performed, and she'd chris-tened the Clare Island Ferry the *Pirate Queen.* Even in the few years since I'd first read *Granuaile* and had the notion to travel around the North Atlantic collecting stories, Grace O'Malley had become better known. In fact, the great excitement around Clew Bay this time was a recent visit by Lucy Lawless, of *Xena, Warrior Princess* fame, who had been here with a film crew only weeks before, shooting one segment of a five-part series on women warriors for the Discovery Channel. Anne had been a consultant for the program, and Mary Gavin Hughes, with her *Shamrock I,* had taken the crew out on the water, even donning a gray wig at one point for a crowd scene.

During the course of all her research and promotion of Grace, Anne and her husband had become very good friends with Jeremy Browne, Lord Altamont, and his wife. One of the fruits of the friendship was a closer pairing of Westport House and the story of Grace O'Malley. The statue, erected four hun-dred years after Grace's death in 1603, was the most visible mark of that pairing. Actually, there were two statues, one of stone, set inside the house, and the other, a bronze cast, on the grounds nearby.

Anne's Jeep was parked in front of the Olde Railway Hotel. We jumped in, but instead of driving to the Wyoming ranch, we swept up the long drive to a magnificent Georgian country house a couple of miles away. Westport House was designed in 1778 by James Wyatt, on the site of an older building, where earlier descendants of Grace O'Malley, the Brownes, had lived. The foundation is said to have been one of the O'Malley castles. One of its greatest beauties is its setting. "The most beautiful view I ever saw in the world, I think . . . It forms an event in one's life to have seen that place, so beautiful is it and so unlike all other beauties that I know of. Were such beauties lying on English shores it would be a world's wonder," Thackeray wrote in 1842. The back of the house, terraced with gardens, slopes down in a landscaped descent of oaks and beeches, a small lake dammed from a stream whose course was altered to make it more picturesque. Now Clew Bay is hardly visible through the magnificent trees.

It being a holiday, the first of the summer, the parking lot was full and dozens of families roamed around both the house and the other attractions. In the lake, giant white swan-shaped boats (called swan pedaloes) glided, propelled by the humans inside. It took a few minutes to hunt up Jeremy Browne, the owner and instigator of the diversification of Westport House into a "leisure park." Finally he came bounding up. A marquess is one step down from an earl, and I felt a little nervous meeting a member of the aristocracy, though Anne had assured me, "He's not like that. You'll like him!"

I did. Tall, white-haired, wearing a sweater and slacks, Jeremy Browne had a boyish enthusiasm and an English accent. After we said goodbye to Anne, he led me into the house for a quick but thorough tour. He was forthright about his family's decision to turn the ancestral home into a paying concern. "In the 1950s we put it up for sale, just to test the market. We had two offers, one for £7500 and the other for £6000—that was to demolish it and sell off the property. It seemed a pity to let go such a house, and so we had to think of something else. We opened the house to the public and since then, gradually, we've been adding attractions, mostly for the kiddies, who get so bored, don't you know, with stately houses."

The new stone-carved statue of Grace O'Malley stood in the front hall, under a magnificent barrel ceiling with an early-nineteenth-century Waterford glass chandelier, next to the staircase. Hanging on the wall was a portrait of Maude Bourke, Grace's great-great-granddaughter through her son Tibbot-ne-Long, later Viscount Bourke. Maude wore a very low cut gown plunging practically to her navel and looked very snobby, as did her bewigged husband, John Browne, in a matching por-trait. Grace, seven feet tall in marble, also showed quite a lot of exposed chest, but her expression was far sterner. She had one hand on a tiller, the other on the handle of her saber.

I had the sense that it wasn't just the kiddies who were a bit bored with stately homes. The Brownes didn't even live in this grand mansion any longer, but down the road. For Jeremy, showing visitors the collections of plate and silver, Waterford glass, paintings, and furniture had paled next to creating his amusement park, tucked discreetly behind trees so little was vis-ible from the windows. Soon we were out of the house, and the next thing I knew I was sitting next to him in the small open car of a miniature train. The engineer pulled the steam whistle and off we chugged. All my life I'd read British novels with lords and ladies in them. In previous centuries they were haughty and proud. In the twentieth century they were sometimes, on the contrary, depicted as terribly modest, even off-hand, about their aristocratic roots. Still, nothing had quite prepared me for the experience of whizzing round a train track with an ebullient marquess who talked openly of restoring the family fortunes as he created a place that everyone could enjoy.

For several years, he told me, he'd been haunting amusement parks in England and Europe, trying to figure out which rides were most popular. After we stepped out of our train car, he led me over to see several of the ones they'd created here, including his favorite, the log flume. It was a modified roller coaster with a western theme; the cars, shaped like rough brown logs, climbed laboriously up a track and plunged steeply into a pool. There was a lot of shrieking at the plunge and a satisfying amount of water flying around.

"I've been thinking of developing more of a seafaring theme here," Jeremy said buoyantly as we watched a car containing a trio of eight-year-old girls inch up the steep track. "Now that we have the statue of Grace, we're beginning to build on her connection with Clew Bay and Clare Island, pirates, castles, all that sort of thing. Pirates are very popular these days, don't you think? I'm imagining a sort of flying gondola ride, with the gondolas as pirate ships, you see? Grace O'Malley, Pirate Queen, pirate galleys, swashbuckling and so on. Great fun, don't you think?"

Grace as entertainment for children? The shocked purist in me vied with the child. After all, I'd grown up in a land of amusement parks. The Pike in Long Beach was once famous all along the West Coast for its ballrooms, swimming hall, and daring rides, like the Jackrabbit roller coaster. Seedy as it became throughout the sixties when I knew and loved it, the Pike was a part of memory's vivid landscape, never displaced by the glossier

and more wholesome nature of Disneyland in Anaheim. Lord
Altamont and I watched as the log car, with three little girls
inside, cranked up to the top of the incline. We fell as silent with
anticipation as they had. In the seconds before they began to
scream with delight and fear as the car tilted and whooshed
down, I remembered that all eight-year-old girls have a pirate
inside. The only difference was that a Pippi Longstocking or
a Grace O'Malley had never had to give up the dream. Both
young Grace and Pippi would have loved a pirate gondola ride, as
I would have.

And Jeremy, who had five daughters, laughed with me to see
the girls, arms held high, come flying down the slope into the
pool, to make a deliriously happy, watery splash of a safe
landing.

THE NEXT morning the clouds were ominous, but I decided
anyway to go back to Westport House and take another private
look at the statue. It was pouring by the time I'd walked through
town; dripping and dark, the grounds were quite deserted. The
bank holiday was over, and the amusement park would only be
open weekends until July. The festive mood of yesterday had
turned drear and melancholy. The wind pulled at my coat; rain
crept up my pants legs, under my collar. It strangely felt a great
deal like my journeys around the North Atlantic several years
ago, when I had been soaked and windblown so much of the
time, and that gave my walk an odd familiarity.

I placed myself in front of the larger-than-life bronze
statue. Rivulets of water ran down her face and neck. The
plaque, and the unveiling, would come in several weeks. Right
now, Grace stood, not exactly as I'd imagined her, on a plinth of

granite. She was bold certainly and brave and farseeing; she was big, she was tough, she looked every inch a warrior and a mother. Yet, her costume of bodice and skirt didn't seem suitable for seafaring, and she had her back to Clew Bay.

I felt ungrateful. After all, I believed so thoroughly by now in the necessity of memorializing women and their achievements. Finally a statue of a maritime woman! A statue of Grace O'Malley, the Pirate Queen! Yet I stood there feeling vaguely disappointed, only because she wasn't my Grace O'Malley, the Grace I had carried in my head all this time. My Grace would have had shorter hair and a gash on her forehead; she would have worn a doublet and hose, had a spyglass to her eye, and been looking out to sea.

At the symbolic end of my journey, *mo thuras*, rituals still failed me. Once again I took a photograph, many in fact, from every angle, and then I trudged out of the beautifully landscaped, summer-wet grounds, the ancient oaks, and chestnuts soughing in the wind, and back into Westport.

There, on the spur of the moment I called a cab and asked the driver to take me out to Rockfleet, to Carraigahowley Castle. On the way he brought me up to date on Clare Island. The Belgians who'd turned the lighthouse into a bed-and-breakfast had moved on, and the property was again in private hands, owned, the driver said, by a titled lady from England. He knew about Xena's recent visit here, too, and the Discovery Channel program.

We discussed the many changes in Ireland over the last decade and he wondered, as did so many here about Americans, whether I had Irish roots. When I told him about my grandfather, he asked me what I was called.

"Sjoholm," he said. "What's that for a name?"

Sea islands

"Swedish," I said.

"But you're Irish? You have relations here, you say?"

"Yes, outside Dunmanway. I had Swedish and Irish grand-parents." I didn't tell him that I'd found the name of Sjoholm, not inherited it. Or that my new name came from sea and island, or that it made a picture in my mind when I said it, of an island sometimes hidden, sometimes visible in the tides. That it felt more nearly mine than my father's adopted name ever had. I certainly didn't tell him that perhaps the Norns had bestowed the name on me—belatedly, to be sure. No need to sound too mystical.

"It's hard to spell," I admitted. "But I still like it."

"Well, now, and wouldn't you, if it's your name?"

"'Tis."

ONE THING about a castle: It doesn't change in just a few years when it's been standing there for centuries. Grace O'Malley's favorite fortress was just as dankly sea-pungent as I remembered it, the stones around its base just as slippery with kelp and spume. It had stopped raining, so I'd asked the driver to leave me and come back in an hour, then I walked around the tower and breathed deep of the bladder wrack and rockweed along the shore of the inlet. I had come a long way to do something—I wasn't sure what—to make an end to my pilgrimage around the coasts of the North Atlantic in search of histories and folklore about the legendary women of the sea. It was long ago now that I'd sat on the rocky shores of Cape Cornwall wondering what those stories might be and how to discover them.

Now I knew that many of these stories had been kept alive in old books and family letters, to be rediscovered by relatives and researchers who believed that they were worth passing on. Grace would always be my favorite, but now I knew she wasn't the only maritime woman of the North Atlantic, just one of the most colorful and best remembered. I imagined that in years to come her historical importance would be recognized, and her popularity would continue to rise. Not too far in the future, perhaps, were a theme park and a movie, and perhaps video games and dolls and other merchandise. Pirates, as Jeremy had said, were very popular these days. Whether Freydís would ever have a statue, whether Janet Forsyth would have a film about her witchcraft trial were open to conjecture. But I felt that I had proved, to my own satisfaction at least, and in my own idiosyncratic way, that women had a centuries-long history with the North Atlantic. "Women and the sea?" I'd been asked over and over. And now I had something behind me when I answered, "Yes."

The tide was coming in. For now, there was just me and the castle and Clew Bay. If I half-closed my eyes, I could see Grace O'Malley's favorite galley anchored out in the small bay. I could hear her swearing cheerfully behind me in the top floor of the castle, spyglass to her eye as she stood watching the clouds blow in from the Atlantic. I gathered a few stones and made a pile, the larger, flatter ones on the bottom, the smaller ones on top, until I'd made a cairn: a signpost, a memorial, a statue of seaweed-spackled stone. I settled back to watch the tide turn the cairn into an island, and then take the stones and submerge them. I took a long, satisfied breath of the salt air and was happy, as I always was, by the sea.

SOURCES AND NOTES

Introduction: Crossing Clew Bay

Since I began researching and traveling, several welcome general books have been published in this field. See Joan Druett's *She Captains: Heroines and Hellions of the Sea* (New York: Simon and Schuster, 2000) and David Cordingly's *Women Sailors and Sailors' Women: An Untold Maritime History* (New York: Random House, 2001). Both these books have chapters on female pirates, as well as other seafaring women around the world.

Chambers, Anne. *Granuaile: The Life and Times of Grace O'Malley* (Dublin: Wolfhound, 1979; revised edition, 1998), I'm deeply indebted to Anne Chambers for her pioneering research on Grace O'Malley. All quotes from English state papers, as well as ballads about Grace come from Chambers's biography. There is a great deal of folklore about Grace O'Malley, and Chambers is careful to distinguish between the legendary aspects of her character and the facts that are known, as other more fanciful writers are not. However, "legendary" doesn't necessarily mean untrue. A rich source in Chambers's research was the folklore collection at the University College of Dublin. In the 1920s and '30s, children all over Ireland were encouraged to interview their relatives about stories from the past. In the case of Grace O'Malley, there were many tales from County Mayo, preserved for four hundred years in folk history, which told of her personal life and great deeds at sea and on land.

Stanley, Jo, ed. *Bold in Her Breeches: Women Pirates Across the Ages* (London: Pandora/HarperCollins, 1995).

Chapter One: Grace O'Malley's Castle

Chambers, Anne. *Granuaile: The Life and Times of Grace O'Malley* (Dublin: Wolfhound, 1979; revised edition, 1998).

Fairburn, Eleanor. *The White Seahorse* (London: Heinemann, 1964). A historical novel about "Graunya O'Malley."

Leask, Harold G. *Irish Castles and Castellated Houses* (Dundalk, Ireland: Dundalgan, 1999).

Chapter Two: The Pirate Queen

Chambers, Anne. *Granuaile: The Life and Times of Grace O'Malley* (Dublin: Wolfhound, 1979; revised edition, 1998).

Yeoman, Peter. *Pilgrimage in Medieval Scotland* (London: B. T. Batsford Ltd, 1999). For a discussion of *an thuras* (alternative spelling: *an toras*) as a form of pilgrimage.

Chapter Three: At the Edge of the Sea Cauldron

Chambers, Anne. *Granuaile: The Life and Times of Grace O'Malley* (Dublin: Wolfhound, 1979; revised edition, 1998). For the story of Howth Castle.

Grant, Katherine. *Myth, Tradition and Story from Western Argyll* (Oban: Oban Times Press, 1925). For stories about the Cailleach, and the source of details about Corryvreckan as the cauldron in which the Cailleach washes her blankets.

Hull, Eleanor. *Folklore of the British Isles* (London: Methuen, 1928). For the story and related quote about the nine daughters of Ægir, who grind out the meal of Prince Hamlet.

Mackenzie, Donald. *Scottish Folk-Lore and Folk Life: Studies in Race, Culture and Tradition* (London: Blackie, 1935). For the most comprehensive survey of the Cailleach as "the Scottish Artemis," and for the suggestion that Muileartach is the Cailleach's ocean form. The verse about Muileartach comes from Mackenzie.

Marwick, Ernest. *The Folklore of Orkney and Shetland* (London: B. T. Batsford, 1975). For the story of the Mither o' the Sea.

McNeill, F. Marian. *The Silver Bough* (Edinburgh: Canongate, 1989). For details on the Cailleach.

Miller, James. *A Wild and Open Sea: The Story of the Pentland Firth* (Kirkwall: Orkney Press, 1994).

Sturluson, Snorri. *Edda*, translated and edited by Anthony Faulkes (London: Everyman, 1987). This text includes the poem about Finnie and Minnie (Fenja and Menja). An important discussion of whirlpools in Norse literature is also found in Giorgio de Santillana and Hertha von Dechend's *Hamlet's Mill: An Essay on Myth and the Frame of Time* (Boston: Godine, 1977). This dense, exciting, and often impenetrable text links stories of whirling quernstones at the edge of the sea to the astronomical fluctuations of the pole star. De Santillana and von Dechend quote the story of the bondswomen from Saxo Grammaticus's *History of the Danes* as well as from Snorri Sturluson. It is their contention that the poem in the voice of the giantess Menja is "the oldest extant document of skaldic literature, antedating Snorri's tale by far." In this chapter and later, I have used the translation of this poem by I. Gollancz, *Hamlet in Iceland* (London: D. Nutt, 1898), preferring it to the Everyman edition. Icelandic scholar Gísli Sigurdssson helpfully pointed me in the direction of *Hamlet's Mill*.

Chapter Four: Raising the Wind

Black, G. F. (collector), and Northcote W. Thomas (editor). *County Folklore Vol. III, Orkney and Shetland Islands* (London: D. Nutt, 1903; facsimile reprint, London: Llanerch Publishers/Folklore Society, 1994). For transcripts of the witch trials and superstitions about witches.

Green, Miranda J. *Dictionary of Celtic Myth and Legend* (London: Thames and Hudson, 1992). For details on Nehalennia.

Larner, Christina. *Enemies of God: The Witch-hunt in Scotland* (Baltimore: Johns Hopkins University Press, 1981). For information on witchcraft trials in Scotland. The quote from *Daemonologie* by King James comes from this source.

Mackintosh, W. R. *Around the Orkney Peat-Fires* (Kirkwall: Orcadian, 1914). For the story of the Westray Storm Witch. For details about clews and sacred threads used by sea witches.

Marwick, Ernest. *The Folklore of Orkney and Shetland* (London: B. T. Batsford, 1975).

McPherson, J. M. *Primitive Beliefs in the North-East of Scotland* (London: Longmans, Green and Co., 1929). The source of the verse, "I knock this rag . . ."

Nicolson, James R. *Shetland Folklore* (London: Robert Hale, 1981). For stories of the eggshell boats and knotted threads of the sea witches.

Scott, Sir Walter. *The Pirate* (Edinburgh: Constable, 1896). See also his journal of traveling through Stromness in *Voyage of the Pharos* (Hamilton: Scottish Library Association, 1998).

Walker, Barbara G. *The Woman's Encyclopedia of Myths and Secrets* (San Francisco: Harper and Row, 1983). For details about the Norns, the Moirai, and St. Brigit.

Chapter Five: Herring Lassies

Anson, Peter F. *Fishing Boats and Fisher Folk on the East Coast of Scotland* (London: J. M. Dent and Sons, 1930).

Telford, Susan. *'In a World a Wir Ane': A Shetland Herring Girl's Story* (Lerwick, Shetland: Shetland Times, 1998).

Chapter Six: A Man's World

Alexander, Michael. *Mrs. Fraser on the Fatal Shore* (New York: Simon and Schuster, 1971). For the story of Eliza Fraser.

Credland, Arthur G. *The Hull Whaling Trade: An Arctic Enterprise* (Beverley, East Yorkshire: Hutton, 1995). For information on Hull's whale-ship owners.

Linklater, Elizabeth. *A Child Under Sail* (Glasgow: Brown, Son and Ferguson, 1977).

Stark, Suzanne J. *Female Tars: Women Aboard Ship in the Age of Sail* (London: Pimlico, 1998).

Troup, J. A. *The Ice-Bound Whalers* (Stromness: Stromness Museum, 1987). For information on the whaling industry in Orkney in the 1830s, specifically the disasters of the 1835-36 season. Christian Robertson's letter regarding the low wages for which men in Stromness would work is also quoted in this book.

Wheelwright, Julie. *Amazons and Military Maids: Women Who Dressed as Men in Pursuit of Life, Liberty and Happiness* (London: Pandora, 1989). For a version of the story of Isobel (Isabelle) Gunn.

Wilson, Bryce. *Sea Haven: Stromness in the Orkney Islands* (Kirkwall, Orkney: Orkney Press, 1992). For many details about the history of the town and its inhabitants, Login's Inn, the Nor'Wast, and the traditional whaling song that I altered.

Chapter Seven: Enchantment

Dennison, Walter Traill. *Orkney Folkore and Sea Legends*, compiled by Tom Muir (Kirkwall, Orkney: Orkney Press, 1995). For stories of the Finfolk, of Annie Norn and Hilda-land and of the selkie wife who reclaims her skin and returns to the sea.

Kalevala: A Prose Translation from the Finnish Epic, translated by Aili Kolehmainen Johnson (Hancock, MI.: Book Concern, 1950). For the story of Ilmatar.

MacAulay, John M. *Seal-Folk and Ocean Paddlers: Sliochd nan Ròn* (Cambridge, UK: White Horse, 1998).

Mackenzie, Donald A. *Scottish Wonder Tales from Myth and Legend* (New York: Frederick A. Stokes Company, 1917; Mineola, NY: Dover, 1997). For a story of the Maid-of-the-Wave.

O'Clery, Helen, editor. *The Mermaid Reader* (New York: Franklin Watts, 1964). For the origin of mermaids as fish-tailed goddesses.

Walker, Barbara G. *The Woman's Encyclopedia of Myths and Secrets* (San Francisco: Harper and Row, 1983). For the names and attributes of sea goddesses.

Williamson, Duncan. *Tales of the Seal People: Scottish Folk Tales* (Brooklyn, NY: Interlink, 1992). Williamson is a storyteller in the north of Scotland. His introduction discusses why the bereaved might wish to believe that seals are relatives.

Chapter Eight: The Lonely Voyage of Betty Mouat

Manson, T. M. Y. *Drifting Alone to Norway: The Amazing Adventure of Betty Mouat, and Tales of Others Who Drifted to Norway* (Brae, Shetland: Nelson Smith Printing, 1996).

Chapter Nine: Seagoing Charm School

Cordingly, David. *Women Sailors and Sailors' Women: An Untold Maritime History* (New York: Random House, 2001). For the story of Mary Patten.

Druett, Joan. *Hen Frigates: Passion and Peril, Nineteenth-Century Women at Sea* (New York: Simon and Schuster, 1998). For stories of nineteenth-century women who traveled with their husband-captains, learned to navigate, and occasionally saved the day.

Druett, Joan. *She Captains: Heroines and Hellions of the Sea* (New York: Simon and Schuster, 2000). For the stories of Tomyris and Artemesia.

Lindgren, Astrid. *The Adventures of Pippi Longstocking* (New York: Viking, 1977).

Mitchell, Alan. *Splendid Sisters: The Story of the Shaw Savill Liners Southern Cross and Northern Star* (London: George G. Harrap, 1966).

Storm, Gale. *I Ain't Down Yet: The Autobiography of My Little Margie*, with Bill Libby (Indianapolis: Bobbs-Merrill, 1981).

Chapter Ten: Halibut Woman

Robinson, Jane. *Wayward Women: A Guide to Women Travellers* (Oxford: Oxford University, 1990).

Taylor, Elizabeth. *The Far Islands and Other Cold Places: Travel Essays of a Victorian Lady*, edited by James Taylor Dunn (St. Paul, MN: Pogo Press, 1997). I drew heavily on Dunn's introduction, and appreciate his work gathering and presenting the story of his remarkable great aunt in this collection of letters and essays.

Wollstonecraft, Mary, and William Godwin. *A Short Residence in Sweden, Norway and Denmark and Memoirs of the Author of 'The Rights of Woman'* (London: Penguin, 1987).

Chapter Eleven: Aud the Deep-Minded

Jacobsen, Jørgen-Frantz. *Barbara*, translated by George Johnston (Norwich, UK: Norvik, 1993).

Jesch, Judith. *Women in the Viking Age* (Woodbridge, UK: Boydell Press, 1991). For the story of Aud the Deep-Minded.

Laxdæla Saga, translated by Magnus Magnusson and Hermann Pálsson (Middlesex, UK: Penguin, 1969).

Marcus, G. J. *The Conquest of the North Atlantic* (Woodbridge, UK: Boydell Press, 1980). For a thorough discussion of Norse navigation, *hafvilla*, and Viking ships.

Schei, Liv Kjørsvik, and Gunnie Moberg. *The Faroe Islands* (London: John Murray, 1991). For a version of the folktale of Barbara of Sumba, as well as information about Gudrún, the Lady of Húsavík. Other information about Gudrún came from Hanus undir Leitinum.

Chapter Twelve: Caught in the Net

Crossley-Holland, Kevin. *The Penguin Book of Norse Myths: Gods of the Vikings* (London: Penguin, 1992). For the "Lay of Hymir."

Davidson, H. R. Ellis. *Gods and Myths of the Viking Age* (New York: Bell Publishing, 1981). For the story of Ruad and the nine maidens.

Hull, Eleanor. *Folklore of the British Isles* (London: Methuen, 1928). For the quote from the eighth-century Irish abbot, "I invoke the seven Daughters of the Sea. . ."

Lacy, Terry G. *The Ring of Seasons: Iceland—Its Culture and History* (Reykjavík: University of Reykjavík, 1998). For a version of the story of Gudríd Símonardóttir. Much of my information came from Steinunn Jóhannesdóttir, whose novel, *Gudríd's Journey*, exploring the first half of Gudríd's life, was published in 2001 in Iceland (Reykjavík: Mal og menning).

Monaghan, Patricia. *The New Book of Goddesses & Heroines* (St. Paul, Minnesota: Llewellyn Publications, 1997) For details about Ran.

Mowat, Farley. *Westviking: The Ancient Norse in Greenland and North America* (Toronto: McClelland and Stewart, 1965). For the quote from *The King's Mirror* on *hafgerdingar.*

Spencer, William. *Algiers in the Age of the Corsairs* (Norman, OK: University of Oklahoma, 1976). For information about Algiers under Turkish rule and the corsairs.

Sturluson, Snorri. *Edda*, translated and edited by Anthony Faulkes (London: Everyman, 1987).

Sykes, Egerton, ed. *Everyman's Dictionary of Non-classical Mythology* (London: J. M. Dent & Sons Ltd., 1962). For the suggestion that Ran's nine daughters suggest the presence of a college of priestesses.

Chapter Thirteen: Iceberg Travel

Bard's Saga, from *The Complete Sagas of the Icelanders* (Reykjavík: Leifur Eiriksson Publishing, 2000).

Bergmann, Gudrún G. *The Mystique of Snæfellsjökull* (Olafsvík: Leidarljós, 1999).

Ellis, Peter Berresford. *Celtic Women: Women in Celtic Society and Literature* (Grand Rapids, MI: William B. Eerdmans, 1995). For the story of Muirenn.

Chapter Fourteen: Leif's Unlucky Sister

Byock, Jesse. *Viking Age Iceland* (London: Penguin, 2001). For the travels of Gudríd Thorbjarnardóttir and other Icelandic women to Rome.

Clark, Joan. *Eiriksdóttir: A Tale of Dreams and Luck* (Toronto: Macmillan, 1994). This beautifully written novel is a convincing look at the harsh reality of life in Greenland and Vínland, and a powerfully imagined portrayal of Freydís Eiríksdóttir.

Fitzhugh, William W., and Elisabeth I. Ward, eds. *Vikings: The North Atlantic Saga* (Washington, DC: Smithsonian, 2000). This book provides the most up-to-date account of the discovery of the site at L'Anse aux Meadows in Newfoundland and the most current research on Viking sites in North America.

Jesch, Judith. *Women in the Viking Age* (Woodbridge, UK: Boydell Press, 1991).

Jochens, Jenny. *Old Norse Images of Women* (Philadelphia: University of Pennsylvania, 1996).

The Vínland Sagas consist of two sagas, *The Greenlanders' Saga* and *The Saga of Eirík the Red*, translated by Magnus Magnusson and Hermann Pálsson (London: Penguin, 1965).

(Recently, the Icelandic historian Helgi Thórlaksson has published research that may prove Glaumbær was not owned by Karlsefni's family in the eleventh century but that their main estate was Reynisnes.)

Chapter Fifteen: A Woman Without a Boat Is a Prisoner

Lacy, Terry G. *The Ring of Seasons: Iceland—Its Culture and History* (Reykjavík: University of Reykjavík, 1998). For some details about Thuridúr Formadur.

Magnúsdóttir, Thórunn. *Sjósókn sunnlenskra kvenna frá verstödvum í Árnessýslu 1697-1980 [Seafaring Women of South Iceland from 1697-1980]* (Reykjavík: MA dissertation, 1984). The portion of the book that deals with how Magnúsdóttir researched her subject was also published in a Danish précis, and delivered as a speech at a meeting of women historians in Oslo in 1983. I summarize her methodology and findings below. Other sections about various women fishers were translated for me from the Icelandic by Daniel Teague, and include some quotes from a book about Thurídur Einarsdóttir by Brynjólf Jónsson, *The History of Skipper Thurídur and the Kambur Farm Burglars*, published in 1941, and in a revised edition in 1975 (in Icelandic).

For her work on women fishing on the south coast of Iceland, Magnusdóttir went to public records that showed in the district how many boats were registered and what sizes they were (since boats are called by the name of how many oars they have, she could calculate with some certainty). She estimated how many rowers it took to man the boats and then looked at the number of male inhabitants in the district. For instance, in 1795 there were eighty-seven boats, requiring a total crew of 560. At that time the district had 370 men between the ages of twenty and sixty. In 1800 there were sixty boats, requiring 465 rowers, but only 434 available men in the district. In 1852 fifty-two boats required 410 people to row them. There were 476 men.

Magnusdóttir counted all men between the ages of twenty and sixty, but assumed that some percentage of these were sick or disabled at any one time. That means that there was a lack of between several dozen to almost two hundred men to row the fishing boats. Magnusdóttir also found from the records that women outnumbered men in every parish. She notes: "A natural conclusion was that women

must have participated in the fishing." Still, she asks, "Are there
dependable sources to show that women worked as fishers? Their
stories are rarely recorded, generally only if they are involved in a
court case or suffer a tragedy, such as drowning with their shipmates.
For instance, Kristine Brandsdóttir, born in 1786, drowned with the
whole crew."

Sigurdardóttir, Anna. *Vinna kvenna á islandi í 1100 ár (Working women
in Iceland for 1100 years)* (Reykjavík: Kvennasögusafn Islands, 1985)
Chapter nine. For material on Halldóra Ólafsdóttir and other women
fishers of Breidafjord, including many women not cited in my text.
Translated for me by Daniel Teague.

Chapter Sixteen: Seawim

Brantenberg, Gerd. *Egalia's Daughters: A Satire of the Sexes,* translated
by Louis Mackay in cooperation with Gerd Brantenberg (Seattle: Seal
Press, 1985).

Fitzhugh, William W., and Elisabeth I. Ward, eds. *Vikings: The North
Atlantic Saga* (Washington, DC: Smithsonian, 2000). For details on
the excavation of the Oseberg ship.

Walker, Barbara G. *The Woman's Encyclopedia of Myths and Secrets* (San
Francisco: Harper and Row, 1983). For details on Frigga.

Chapter Seventeen: Trouser-Beret

The Sami are an indigenous people who form an ethnic minority in
Norway, Sweden, Finland, and Russia, and who have occupied the
region north of the Arctic Circle for probably around four thousand
years, and possibly earlier. With around forty thousand Sami, Norway
has the largest population. Until the 1600s the Sami and the few
Norwegian settlers lived side by side. More intensive colonization by
the Norwegians, especially along the coast, led to assimilation and
active suppression. By the end of the 1800s use of the Sami language

348 THE PIRATE QUEEN

was restricted, and by 1902 a law was passed forbidding the sale of land to anyone who did not speak Norwegian. Norway, which had been ruled by Denmark since the Middle Ages, became independent in 1814, but was pressured into a political union with Sweden, which did not cease until 1905. One of the side effects of the country's nationalism was an attempt to culturally eradicate its ancient ethnic minority. Only in the 1960s, with the rise of indigenous peoples' organizing efforts worldwide, did the Sami begin to assert their rights. In 1988 the Norwegian Parliament adopted a new Article to the Constitution that acknowledged and preserved Sami rights and paved the way for the creation of a Sami Parliament, which opened in 1989.

No material on Trouser-Beret exists in English. In addition to conversations with Hilgunn Pedersen , I benefited from a section titled "Arbeidsdeling hos samene" ("Division of Labor Among the Sami") in a volume of local history, *Lødingen, Tjeldsund og Tysfjords Historie 1700-1870, volume V: Fra Vidstrakt Prestegjeld til Storkommune*, edited by Alf Ragnar Nielssen, authored by Alf Ragnar Nielssen and Hilgunn Pedersen (Lødingen: Tjeldsund og Tysfjord Kommuner, 1994), as well as other genealogical notes about Beret Paulsdatter given to me by Pedersen. Buks-Beret is also known as Boks-Beret, Boksberret, and Bokseberet, depending on dialect. Bukse means trousers in Norwegian.

The following Norwegian sources were helpful: *Dundor-Heikka og flere lappers historier* by Inga Bjørnson (Oslo: Alb. Cammermeyers Forlag, 1915) and "Det tradisjonelle kjønnsrollemønster i Nord-Norge" by Håvard Dahl Bratrein in *Drivandes Kvinnfolk* (Tromsø: Universitetsforlaget, 1976). *Rundt Norge* by Dr. Yngvar Nielsen is the oversize travel book referred to in the chapter (Kristiania: Mallings Bokhandel, 1882). *Samekulturen* by Ornulv Vorren and Ernst Manker (Tromsø: Universitetsforlaget, 1976) had useful information on the Sea Sami of the Tysfjord.

Brøgger, A. W., and Haakon Shetelig. *Viking Ships* (Oslo: Dreyer, 1951). For information on Sami boat building. The quote by Nansen on the "women's boat" is also from this book.

Chapter Eighteen: Statue of a Woman
Staring Out to Sea

Druett, Joan. *She Captains: Heroines and Hellions of the Sea* (New York: Simon and Schuster, 2000). For information on Viking longships and Saxo's story of Alfhild.

Jesch, Judith. *Women in the Viking Age* (Woodbridge, UK: Boydell Press, 1991). For the skaldic verse about the admiring widow, taken from a series of verses by Thjódólf Arnórsson that describe King Harald's navy leaving Trondheim, Norway.

Olaus Magnus. *A Description of the Northern Peoples, Volume I*, translated by Peter Fisher and Humphrey Higgens, edited by Peter Foote (Original publication 1555, in Latin; London: Hakluyt Society, 1996). For the story of Alvid.

Saxo Grammaticus. *The Nine Books of the Danish History of Saxo Grammaticus*, translated by Oliver Elton (London: Norroena Society, 1907). For the story of Alfhild, Rusla, and other female warriors.

ILLUSTRATION CREDITS

Cover
Rockfleet Castle photograph © Suzanne Arnold
Sea photo © Royalty-Free/CORBIS

Frontmatter
Title page, Rockfleet Castle photograph © Suzanne Arnold

Introduction
Page xxi, photograph courtesy of the author
Page xxiii, reprinted from Anne Chambers, *Granuaile: The Life and Times of Grace O'Malley*, Wolfhound Press (Dublin, Ireland)

Chapter One
Page 13, drawing courtesy of Ron Druett © 2000

Chapter Two
Page 22, © Suzanne Arnold
Page 35, reprinted from Anne Chambers, *Granuaile: The Life and Times of Grace O'Malley*, Wolfhound Press (Dublin, Ireland)

Chapter Three
Page 53, reprinted from Peter Foote, ed., *A Description of the Northern Peoples* by Olaus Magnus, The Hakluyt Society (London, England)

Chapter Four
Page 59, cover illustration reprinted from Klausmann, Meinzerin, and Kuhn, *Women Pirates: and the Politics of the Jolly Roger*, Black Rose Books Ltd. (Buffalo, NY)
Page 67, illustration by W. Fraser and S. Sangster; reprinted from Sir Walter Scott, *The Pirate*, Archibald Constable and Company (Westminster, England)

Chapter Five

Page 77, courtesy of the Scottish Fisheries Museum

Page 84, courtesy of William Smith

Page 87, from the Stromness Museum

Page 89, illustration by John McGhie courtesy of the Scottish
Fisheries Museum

Chapter Six

Page 108, illustration from *Narrative of the Capture, Sufferings and
Miraculous Escape of Mrs. Eliza Fraser*, Charles Webb (New York,
NY); reprinted from Michael Alexander, *Mrs. Fraser on the Fatal
Shore*, Phoenix Press (London, England)

Page 110, illustration from John Ashton, ed., *Modern Street Ballads*,
Chatto and Windus (London, England); reprinted from Suzanne
J. Stark, *Female Tars: Women Aboard Ship in the Age of Sail*,
Pimlico (London, England)

Chapter Seven

Page 122, drawing by John Duncan, A.R.S.A; reprinted from Donald
A. Mackenzie, *Scottish Wonder Tales from Myth and Legend*, Dover
Publications, Inc. (Mineola, NY)

Chapter Eight

Page 128, photo courtesy of the author

Page 132, courtesy of the Illustrated London News Picture Library

Page 134, courtesy of the Shetland Museum

Chapter Ten

Page 166, courtesy of the Pogo Press, Incorporated

Page 168, reprinted from *Faroe Isles Review*, issue 1, Bókagarður
(Tórshavn, Faroe Isles)

Chapter Twelve

Page 195, engraving by Flameng, 1869; reprinted from Joan Druett,
She Captains: Heroines and Hellions of the Sea, Simon & Schuster
(New York, NY)

Chapter Fourteen

Page 236, courtesy of Gunnar Marel Eggertsson

Page 248, "Gudrídur Thorbjarnardóttir," Asmundur Sveinsson
   © Heirs/Myndstef 2004

Chapter Fifteen

Page 265, courtesy of the National Museum of Iceland

Page 270, photo courtesy of the author

Chapter Seventeen

Page 289, photograph by Annie Giæver; reprinted from Bente
   Foldvik, *Jenteliv uten vaskemaskin,* Nordlys

Page 298, reprinted from Johannes Shefferus, *The History of Lapland,*
   Bokförlaget Rediviva (Stockholm, Sweden)

Chapter Eighteen

Page 303, from Ellms, *Pirates Own Book,* Boston 1837; reprinted from
   Joan Druett, *She Captains: Heroines and Hellions of the Sea,* Simon
   & Schuster (New York, NY)

Page 311, reprinted from Peter Foote, ed., *A Description of the
   Northern Peoples* by Olaus Magnus, The Hakluyt Society
   (London, England)

Page 320, photo courtesy of the author

Epilogue

Page 333, courtesy of the author's private collection

ACKNOWLEDGMENTS

MANY OF the stories I went looking for and happened upon as I traveled around the North Atlantic have been kept alive by folklorists, writers, and relatives of seafaring women. I relied heavily on their passion for research and dedication to memory. My greatest thanks, therefore, to all the writers and storytellers I encountered along the way, for the pleasure of their company and for their belief that what women have accomplished matters to us all.

In Ireland, I'm extremely grateful for the help of Anne Chambers, Mary Gavin Hughes, and Jeremy Browne, Lord Altamont, who know and love Clew Bay and who increased my understanding of the pirate queen who once lived there. Many thanks also to Mary McGreal of the Mayo County Tourist Office in Westport, Ireland and to Mary O'Malley of the Granuaile Heritage Centre.

In Scotland, I'd like to thank Ellen Galford and Ellen Kelly for taking me to Anstruther to the Scottish Fisheries Museum, and Linda Semple for digging up an old copy of *The Pirate*. In Stromness, Orkney, I was fortunate to meet Gunnie Moberg and Anne Robertson, which led me to the fudge factory and Jim Robertson. A great thank you to Jim Robertson for the tour, the talk, and the fudge. Bryce Wilson, honorary curator of the Stromness Museum, offered useful corrections to the chapter on his wonderful town.

In Shetland I am grateful to Tommy Watt of the Shetland Museum and to Douglas Sinclair of the Lerwick Library, as well as to the incomparable Dorothy Thomson and to Mary Isbister. I thank Jeanne Pratt, author of the "Instructions to Hostesses" for her illuminating notes on shipboard life and work.

Hanus undir Leitinum very kindly took the time to show me around Húsavík in the Faroe Islands and to give me a sense of Gudrún Sjúrdardóttir's world.

In Iceland I appreciated having two weeks at Gúnnarshus, in the apartment maintained by the Writers' Union of Iceland, and thank Jónína Michaelsdóttir and Ragnheidur Tryggvadóttir for helping make that possible. Inga Jóna Thórdardóttir, Brynja Benediktsdóttir, Erla Hulda Halldorsdóttir at the University of Reykjavík Library, Gísli Sigurdsson, Gulli and Gudrún Bergmann, Jónas Kristjánsson, and Ellen Ingvadóttir all contributed to my understanding of Icelandic history and women's roles in seafaring and fishing. Daniel Teague was an able translator of some of this history. Steinunn Jóhannesdóttir's research on Turkish Gudda sparked my own curiosity, and I thank her for sharing her knowledge with me. I'm very grateful to Thorunn Magnusdóttir, for her scholarship and great generosity, as well as to Gudrún Bergmann for encouragement to do something unexpected.

My conversations with Joan Clark in St. John's, Newfoundland, and Dr. Birgitta Linderoth Wallace in Halifax, Nova Scotia about Freydís Eiríksdóttir helped me to understand some of the many fascinating issues surrounding this historical figure. Scholarship on the Vínland Voyages (and much to do with Vikings in general) is vast and sometimes conflicting, and all mistakes of interpretation are, of course, my own. However, I give particular thanks to Dr. Wallace for her comments on my chapter about Freydís.

My friends in Tromsø, Norway, Ragnhild Nilstun and Øystein Aspaas, were convivial hosts and Ragnhild has been a keen reader as well. I thank her especially for first pointing me in the direction of Trouser-Beret. Gerd Brantenberg opened her home to me with good humor and kindness. Lars Børge Myklevoll of the Arran Center in Drag, Norway contributed to my knowledge of Trouser-Beret and her place in Sami history. But for Hilgunn Pedersen and her help, I would never have been able to write about her ancestor. I would also like to thank Norwegian Coastal Steamer, Inc.

The Seattle Arts Commission helped jump-start this project and I thank them. I am also grateful to the trustees of Brisons Veor, the writers' retreat at Cape Cornwell where I first read about women pirates and began dreaming about Grace O'Malley. Parts of this book were written at Soapstone, a writers' retreat in Oregon, and at the Baltic Writers and Translators Centre in Visby, Gotland. I am grateful for the time and space they offered.

Nancy Pollak, the Canadian friend with whom I almost met a watery end in the Inside Passage, encouraged me greatly in her readings of the manuscript in different stages. I also appreciate the support and comments of Jeanne Barrett, Judith Barrington, Betsy Howell, Rachel Lodge, Brenda Peterson, Louise Quayle, and Anna Wingfield. Tere Carranza contributed in many essential ways to the journey that was the basis for this book. Katherine Hanson was a resource, as always, regarding Scandinavia, and I thank her for many interesting conversations regarding Norns and the Norse pantheon of gods and goddesses.

I'd also like to thank Jennie Goode for graceful copyediting and heroic fact-checking, and Jenna Land Free for assistance with tracking down illustration permissions. I'm grateful to Suzanne Service for her maps and Patrick David Barber for book design and cover. To my niece, Jennifer Wilson, many thanks for designing the website piratequeen.org. To Ingrid Emerick, my editor at Seal, great thanks for enthusiasm and vision.

ABOUT THE AUTHOR

Barbara Sjoholm is the editor of the anthology *Steady As She Goes: Women's Adventures at Sea*. Her essays and travel narratives have appeared in the *American Scholar*, the *New York Times*, *Smithsonian*, and slate.com. As Barbara Wilson, she is the author of numerous books, including the award-winning memoir *Blue Windows: A Christian Science Childhood*, and *Gaudí Afternoon*, which won a British Crime Writers Award for best thriller set in Europe, and was filmed in Barcelona by Susan Seidelman. She has translated several books from Norwegian and was awarded a Columbia Translation Prize for her work on Cora Sandel's short stories. She lives in Seattle.

Visit the book's website at *www.piratequeen.org*.

SELECTED TITLES
FROM SEAL PRESS

Steady As She Goes edited by Barbara Sjoholm. $15.95, 1-58005-094-8. This collection of harrowing adventure yarns and illuminating boating tales will appeal to anyone who has ever dreamed of running away to sea.

Give Me the World by Leila Hadley. $14.95, 1-58005-091-3. The spirited story of one young woman's travels by boat and by land with her six-year-old son.

Going Alone: Women's Adventures in the Wild edited by Susan Fox Rogers. $14.95, 1-58005-106-5. Explores the many ways women find fulfillment, solace, and joy when they head out alone into the great outdoors.

The Curve of Time: The Classic Memoir of a Woman and her Children Who Explored the Coastal Waters of the Pacific Northwest, second edition by M. Wylie Blanchet, foreword by Timothy Egan. $15.95, 1-58005-072-7. The memoir of a woman who acted as both mother and captain of the boat that became her family's home during the summer.

No Hurry to Get Home: The Memoir of the New Yorker *Writer Whose Unconventional Life and Adventures Spanned the Twentieth Century* by Emily Hahn. $14.95, 1-58005-045-X. Hahn's memoir captures her free-spirited, charismatic personality and her inextinguishable passion for the unconventional life.

The Unsavvy Traveler: Women's Comic Tales of Catastrophe edited by Rosemary Caperton, Anne Mathews, and Lucie Ocenas. $15.95, 1-58005-058-1. Twenty-five gut-wrenchingly funny responses to the question: What happens when trips go wrong?

A Woman Alone: Travel Tales from Around the Globe edited by Faith Conlon, Ingrid Emerick, and Christina Henry de Tessan. $15.95, 1-58005-059-X. A collection of rousing stories by women who travel solo.

Seal Press publishes many outdoor and travel books by women writers. Please visit our website at www.sealpress.com

9 781580 051095